Our Knowledge of the Past
A Philosophy of Historiography

How do historians, comparative linguists, biblical and textual critics, and evolutionary biologists establish beliefs about the past? How do they know the past? This book presents a philosophical analysis of the disciplines that offer scientific knowledge of the past. Using the analytic tools of contemporary epistemology and philosophy of science the book covers such topics as evidence, theory, methodology, explanation, determination and underdetermination, coincidence, contingency, and counterfactuals in historiography. Aviezer Tucker's central claim is that historiography as a scientific discipline should be thought of as an effort to explain the evidence of past events. He also emphasizes the similarity between historiographic methodology and Darwinian evolutionary biology. This is an important, fresh, new approach to historiography and will be read by philosophers, historians, and social scientists interested in the methodological foundations of their disciplines.

Aviezer Tucker is a research associate at the Australian National University.

Our Knowledge of the Past

A Philosophy of Historiography

AVIEZER TUCKER

Australian National University

CAMBRIDGE
UNIVERSITY PRESS

PUBLISHED BY THE PRESS SYNDICATE OF THE UNIVERSITY OF CAMBRIDGE
The Pitt Building, Trumpington Street, Cambridge, United Kingdom

CAMBRIDGE UNIVERSITY PRESS
The Edinburgh Building, Cambridge CB2 2RU, UK
40 West 20th Street, New York, NY 10011-4211, USA
477 Williamstown Road, Port Melbourne, VIC 3207, Australia
Ruiz de Alarcón 13, 28014 Madrid, Spain
Dock House, The Waterfront, Cape Town 8001, South Africa

http://www.cambridge.org

First published 2004

Printed in the United States of America

Typeface ITC New Baskerville 10/13.5 pt.   *System* LᴀTEX 2$_\varepsilon$ [TB]

A catalog record for this book is available from the British Library.

Library of Congress Cataloging in Publication Data
Tucker, Aviezer, 1965–
Our knowledge of the past : a philosophy of historiography / Aviezer Tucker.
p. cm.
Includes bibliographical references (p.) and index.
ISBN 0-521-83415-5
I. Title
2003060237

ISBN 0 521 83415 5 hardback

To Veronika

Pravda vítězí!

But in the meanwhile, we must be patient . . .

Contents

Introduction: The Philosophy of Historiography   *page* 1

1. Consensus and Historiographic Knowledge   23
2. The History of Knowledge of History   46
3. The Theory of Scientific Historiography   92
4. Historiographic Opinion   141
5. Historiographic Explanation   185
6. The Limits of Historiographic Knowledge   208
7. Conclusion: Historiography and History   254

References   263
Notes   279
Index   287

Our Knowledge of the Past

A Philosophy of Historiography

Introduction: The Philosophy of Historiography

This book studies our knowledge of history, its nature, historical development, epistemic limits, and scope. In ordinary language "history" is ambiguous. It may mean past events or the study of past events (Dray, 1993, p. 1). In its original Greek *historie* is etymologically related to the verb "to see" and consequently to inquiry and knowledge. In other languages, "history" means a story (Le Goff, 1992, pp. 101–3). Arthur Marwick (1993, p. 6) distinguished five different uses of "history." In addition to past events and the activity of research into past events, Marwick added the interpretations that result from research, the accumulated knowledge of the past, based on those interpretations, and what is considered significant of the accumulated knowledge of the past.

Ordinary language aside, in this book I use a terminology designed to fit its epistemic focus: By history I mean past events. *Historiography* is composed of representations of past events, usually texts, but other media such as movies or sound recordings may also represent past events. *Historians* like Ranke or Mommsen wrote about history, they produced historiography. *Historiographers* like Momigliano and Iggers wrote about historiography, about the works of historians like Thucydides and Ranke. *Scientific historiography*, the main topic of this book, is historiography that generates probable knowledge of the past. *Historiographic interpretation* is the final historiographic product that is ready for popular consumption in the form of textbooks and "the history of" popular books.

Historiographic interpretations include knowledge generated by scientific historiography, but also ethical, aesthetic, political and other value judgments. The artistic and rhetorical interpretations of the results of historiographic research, of scientific historiography, ought to be distinguished from the logical structure of historiographic research (Lloyd, 1993, p. 53). Interpretations decide which parts of scientific historiography are sufficiently significant to be included in textbooks, and what kinds of value judgments should be passed on them. Different historiographic interpretations may incorporate an identical core of scientific historiography but "spin" it in different directions. For example, different historiographic interpretations of the New Deal in the United States may agree on what happened, on its causes and effects, the scientific core of interpretation. But one interpretation may consider it a positive development, the creation of a more civilized and moral United States with greater economic security. Another interpretation may consider it a degeneration of American individualism and liberty and its replacement with state paternalism and individual irresponsibility. Accordingly these two interpretations would emphasize different parts of scientific historiography, the first would discuss improvements in the standard of living of unemployed workers and the second would stress the growth in the size of the federal government.

The distinction between history and historiography parallels that of nature and science. The philosophy of science studies science and its relations with the evidence. It cannot study exclusively nature directly, or it would be a science. Similarly, scientific historiography studies history through its evidential remains. Philosophy can study the epistemology of our knowledge of history, the relations between historiography and evidence. This subfield of epistemology is then the *philosophy of historiography*. The philosophy of historiography has nothing to say about history directly, or it would be historiography. As a philosophy of historiography it deals exclusively with philosophical questions that can be elucidated, analyzed, or answered by a rigorous examination of historiography. Problems for which historiography is irrelevant may be philosophical, but are beyond the scope of the philosophy of historiography.

THE PHILOSOPHY OF SCIENTIFIC HISTORIOGRAPHY

The philosophy of scientific historiography, like other philosophic meta-disciplines such as the philosophy of science or the philosophy of law may be divided into *phenomenological, descriptive,* and *prescriptive* modes of inquiry. *Phenomenological meta-disciplinary inquiry* is a rigorous examination of the consciousness of disciplinary practitioners such as scientists or historians. Meta-historiographic phenomenology asks questions such as: How do historians perceive their enterprise? Self-consciousness can be incomplete and even misleading. Scientists and historians like to present their enterprise to themselves and outsiders as fitting prevailing cognitive values and ideals, even if their actual practices do not reflect these values at all. Many scientific innovators have not been fully or correctly conscious of their own methodologies. The explicit values to which scientists pledge allegiance are not necessarily the actual implicit values that affect and guide their scientific work (Laudan, 1984, p. 55). For example, Newton presented his methodology in terms of the contemporary dominant inductive philosophy of science, though Newtonian physics is clearly not inductive. Historians and philosophers of science are more interested in understanding Newtonian science than in what exactly Newton thought of his enterprise (Cohen & Westfall, 1995, pp. 109–43).

Philosophic descriptions attempt to present what disciplines like historiography are actually like. Any philosophic description is theory laden. I found some of the theories and concepts of recent epistemology and philosophy of science particularly useful for describing historiography. The history of historiography is the foundation for the philosophical description of historiography, just as the history of science is the basis for the philosophic description of science. In including the part of historiography that is devoted to representing the history of writing about the past, the philosophy of historiography partly overlaps with historiography proper. *Philosophical meta-disciplinary prescription* considers normatively what are the proper practices for a discipline such as historiography. It posits some meta-historiographic normative principles or ideals that may be a description of the practices of a "successful" part of the discipline or another exemplary discipline, whether or not this description is accurate.

Though phenomenology, description, and prescription are equally legitimate foci of inquiry, description is more important for the purpose of this book, the analysis of historiographic knowledge. The nature of the historiographic enterprise is independent of the professional self-consciousness of historians. Indeed, I will demonstrate that this self-consciousness is often false. Understanding historiography or science requires understanding what historians or scientists are doing, not what they think they are doing (Goldstein, 1996, pp. 195–6). Textbooks and ex post facto accounts by participants present a distorted image of actual practice: "Historiography is what historians write as historians, not what they say they do" (Goldstein, 1996, p. 256). For example, in their 1898 book, Langlois & Seignobos (1926) codified what many of their contemporaries considered Ranke's method. Langlois & Seignobos assumed an outdated philosophy of science that was inductive and empiricist: They divided the sciences between those that depend on direct observations, and those like historiography and geology that cannot observe the events they study, but have to infer them from written documents and other material traces of the past. They were wrong in their understanding of science, as physicists and chemists are not able to observe electrons any more than historians can observe historical events. Yet, these anachronisms should not obscure the fact that Langlois & Seignobos described correctly the similarities between how historians and textual critics obtain knowledge. As I demonstrate in this book, both attempt to prepare a complete genealogical table, a *stemma codicum*, that should connect the plural similar evidence with its common cause, may it be a historical event or a textual archetype that generated several exemplars (pp. 80–3, 95). A younger generation of historians, including the founders of the Annales school, were right to criticize their almost exclusive identification of evidence with written texts. But if we broaden Langlois & Seignobos's concept of evidence to include nondocumentary and material evidence, their analysis of historiographic practice as distinct from their philosophic self-consciousness is still correct. Similarly, Murphey (1973, pp. 57–8) noted that despite Beard and Becker's presentation of their historiography as distinct from Ranke's paradigm, and their distinctive claim that all historiography is underdetermined by the biases and perspectives of historians, their actual historiographic procedures and practices were not significantly different from those of Ranke.

As Kant put it, "Ought implies can." Before philosophers can tell historians what they should do, they should get a good idea of the epistemic limits of all possible historiography. A sophisticated analysis of the epistemic scope of scientific historiography is the only method through which it may be possible to evaluate the epistemic limitations of all historiographic knowledge. A relevant prescription must also be founded on a thorough understanding of existing historiography to avoid reproaching historians for not practicing what at least some of them already do. It is rash to ask whether historiography fits certain standards before we know what are the intrinsic standards of historiography. A prescriptive discussion of historiography would be premature.

Before embarking on the project of describing and explaining historiography, it is important to caution against confusing description with phenomenology and prescription. These confusions led to mistakes when philosophers of historiography believed they had solved one problem, while in fact they discussed a different problem altogether. When philosophers of historiography confuse description with phenomenology, they think they describe historiography, while in fact they describe what historians think of their practice. This confusion may result from a meek acceptance of historiographic self-consciousness, the assumption that historians must know what they are doing. When philosophers accept at face value the self-consciousness of historians, historiography appears usually more rational and coherent than it actually is. When historians like Elton (1969) or Carr (1987) wrote historiographic manuals they rationalized what they perceived as their own practices and criticized as deviant what they took to be those of their competitors. Other historians adopted what they perceived as the prevailing epistemic paradigm as a model for their own professional self-consciousness. However, Ranke's "inductive empiricism" just as the "relativism" of some contemporary historians do not reflect more than what historians have taken contemporary epistemologies to legitimize.

When philosophers of historiography confuse description with prescription, they prescribe while they think they describe. This confusion may arise out of insensitivity and lack of attention to historiography, assuming that historians must behave as a rule according to prescriptive standards set by the philosopher. The logical-positivist project in the philosophy of historiography was actually prescriptive. Hempel

(1965) endorsed on a priori grounds a logical model as the one and only correct form of explanation and then applied it to historiography as its description. Hempel did not bother to actually examine historiography because he thought it either followed his model or was bad historiography.

HISTORIOGRAPHIC KNOWLEDGE

The description of scientific historiography, of the nature, types, and scope of historiographic knowledge, requires an investigation of the history of scientific historiography, of historiographic research. At the beginning of the nineteenth century, historians adopted new communal methodologies that are often referred to as scientific or critical historiography. By communal methods I mean:

Agreed means of obtaining evidence; accepted strategies for the marshalling and deployment of evidence; conventions adhered to in the criticism of claims and the conduct of controversy; shared assumptions about the division of labor and distribution of authority in inquiry; etc. (Jardine, 1991, p. 78)

With the aid of these and other theories and methodologies, historians have been able to produce historiographic knowledge. This knowledge, such as it is, is the subject matter of the philosophy of historiography.

Leon Goldstein (1976, pp. 140–1) introduced an important distinction between the superstructure and the infrastructure of historiography. The superstructure of historiography is the finished product of historiographic research, ready for consumption by nonhistorians, usually in narrative form. The historiographic infrastructure is historiographic research, interaction with evidence, the bulk of the professional activity of historians. Goldstein warned against basing a philosophy of historiography on the superstructure of historiography. Hanson (1958) may have been the first to criticize the philosophy of science for analyzing the finished systematic theoretical result of scientific research, rather than the process of scientific research. Kuhn (1996, pp. 136–8) warned against basing a philosophy of science on textbook science. Textbooks misrepresent the process of investigation and the historical evolution of research and theorization. They make it appear more consistent, coherent, and progressive than it actually is. Likewise, in the philosophy of historiography:

> ...Philosophical writers have virtually ignored...problems concerning the emergence or constitution of the historical past in the course of historical inquiry...because the history books they tend to read, full blown accounts of much-studied periods, tend to obscure them. Such a book would tend to present what is essentially the generally accepted tradition of those historians who work on the period in question as if it were a description of the real past. The author of the work may disagree on this or that point with the established opinion, and where he does he may be inclined to deal more explicitly with the evidence he thinks supports his deviation; but, for the most part, his book will be a presentation of what he thinks happened with very little interruption of the account in order to deal with evidence. Of course, he will constantly be referring to evidence, either in published collections of material or in archival sources, but mostly these references will be understood only by his professional colleagues.... Writers of philosophical essays on history...may note...that the historian's account must...be based upon evidence, but...have not the slightest idea of precisely how – unless it be that widely held but totally erroneous idea that he finds his facts in old texts and copies them out. For the most part we [philosophers] follow the account, attend to the descriptions it contains, note the evaluations historical critics sometimes make of the men and events they write about, and, above all, keep a wary eye out for how things get explained. It is very easy, indeed, on the basis of such reading, to take the historical past for granted in some realistic way and treat it as something there to be described and explained. (Goldstein, 1976, pp. 50–1)

Goldstein (1976, pp. 139–82; 1996, pp. 86, 183) and Marwick (1993, p. 195) argued against placing textbook narratives that compose the historiographic superstructure at the center of the philosophy of historiography. The superstructure does not reflect the historiographic process of inquiry, the relation between historiography and evidence; rather, it represents the stylized results of inquiry. It is impossible to reconstruct the epistemology of historiography from studying its superstructure, as it is impossible to evaluate a scientific article from reading its abstract or conclusion. Since this book pays little attention to the superstructure of historiography, it pays even less attention to the debate whether it has the structure of a narrative or not.

Limiting the purview of philosophic problems that we discuss to those that can be decided by an analysis of historiography permits us to dispose of debates that do not belong to the philosophy of historiography. Perhaps the most essential distinction between the schools of philosophy that became known as "analytic" and "continental" concerns the theory of meaning: How do words or propositions receive their meanings? Analytic philosophers argue that words or sentences receive their meanings from their relations with the world. Continental philosophers tend to claim that words receive their meaning through their relations with other words. The original poststructuralist interest in history was a reaction against criticisms that it ignored historiography, which in some circles meant Marxism (Attridge et al., 1987). But the core of the debate about poststructuralism is about the nature of language and its relation, or lack thereof, with the world. The presence of poststructuralist or narrativist interpretations of the superstructure of historiography is hardly surprising since this set of literary theories and methods were constructed to interpret any text or textlike structure, from my tax returns (tragic) to my career (comic) to this sentence (ironic). However, the decisive battle in the war of theories of meaning will not be fought in the disputed margins, but in the sustaining cores. The relevant field for this battle is the philosophy of language and not the philosophy of historiography. In a sense this book calls for the liberation of the philosophy of historiography from imperialist ambitions of partisans of other philosophical debates (Tucker, 2001).

The chief inquiry of this book is into the relations between historiography and evidence. Rachel Laudan (1992, p. 57) opined that the philosophy of historiography lost its relevance for mainstream philosophy because it continued to focus on the *forms* of historiographic theories and explanation, while the research program of the philosophy of science shifted to focus on issues of *validation* whether scientific theories are well founded and justified and how they change (Laudan, 1992, p. 57). Peter Kosso (1992) suggested that the relation between evidence and historiography is not substantially different from the relation between evidence and theory in biology, geology, or physics. A misleading analogy between historiographic descriptions of past events and scientific descriptions of evidence led to the common mistake that since historians cannot observe historical events, knowledge of history can never be scientific. Yet, descriptions of historical events in historiography are as theoretical as descriptions of electrons are in physical theory. Historiographic evidence such as written documents or material remains is just as observable as scientific evidence. Murphey likened George Washington to the electron, "an entity postulated for the purpose of giving coherence to our present experience . . . each is unobservable by us" (Murphey, 1973, p. 16).

Arguably, contemporary epistemology began with Quine's (1985) naturalized epistemology. Quine suggested that how we arrive at our beliefs is relevant for answering the normative question of how we should arrive at them. Quine recommended that epistemology focus on descriptions of the links between observation and science. Description is better than rational reconstruction because it is better to discover how science in fact developed than to "fabricate a fictitious structure." Epistemology should study the relation between input and output, evidence and theory (Quine, 1985). Such a research program in the philosophy of historiography should examine the relations between evidential input and historiographic output. There can be three approaches to such a philosophy of historiography: *Determinist* philosophy of historiography would claim that historians infer from evidence with historiographic theories and methods a single historiographic "output." Historiographic determinists could recognize that different subfields of historiography have different "inputs," different types of theories, methods and evidence. But they would claim that all historiographic outputs are consistent, creating together a jigsaw puzzle picture of the past. Historiographic *indeterminists* would claim that whatever consistency and regularity we find in historiographic judgments result from political, ideological, or socio historical factors that influence groups of historians. Otherwise, evidence does not affect historiography. Historiographic *underdeterminism* would claim that historians are constrained by the evidence and their theories to choose among a finite range of possible historiographies. One of the goals of the philosophy of historiography should be to discover whether historiography is determined, indeterminate, or underdetermined.

This distinction between determined, underdetermined, and indeterminate parts of historiography should not be confused with a distinction between chronicle facts and explanations of events. Some dry pieces of historiographic chronicle are underdetermined because of the paucity of evidence, for example, whether Czechoslovakia's Foreign Minister Jan Masaryk was assassinated or committed suicide in 1948, or how popular the Communist takeover of Czechoslovakia was in February of that year. Some explanations of events are determined for example, that the rise of Nazism caused the Second World War, or that the global economic recession of the thirties was a contributing cause of the rise of Nazism. Any speculation about the religion of cavemen who left material remains in the shape of buxom women is indeterminate.

PHILOSOPHY OF HISTORIOGRAPHIC INTERPRETATION

The philosophy of historiography may be divided into the philosophy of scientific historiography, which is a branch of epistemology, and the philosophy of historiographic interpretation that is closely related to ethics, political philosophy, and aesthetics. This book is exclusively about the philosophy of scientific historiography. Yet, it should be noted that there is much work to be done in the philosophy of historiographic interpretation, since the last thorough philosophical discussion of historiographic interpretation is almost a century old. The Neo-Kantian Rickert (1962) and Simmel (1977) differentiated two kinds of values in what I call historiographic interpretation: Ethical values judge whether historical events were beneficial or harmful, worthy of praise or blame. Other values decide whether historical events are significant or meaningful and therefore worthy of mention in historiography. The Neo-Kantians argued that ethical values are not distinctively historiographic. Historians borrow them from ethics.

Historians cannot mention everything they think they know about the past. Their selection of what is meaningful and significant is value laden. Rickert (1962, pp. 19, 86) thought that only human events can be meaningful in this sense, whereas the natural sciences deal with meaningless events. The Neo-Kantians did not consider that all branches of knowledge must be selective in their presentation of what they think they know of the world. All such selections must be value laden. The selection of which problems and evidence to study in the sciences, including historiography, is often associated with research programs or paradigms. While such research programs are present in historiography, some historiographic interpretations select what they consider to be meaningful knowledge of history according to external values that direct them to consider the history of a group they identify with or are otherwise interested in as meaningful. They write historiographic interpretations of the histories of nations or of the world, of global trade or postcolonialism, of genders or children, of everyday life or of high culture, of religion or science. Rickert suggested that the values historians and other "cultural scientists" use are not individual, but cultural. Historians do not question the values they receive from their culture but apply them to understand history within their preconceived cultural axiological frameworks. "What is historically essential must be *important* not only for this or that particular historian, but for *all*" (Rickert, 1962, p. 97). In Rickert's opinion, what is important for all the members of a culture is historiographically objective (p. 136). Historiographic objectivity is relative then to the culture from which it emerges. Greater objectivity and better historiographic interpretations can be achieved by the adoption of a Kantian, universally valid, system of values that would generate a truly universal historiographic interpretation (p. 140). Though I am sympathetic to Rickert's conclusion and though there is insufficient philosophical discussion, descriptive as well as normative, of historiographic interpretations, there is no room in this book for discussions of historiographic interpretations.

It is important though, to emphasize the distinction between the philosophy of scientific historiography, which is a branch of epistemology, and the philosophy of historiographic interpretation, which is a branch of value theory. Walsh (1966) distinguished what historians consider historiography from interpreted, constructed, historiography for the "plain man." Historians, according to Walsh, consider their vocation as the solution of "particular puzzles" (p. 58). The plain man is interested in the contemporary meaning of historiography. All historians and reasonable people would agree that the French Revolution took place in 1789, but their interpretations of it may depend on their nationality and political opinions. Solving puzzles is indeed the normal activity of scientists according to Kuhn (1996). But Walsh underestimated the scope of scientific historiography when he associated professional historiography exclusively with the collection of true particular facts, the minutiae of history, and interpretation with outlining the bigger picture. Great scientific historians like Ranke, Burckhardt, or Mommsen inferred the bigger picture scientifically and did not restrict themselves to minutiae. Within a paradigm, what Kuhn called normal science can indeed concentrate on solving puzzles, but those puzzles deal with explanation and generalizations as much as with the establishment of facts. According to Walsh, professional historians resist the call to interpret history or to recognize, as Walsh did that willy-nilly they interpret history because they spend their professional life tracking new evidence or finding new ways to use existing evidence to establish facts that they publish in professional journals, and frown on books of larger scope that make value judgments. Walsh suggested that historians are unaware of their own value judgments because they share them. "There are no really first-class historians in the country who do not share liberal views, a fact which reflects the settled political and social conditions in which we live. As a result, non-conformist history, of the Marxist variety for example, tends to be technically crude, so much so that it invites no serious interest" (Walsh, 1966, p. 67). British Marxist historians like Eric Hobsbawm, E. P. Thompson, and Christopher Hill falsified Walsh's claim while he was making it in 1960. There is a politically, nationally, and otherwise heterogeneous historiographic community that agrees on what it considers to be knowledge of history. Historians, Marxist and Liberal for example, who can agree on some knowledge claims, disagree in their interpretations. Historians are aware of each other's different interpretations and are able to distinguish interpretation from knowledge in a single text. There are many different interpretations of events like the French Revolution. Reading more than a single interpretation of similar scientific historiographic content suffices to distinguish interpretations from the core of scientific knowledge that diverse historians share.

Since the historiographic textbooks, which too many philosophers of historiography took to represent typical historiography, do not distinguish historiographic knowledge from interpretation, too many philosophies of historiography confuse questions of knowledge with questions of values. For example, Danto (1985) claimed that historiography is distinguished from science by its use of what he called "narrative sentences," that have two or more temporal references. For example, "the First World War began with the assassination of Archduke Ferdinand in Sarajevo," refers at once to that fateful day in 1914, as well as to five more years of war. Obviously, no exhaustive and true description of that day written in 1914 could have included the above true proposition. In Danto's opinion, such sentences can also be found in literature. But in the natural sciences each sentence has only a single temporal reference. Pace Danto, narrative sentences can be found in scientific just as in historiographic texts. Descriptions of events such as the presence of certain humanoid species in Africa a million years ago and the origins of the solar system or the universe refer at once to the events and to processes that resulted in the human race. Narrative sentences can be used in any scientific account of an event that partakes in a larger process.

More significantly, Danto's analysis of narrative sentences conflates separate issues in the philosophy of scientific historiography and in the values underlying historiographic interpretations. Epistemically, we can distinguish the evidence for historical processes from the evidence for events that compose such processes. Clearly, in 1914 there was sufficient evidence to infer knowledge of the circumstances of the demise of Archduke Ferdinand at the hands of Serbian nationalists, but there was no evidence to infer any description of the larger process that would include those events and receive the name: the First World War. Sufficient evidence for the process would be available only after the process would be complete, after 1919. We can possess knowledge of events, without thereby knowing some of the processes they are parts of.

But this narrative sentence is also about the significance of the event, the assassination of Archduke Ferdinand. This, of all other assassination and unnatural deaths among the Habsburgs, is meaningful because of its effects. Had it not resulted in the outbreak of the First World War, it would have been considered less important and would not have been mentioned so often in historiographic interpretations. The significance of this event was not obvious immediately. A historian writing in 1914 while having full knowledge of current events could not have known its full significance, just as contemporary historians cannot yet know the full significance of the terrorist attacks on the United States on September 11, 2001 (Judt, 2001). Since the historical process is open ended, we can never be sure that a seemingly insignificant event will not acquire significance as a result of participating in a process we are unaware of currently. For example, in the history of science we find arcane mathematical models whose discovery had been considered insignificant until a scientist used them in a successful theory. All narrative sentences refer to a process composed of distinct events. But scientific historiography uses narrative sentences to inform us that an event it describes is connected with a process. Historiographic interpretation uses narrative sentences to inform the reader of the significance of the event it describes, given certain values.

Walsh (1966) argued that the difference between science and historiography lies in the criteria used to select which facts are more important than others. Scientists, according to Walsh, select facts according to their causal efficacy. The greater and more extensive are the effects of a class of facts or a particular fact the more important and worthy of mention they are. Though this criterion of causal efficacy is present in historiography as well, it is supplanted, according to Walsh by many other criteria that judge facts important from a contemporary perspective, depending on our identities and values. For example, historians of philosophy are interested in stoic and medieval logic because it anticipated twentieth-century truth functional logic. Walsh's vision of science, as well as historiography is farfetched. Scientists and historians do not pick facts as a farmer may pick ripe fruit off a tree. There are no given scientific or historiographic ready-to-eat facts that scientists or historians just need to select and put together in their disciplinary basket. If we take facts to be units of knowledge of which we are almost entirely certain, then knowledge of facts follows research and is theory laden because what scientists and historians take to be facts depends on their theories, research programs, and the constraints of the evidence. Historiographic, and for that matter scientific, interpretations indeed use various value judgments to select which aspects of scientific research to attempt to communicate to lay readers. But here too, the scientific and historiographic criteria for interpretations are not significantly different. Present effects and similarity with significant aspects of the present are just as significant in science as they are in historiography. For example the interest in extinct humanoid species is motivated both by their effect on the evolution of our own species, or in the case of species that did not affect our own, like the Neanderthals, their similarity and difference from our own species that teach us something about our specificity in our immediate biological context.

PHILOSOPHY OF HISTORY

There are strong epistemic reasons to deny that the philosophy of history, which encompass propositions about history that do not depend on historiographic research and evidence, is a form of knowledge of history. The epistemology of the philosophy of history is distinct from scientific historiography in being idealistic, in purporting to gain knowledge of history that does not depend on evidence and scientific methods of examining it. To use Kantian (1998) terminology, the philosophy of history depends on the possibility of synthetic a priori knowledge of history. The distinctly idealist model for synthetic a priori knowledge of history is of self-knowledge: We know things in the world objectively by using our senses. We know ourselves objectively by what we do and what other people tell us about ourselves. But we also obtain self-knowledge subjectively through intuitive self-consciousness. Though scientific knowledge is objective, we are often more certain of the second, subjective, and immediate kind of knowledge. For example, we know the mind of a child is different from that of an adult often on the basis of our insight into our younger selves, rather than on the basis of empirical research in child psychology. If we could gain knowledge of history that resembles self-consciousness, we would achieve certain knowledge of history without scientific historiography. To do so, the philosophy of history must be that part of the historical process that is conscious of itself. When we know ourselves we are the subject and object of knowledge, united in self-consciousness. Perhaps we can know history similarly in philosophical self-consciousness. "Vico and those who continue along his line of thought, including Hegel, Marx, Croce, and Collingwood, have tried to base the very possibility of historical knowledge on the identity of subject and object" (Rotenstreich, 1958, pp. 38–9). Philosophies of history claimed to be the self-consciousness of what philosophers took to be history. Philosophers of history have constructed fancy metaphysical entities like "ideal eternal history," "the spirit," "organic civilizations," "clashing civilizations," and so on, to designate what they took to be the essence of history. It is difficult, however, to make sense of these metaphysical constructs or find out a method for examining whether or not they exist. Nathan Rotenstreich argued against the claim that philosophical consciousness of history, as a part of its object, the historical process, is in a privileged epistemic position for acquiring certain and unmediated knowledge of history. Pace Hegel, though philosophy of history is a part of the historical process, it does not constitute its self-consciousness (Rotenstreich, 1958, pp. 142–3). Mutually inconsistent

philosophies of history seem to have been reflecting the consciousness of their particular eras rather than of the whole of history: the
decline of the Roman Empire and Augustine; the decline of the Arab
empires and Ibn Khaldun; the enlightenment and Kant; Romanticism
and Herder; the French Revolution and the rise of nationalism and
Hegel; the Industrial Revolution and Marx; the progress of science and
Comte, Spencer, and Mill; the post–World War I demise of the German
empires and their crisis of modernity and Spengler; the fall of the
British Empire and Toynbee; the perceived loss of United States world
economic hegemony facing Japanese and German competition and
Paul Kennedy (1989); the end of the Cold War and Francis Fukuyama
(1992); the ethnic wars that followed the fall of the Soviet Empire and
the rise of fundamentalism and Samuel Huntington (1997).

If the philosophy of history is *the* self-consciousness of history; not
just *a* consciousness of history or how history appeared to people who
lived at a certain place and time, philosophers of history must occupy
a privileged position within the historical process: "Total truth would
be obtained only from the perspective of a present which never ceases
to be present, i.e., from the end of history" (Rotenstreich, 1958, p. 48).
From the temporal vantage point of the end of a process, whether it
is linear or cyclical, it is possible to discern its direction and meaning. Therefore philosophies of history from the Hebrew prophets to
Fukuyama, through Vico, Hegel, Marx, Toynbee, and Kennedy have
had to include apocalyptic themes in their philosophy to justify their
claim to understand the whole historical process. Alternatively, it may
be possible to understand history from the present if there is no significant historical change. For example, Huntington's (1997) clashing
cultures were, are, and will be the essence of a static history. However,
these philosophies of history "proved" that they are situated at the end
of history, or the absence of change in history, by relying on themselves,
they begged the question. So far, it seems that the end of history is a
horizon that constantly recedes as we approach it. Philosophers of history have not been in a privileged position to be the self-consciousness
of history, though the best of them (e.g., Augustine, Ibn Khaldun,
Hegel, Marx, Fukuyama) reflect their local historical consciousness
and therefore are important for understanding the intellectual history of their era.

It had been presumed from about the end of the Second World
War to the end of the Cold War that Toynbee was the last philosopher

of history (Dray, 1981, pp. 79–87; 1993, p. 2). But the radical historical changes that took place from 1989 to 1991 generated a booming market for philosophy of history. Apocalyptic philosophies of history promise that history is ending, and therefore the present or immediate future is the end, the meaning, of history. Many people find such thoughts comforting. If we are at the end of the historical process, there will never be new circumstances to adapt to. If we know where we are going to, the end of history, we will understand the meaning of the past, where we came from and the present. Questions of historical destiny are likely to rise during periods of radical historical change. It is no coincidence that great historical changes tend to be accompanied by the introduction of new philosophies of history that embody the ethos of the era. The debunking of philosophy of history by philosophers like Berlin (1960) and Popper (1964) and historians like Langlois and Seignobos (1926, pp. 1–2) may account for its post-1989 reemergence from academic political science. Philosophy of history will continue to be popular among the religiously inclined and epistemically unconcerned because it purports to tell us our destiny, where we come from and where we are going, and what it all means. These universal questions are felt more acutely during periods of historical discontinuity. Yet, despite periodic popular fascination with questions that cannot have a scientific answer, there is no synthetic a priori knowledge of history. When philosophers consider history, they must do so through and in relation to historiography.

THE RESEARCH PROGRAM

Collingwood (1956), Murphey (1973), and Goldstein (1976) made an obvious observation that was ignored by many philosophers of historiography. Historiography makes no observations of historical events, but presents descriptions of such events in the presence of evidence. There are no given historical facts that historians can select to compose their narratives more or less objectively. Historiography "is a science whose business is to study events not accessible to our observation, and to study these events inferentially, arguing to them from something else which is accessible to our observation, and which the historian calls 'evidence' for the events in which he is interested" (Collingwood, 1956, pp. 251–2). An epistemic and empirical research program in the philosophy of historiography should therefore examine the relations between evidence and historiography. The immediate, primary, subject matter of historiography is evidence and not events.

In a broader epistemic perspective, historians attempt to receive and transmit information that was generated in the past. Fred Dretske (1981) attempted to understand knowledge in general as beliefs caused or sustained by information. Dretske used information in the sense it is used in information theory, as the elimination of uncertainty. Information is transferred from a source, a historical event in our case, to a receiver, a historian for example through the evidence. Received information that is independent of the source is considered noise. Information theorists call information generated by the source that is lost and not transferred, "equivocation." Every historical event generates many information signals, most of them are gradually lost, they are overtaken by equivocation, memories fade, eyewitnesses die, and documents are destroyed and lost. Conversely, the information signals that are received by historians in the present are contaminated with noise, forgeries, later additions, and so forth. When historians attempt to study an event, they must try to separate noise from signal, and infer more information from the information they receive with the assistance of background information and theories. Dretske (1981, p. 71) used the term "nested information" to refer to information that is generated from a signal that connects a source event with a present reception, in conjunction with nomic regulations. For example, if no books are published before there is a literate reading public (a nomic regulation), information about the presence of books at a given period and place contains also nested information about literacy. Following Dretske's epistemic framework, the philosophy of historiography should examine how historians separate information from noise and extract nested information.

In the philosophy of science there are two chief approaches to the relations of theory and evidence. According to one, evidence confirms theories; competing theories are differentiated according to the degree of confirmation that the evidence confers on them. The other approach suggests that theories explain the evidence; theories are differentiated according to how well they explain the same evidence. The theory that best explains the evidence is selected. A third approach considers the previous two to be complimentary: The best explanations of the evidence are also most confirmed by it. Accordingly, accepted historiography may either be confirmed by the evidence, or be the best explanation of the evidence, or both. This book elucidates the relations between historiography and evidence as the key for understanding the nature, limits, and scope of scientific knowledge of the past. The philosophy of historiography must demarcate first an empirical base for the search for historiographic knowledge. Once a likely concentration of historiographic knowledge is located, it is possible to examine its epistemology, scope, and limits. The philosophy of historiography would then be the best explanation of scientific historiography.

In arguing that there is knowledge of history that can be taught, I critique two alternative positions, skepticism and esotericism. *Historiographic skepticism* holds that there is no knowledge of history. Historiography is indistinguishable from fiction, and often reflects ideological and other biases of its authors and their cultures. It is impossible to know with any degree of certainly what happened in the human past (Jenkins, 1991). *Historiographic esotericism* holds that historians do possess knowledge of history, but it is impossible to explicitly explain how or why. Therefore historians cannot teach how to obtain knowledge of history anymore than statesmen of great virtue can teach it to their children and pupils according to Plato. Historiographic wisdom would resemble Socratic virtue; gourmet baking and beer brewing, an art that cannot be reduced to any "recipe"; sets of theories and methods that can be described, replicated, and explained abstractly, or explicitly taught to novices. Instead, such art is the outcome of talent, common sense, insight, and above all practical experience. Historiography would not be a science that can be taught in a class room, but an art that requires a long apprenticeship before joining a guild (Berlin, 1960; Martin, 1989). However:

The problem of hidden epistemologies is that they can mislead practitioners into believing that 'common sense' [for which we should read 'the currently prevailing idea of naive empiricism'] or personal emphatic insight or rhetorical persuasiveness are the only possible arbiters of interpretation and explanation. In that case the rational idea of 'truth' is rejected in favor of pre-rational or irrational 'understanding', which cannot be shared widely. (Lloyd, 1993, p. 4)

First, I examine where knowledge of history is likely to be present. Second, I examine this knowledge as it emerged historically. Third, I analyze how this knowledge is obtained. Fourth, I examine the limits of historiographic knowledge. Finally, I study the possible reasons for limits on scientific historiography. The first chapter in this book lays the epistemic foundations by arguing that heterogeneous uncoerced and large consensus on historiographic beliefs is a likely indicator of knowledge. Therefore, the empirical basis for our examination of knowledge of history should be those parts of historiography where there is a heterogeneous consensus on beliefs on history. The second chapter examines how historiography achieved such a consensus on beliefs about the past in the first half of the nineteenth century. The theories and methods that led to consensus on beliefs were developed earlier in biblical criticism, classical philology, and comparative linguistics. After the establishment of scientific historiography, evolutionary biology and archeology adopted these theories and methods. Together, they constitute a scientific revolution that lasted from the late eighteenth to the late nineteenth centuries. Leopold Ranke assembled, institutionalized, successfully practiced and transmitted to the next generation the theoretical core that generates historiographic consensus. Like Newton, the significance of Ranke is not in what he thought of his enterprise, but in what he actually achieved, the establishment of scientific historiography, its core theories and methodologies, the founding of a paradigm. The misleading quote on the task of historiography "only to show what actually happened [*wie es eigentlich gewesen*]" is mentioned often in relation to Ranke by people who rarely read his actual research. Ranke was the first to assemble a group of core theories and methods that define scientific historiography. These theories have been refined and supplanted during the subsequent development of historiography.

The central third chapter examines how historians, comparative linguists, textual critics, and evolutionary biologists have been reaching consensus about their beliefs about the past, what have been their theories and methods. Philosophers who were innocent of historiography looked in vain for the elusive theoretical background of historiography in the social science and common sense generalizations. That theoretical background lay all the time under their noses, but they looked in all the wrong places, probably because they examined textbook historiography instead of historiographic research. Philosophers of historiography like philosophers of science found it difficult to identify local historiographic methodologies that are routine and habitual and are neither discussed nor articulated, yet are passed on from one generation of historians to the other (Jardine, 1991, p. 90). The actual theories and methods that historians use habitually are about the transmission of information over time, from event to evidence. How does one distinguish noise from information? I argue that the theories and methods of historiography as well as biblical criticism, classical philology, comparative linguistics, and evolutionary biology all engage in inference from evidence to a common cause, an original text, a proto-language, a description of historical events, or a description of an extinct species. These sciences prove first that a hypothetical common cause is the best explanation of similarities within the evidence (between texts, languages, descriptions of events, or species), and second that a particular common cause is the most probable among possible competing common causes. I describe these theories and methods formally, in Bayesian terms borrowed from the philosophy of science.

The fourth chapter examines those areas of historiography where there is no consensus, where the historiographic community fragments into schools and subschools or factions. The absence of consensus in some areas of historiography indicates at the very least that the core theories that define the historiographic community are insufficient for inferring in conjunction with evidence a single determinate historiography. Longterm disagreements do not usually result from different evidence, because following the recognition of a disagreement, historians tend to proceed with a presentation of evidence that would then be shared. Historiographic core theories constrain the possible range of interpretations, but parts of historiography are still underdetermined. Unlike in science, where the evidence is idealized to fit the theory, in underdetermined historiography additional imprecise theories associated with schools are modified ad hoc to fit particular evidence. Since these modifications are rarely made explicit and historians use identical terms, for example, the French Revolution or the Middle Ages, which have similar syntactic functions, garbled communication may ensue. The philosophical project is to understand why we find school divisions and theoretical fragmentation within a united historiographic community that shares a paradigm? Why do historians adapt some of their theories to the evidence rather than the other way round, causing increasing theoretic fragmentation?

Chapter five is devoted to historiographic explanation. I argue that there is no epistemic difference between historiographic explanations and other historiographic hypotheses. They are determined or underdetermined according to their relation with the evidence. Further analysis and the long and arduous debates over the covering law model are epistemically redundant. Chapter six attempts to gauge the epistemic limits and scope of scientific historiography. It examines and rejects various philosophical arguments for and against the possibility of scientific historiography. Then it examines in detail the claim that since historiographic descriptions of events are in some sense unique, there cannot be a confirmed and general scientific theory of history.

The question concerning our knowledge of the past should be of equal concern to philosophers, historians, students of biblical criticism, classicists, comparative linguists, evolutionary biologists, and social scientists. I wrote this book with all these readerships in mind.

Philosophers find often that formal representation, Bayesian probability in our case, clarifies and concentrates the discussion. Some historians and many classicists may not be as used to this form of representation as their philosophical colleagues. To communicate with them, I introduce this formal representation without assuming any previous acquaintance with it. When I use formal representation, I express the same concepts in words, for the benefit of readers who are not accustomed to formal notation.

Since I believe that the philosophy of historiography, of our knowledge of the past, must be grounded in the scientific practices of historians, comparative linguists, and evolutionary biologists, I discuss and offer many examples from the histories of these sciences. In addition to providing empirical proof for my philosophical analysis, these examples demonstrate the relevance of my analysis for the everyday practices and concerns of scientists who attempt to obtain knowledge of the past.

1

Consensus and Historiographic Knowledge

KNOWLEDGE OF HISTORY VS. SKEPTICISM
AND ESOTERICISM

In the Meno Plato (1981) asks what virtue is and whether it can be taught. Plato's Socrates concludes that virtue is knowledge, but this knowledge cannot be taught because the people who obviously possess it have not been able to pass it on to their children and pupils. This book asks similar questions: What is knowledge of history? Who possesses such knowledge? Can this knowledge be taught? "The best proof that history is and must be a science is that it needs techniques and methods, and that it can be taught" (Le Goff, 1992, p. 179). I start in the middle, by asking who is likely to possess knowledge of history. If it is possible to identify a group of people who are likely to possess knowledge of history, the examination of the practices of this group in chapter two should provide an empirical basis for learning what is historiographic knowledge in chapter three, how it is obtained and what is its theoretical and methodological core. I argue in this chapter that consensus on historiographic beliefs in uncoerced, heterogeneous, and sufficiently large groups of historians is indicative of knowledge of history. First, I distinguish my concept of consensus from others that have no epistemic significance. Second, I explain why the unique heterogeneity of the group that reaches a consensus on beliefs favors knowledge as the best among competing explanation of the consensus. Then, I examine the significance of cognitive values in reaching a consensus of beliefs about the past. Finally, I distinguish groups of historians who are likely to possess knowledge of the past from those who are outside of the consensus that is founded on common cognitive values that are likely to be conducive to attainment of knowledge.

CONSENSUS AND KNOWLEDGE

It is surprising to note that historians of diverse interests, historical periods and contexts, creeds, nationalities, political opinions, and other collective identities have independently reached similar beliefs about history and have adopted many of the beliefs about history that resulted from the research of others. Bearing in mind the radical heterogeneity of historians, it would have been reasonable to expect historians to disagree about political or religious historiography as much as they disagree about politics and religion.

Philosophers have often noted that science displays an uncommon degree of consensus among its practitioners. Those parts of historiography that display similarly high levels of consensus among historians may share their epistemic status with science. Consensus is valued in science because it is the result of the achievements of what Kuhn (1996) called a paradigm, a theoretical framework so persuasive that scientists choose to work within it in what Kuhn called normal science. Arguably, consensus on historiographic beliefs may be caused by the achievements of a historiographic paradigm that generates historiographic knowledge.

However, consensus in the sciences is not a goal in itself (Goldman, 1999, 70–1; Roth, 1987, pp. 127–8). Consensus on beliefs is neither a sufficient nor a necessary condition for presuming that these beliefs constitute knowledge (Goldman, 1999, p. 357). Communities have been agreeing on many silly beliefs.

A consensus on beliefs in a group over a certain period of time is a concrete event that can be explained by different competing hypotheses. From an epistemic perspective, the most interesting such hypothesis would suggest that shared knowledge is the best explanation of a consensus on beliefs.[1] The epistemic significance of this hypothesis does not privilege it otherwise; it certainly does not make it true. Alternative hypotheses may explain better a concrete consensus on beliefs. For example, a consensus may be reached as a result of shared biases, common political interests, or coercion. The philosophy of historiography is interested then in comparing the hypothesis that consensus among historians reflects shared knowledge against myriad alternative hypotheses that explain this consensus by the historians' shared class background, shared professional interests, the ever present *zeitgeist,* or for that matter the constellations of the zodiac. Obviously, not all competing hypotheses are of equal merit.

The evaluation of the hypothesis that connects common knowledge with a consensus on beliefs does not require taking sides in the contentious philosophical debate on the definition of knowledge, beyond its independence of the consensus it should explain, since if we define knowledge in terms of consensus on beliefs, the argument is vacuous. A version of the classical definition of knowledge as justified true belief, or a revised version of it as a true belief that was fashioned by a reliable process, or Dretske's (1981, p. 86) proposal that knowledge is belief caused or sustained by information, would all do quite as well. If it can be proved that common knowledge is the best explanation of a concrete consensus on beliefs, this consensus would mark a region where knowledge is likely to be present. This is a useful preliminary procedure for locating knowledge before examining the justification of beliefs, or the reliability of the process, or the flow of information that leads to the beliefs in the rest of this book.

CRITIQUE OF CONSENSUS AS A PROCESS

Philosophers, such as Habermas, who consider consensus philosophically significant, as an indicator of truth and more, are aware of the fact that consensus may emerge for a host of different reasons. If by consensus we mean actual agreement between real people, it may be based on shared mistakes or coercion. Habermas limited his philosophic discussion of consensus to what he considers its ideal rational type, achieved exclusively by force of argumentation. Rescher (1993, p. 13) correctly criticized the philosophic significance of Habermas's concept of consensus because it begs the question of rationality. Habermas attempted to use consensus to elucidate rationality, but he must assume what is rationality to discover which consensus matters in the first place for the discovery of rationality. Any account of epistemic consensus that reduces consensus to a process that should generate the proper, significant, type of consensus similarly begs the question. If a consensus is epistemically significant only if it follows a particular process, then the process is important, not the ensuing consensus. It would be necessary to study the process that leads to consensus, to examine its rationality, to conclude whether it resulted in knowledge or not. Evans (1999, p. 99) argued against the significance of consensus among historians: Academic historians have proved themselves to be easily corruptible. Professional historians in Nazi Germany reached a consensus that was clearly flawed. The only consensus that matters is one based on good rules of professional conduct. Therefore, a discussion of consensus is superfluous. Evans suggested that instead of consensus among historians, it is necessary to examine the rules of historiographic inference that allow good historians to agree. Arguments for a particular kind of consensus generating process (Lehrer & Wagner, 1981) or against it (Caws, 1991; Levi, 1985) are irrelevant for debating the epistemic significance of consensus. They debate the epistemic usefulness of a mooted process for decision making.

It is possible to avoid the reduction of consensus to a process by discussing ideal, rather than actual consensus. The study of an ideal consensus in an ideal situation permits one to ignore actual cases of consensus that were irrational or founded on false beliefs as deviations from the ideal. The later Habermas followed Peirce's tradition in attempting to understand truth by analyzing an ideal speech situation, pragmatic conditions for the achievement of consensus. If "consensus" is used in the Habermasian sense of an ideal consensus under ideal circumstances that allow a process of unconstrained rational consideration, consensus is reduced to the outcome of unbridled rationality. Unbridled rationality does not require a consensus, if a single individual or a machine possesses all the relevant evidence, background knowledge, and pure rationality, that individual or machine will achieve a rational result by itself. A consensus is unnecessary for the achievement of a rational result. Again, a concrete consensus would be insignificant for determining truth since at most it would approximate the ideal process. Rescher (1993, pp. 55–7) concluded that consensus has no intrinsic value that people should strive to achieve.

Rescher's rejection of Habermas's project of understanding rationality and truth through consensus led him (1993, pp. 17–20) to argue that consensus is philosophically insignificant. Still, Rescher (1993, pp. 37–8) acknowledged that scientists find consensus useful for correcting individual mistakes in measurement and for assuring replication and verifiability (in the sense of precise description). Rescher argued further that consensus among experts and practitioners on a belief is "a decisive probative consideration" in its favor. Because "agreement is indicative of an *invariance* of sorts: it reflects the fact[2] that, not withstanding the variation of the particular epistemic stance of different individuals, people's efforts at epistemic problem solving favor one particular outcome. And this sort of invariance is clearly a positive evidential factor" (Rescher, 1993, p. 61). I endorse Rescher's criticism of attempts to reduce consensus to the proper outcome of real or ideal processes. But it is also necessary to clarify and develop Rescher's acknowledgment that consensus can be a positive evidential factor and therefore has an instrumental value in discovering groups that share knowledge. I find Rescher's suggestion that scientific consensus corrects individual mistakes and biases particularly interesting.

THE EPISTEMIC SIGNIFICANCE OF CONSENSUS ON BELIEFS

A concrete consensus on a set of beliefs by a community at a given historical period may be explained by different factors according to various hypotheses. A particularly interesting hypothesis from an epistemic perspective is the *knowledge hypothesis* that holds that given background conditions, a consensus on beliefs reflects common knowledge. If all the alternative hypotheses to the knowledge hypotheses are false or are not as good in explaining a concrete consensus on beliefs, the knowledge hypothesis is the best explanation of the consensus. In such a case, consensus becomes a plausible, though fallible, indicator of knowledge. Though knowledge may be a better explanation of a consensus than all existing competing explanations, this explanation is still fallible because a better hypothesis than the knowledge hypotheses can never be excluded.

One may object that the number of alternative hypotheses to the knowledge hypothesis is infinite. "All sorts of methods can yield consensus: brain-washing, the threat of the rack or burning at the stake, totalitarian control of the sources of information" (Goldman,

1987, p. 120). But it is unnecessary to examine all the logical alternatives to decide whether a concrete consensus on beliefs is a probable indicator of knowledge. In concrete cases of consensus on beliefs, the actual number of mooted alternative hypotheses to the knowledge hypothesis is usually quite manageable because alternative explanations are usually connected with general theories in the sociology of knowledge or social constructionism, whose number is manageable. The knowledge hypothesis does not have to prove its absolute truth, only its comparative advantage over its existing competitors.

I argue that if a consensus on beliefs satisfies the following three conditions, the gap between the likelihood of the consensus given the knowledge hypothesis and its likelihoods given competing hypotheses increases significantly; the group that shares a consensus on beliefs should be:

1. Uncoerced.
2. Uniquely heterogeneous.
3. Sufficiently large.

UNCOERCED

Coercion is no foundation for real consensus, but for "unwilling acquiescence" (Caws, 1991, p. 379). The coercion of individuals may take many forms. Some may be intimidated by threats. Others may be manipulated by their economic dependence. Still others may be browbeaten. These types of influences may lead to the establishment of a discursive hegemony of a particular segment of the population. But short of totalitarian power, they are insufficient for coercing a consensus on beliefs. Some people are not easily intimidated, others have a strong character and do not react to threats, and many people take their own opinions sufficiently seriously to express them irrespective of the effect it may have on their personal fate. Historical experience demonstrates that the establishment of even a local coerced consensus on public expressions of belief in a state-sanctioned dogma requires extensive and extreme use of violence. The Inquisition and the Soviet NKVD secret police enforcement of dogmas required more than intimidation and institutional hegemony. They had to kill and imprison those who would not be coerced by other means to silence them. The overt public consensus in the Soviet Union on Lysenko's theory of biological adaptation did not imply the presence of knowledge. Soviet scientists did not consider the merits of the theory, but the high probability of a long incarceration in the Gulag if they denied it. Indeed, since some scientists defied this official dogma despite the threat, temporary and local consensus was achieved ultimately only by the physical elimination of dissent (Lakatos, 1978, p. 7). Nontotalitarian environments contain many positive and negative sanctions for publicly espousing this or that belief. These sanctions probably skew the aggregate public reporting of views of individuals, in comparison with what honest reporting of their beliefs would have looked like. Such sanctions can coerce public expressions of beliefs by weak, opportunistic, or economically dependent individuals but cannot coerce a consensus.

UNIQUELY HETEROGENEOUS CONSENSUS ON BELIEFS

The unique heterogeneity of a consensus group generates the strongest argument against alternative hypotheses to the knowledge hypothesis. Consensus in a heterogeneous group eliminates competing hypothesis to the knowledge hypothesis, as uniformity of results in a heterogeneous group can confirm hypotheses in controlled scientific experiments. When it is impossible to either control extraneous intervening variables in a laboratory setting or select a random sample and subject it to statistical analysis, scientists attempt to control extraneous variables by selecting an experimental group composed of members who do not share any of the properties they attempt to control. For example, when a pharmaceutics manufacturer wishes to examine the effectiveness of a new drug, it is impossible to select a random sample of humanity, infect it with a disease, inject it with the cure, and see what happens. Nor is it possible to find the effects of age or gender on the progress of the disease and cure by manipulating at will the age and gender of human guinea pigs. Instead, scientists select a heterogeneous group of people who are already infected with the disease but otherwise do not share properties that could be responsible for their recovery, such as age, genetic makeup, socioeconomic background, medical history, and so on. If after taking the new medicine all the members of the heterogeneous experimental group are cured, the medicine is the best explanation of the cure, rather than the various factors that members of the group do not share. If all the members of the experimental group are cured except a subgroup that is homogeneous in say, sharing the stage of development of the disease or in having a particular genetic makeup, it is still warranted to assign the cure to the new drug, because the best explanation of the exceptional, dissenting, group is its homogeneous makeup. As long as the cured group is uniquely heterogeneous, if all the subgroups of patients who are not cured are homogeneous in certain relevant respects, the best explanation of the cure is the medicine.

In the absence of coercion, the more heterogeneous is the consensus group, the easier it is to refute alternative hypotheses to the knowledge hypothesis that link properties that only some members of the consensus group share with the consensus on beliefs. Alternative hypotheses may attempt to explain a concrete consensus on beliefs with particular power relations, or political interests, or ideological convictions, or gender bias, or cultural contexts. But if the consensus group is composed of some persons who are not connected to each other in any power relationship, others who do not share political interests and ideologies, of both genders and many cultures, such hypotheses are less probable than the knowledge hypothesis.

The evaluation of a consensus group as sufficiently heterogeneous depends on existing alternative hypotheses to the knowledge hypothesis. To be considered sufficiently heterogeneous, members of the consensus group should not share any of the properties that plausible alternative hypotheses single out as explanations of that concrete consensus. A group that has been considered heterogeneous may lose this status if all its members share a biasing property that a new hypothesis posits as the explanation of the consensus. For example, feminist philosophers of science developed hypotheses that connect male biases in scientific communities in medicine and biology with their scientific beliefs (Longino, 1990, pp. 103–214; Okruhlik, 1994). Before the introduction of feminist philosophy of science, historians and philosophers of science had not considered the exclusively male composition of certain scientific groups significant for the explanation of their consensus on certain beliefs. It is possible to guard only biases that are connected with alternative hypotheses to the knowledge hypothesis. It is always possible that a relevant bias has been overlooked and the knowledge hypothesis is false despite the apparent heterogeneity of the consensus group. Confidence in the knowledge hypothesis is directly related to the variety and diversity of alternative hypotheses. The more varied alternative hypotheses there are, the easier it is to guard against bias.

People may reach a consensus on beliefs because of their various biases, rather than despite them. A complex alternative to the knowledge hypothesis may combine conjunctions and disjunctions of different factors to explain together the heterogeneous consensus. An analysis of the consensus group may discover separate subgroups that share their beliefs because of their different biases. Miriam Solomon (2001) advocated such an explanation of scientific consensus on beliefs. Solomon suggested that individual scientists choose among competing theories according to their different biases. Scientific consensus on beliefs results from different biases, decision vectors, in her terminology, that somehow have the same effect. Better scientific theories are affected by a greater variety and distribution of biases than theories that follow a more narrow range of biases. Solomon did not regard biases, decision vectors such as ideology or pride, deference to authority or agreement with scriptures as impediments to the achievement of scientific knowledge, but as inevitable necessary prerequisites for scientific progress. If Solomon is right, historians and scientists do not agree despite their different genders, cultures, religions, interests, and so forth, but exactly because they are men and women of different cultures and of various interests. Solomon collapsed the distinction among evidence, empirical vectors in her terminology, cognitive values, theoretical vectors in her terminology, and biases, which she calls social vectors. Altogether, Solomon (2001, pp. 62–3) estimated there are 50 to 100 decision vectors of all kinds that affect theory choice by themselves or in interaction with each other.

Solomon suggested that diversity of biases is the best explanation of consensuses on beliefs among scientists. This explanation is possible, but ceteris paribus is not as plausible as the knowledge hypothesis. Scientific theories are constantly in the process of acceptance and rejection by new scientists who enter science or become acquainted with a theory they were unfamiliar with earlier. If Solomon is right, each new scientist brings into the mental act of theory acceptance a new set of individual biases, yet somehow they all result in the same set of beliefs. Ceteris paribus, the likelihood of consensus on beliefs in a heterogeneous group is higher given common knowledge than given diverse biases because of the low probability that all existing biases will favor the same set of beliefs. Take for example conflicting interests. The knowledge hypothesis suggests that a consensus is likely given that historians with conflicting interests set these interests aside to form beliefs according to what they know. Solomon would claim that consensus on beliefs is likely given conflicting interests. This is possible though unlikely, since it is more probable that causally efficacious conflicting interests would lead to different beliefs. For example, partisan interpretations of the histories of conflicts in places such as Northern Ireland or the Middle East are inconsistent because their authors have conflicting political, national, and religious interests and identities. If historians are capable of reaching consensus on many beliefs about the history of these conflicts, it is more likely given shared knowledge than given their conflicting interests.

Solomon is able to bring empirical examples for her claim because her concept of "consensus" is vague: "Consensus is typically not all encompassing... since usually some dissent remains. The decision whether or not to call a state of affairs 'consensus' or 'dissent' is to some extent arbitrary" (Solomon, 2001, p. 118). Solomon used "consensus" mostly as synonymous with majority opinion or the opinion of an academic establishment, not as unity of opinions. Even sophisticated and convincing externalist interpretations of the history of science (Shapin & Schaffer, 1985) would find it difficult if not impossible to explain large and heterogeneous consensus on beliefs as the result of external political and other interests and biases, not just at the initial stage of scientific innovation and immediate reception, which must emerge somewhere sometime, but also in the many subsequent cases of belief acceptance by an increasingly diversified population of varying interests and biases.

For the multiple biases thesis to be right, the likelihood of the consensus given a bias, multiplied by its likelihoods given all the other biases must still be higher than its likelihood given shared knowledge.[3] *Ceteris paribus*, the knowledge hypothesis, is also simpler and of a wider scope than complex alternative theories (Tucker, 2003).[4]

A consensus on beliefs may emerge as a result of different theoretical assumptions of a heterogeneous theoretical background. For example a consensus on the date of an archeological artifact may emerge as a result of carbon dating, analysis of the architecture of the remains of the house where it was found, its materials and techniques, the discovery of coins nearby, and analysis of the language in which texts found there were written. Accordingly this consensus is founded on various theories from physics, archeology, numismatics, and comparative linguistics (Kosso, 2001; Wylie, 1999). When scientists use different theories to reach an identical conclusion, the theories mutually confirm each other as well as the conclusion. These theories "bootstrap" each other, to use Glymour's (1980) expression. The best explanation of such consensus is still the knowledge hypothesis.

In the real world, there is no universal consensus on beliefs because some people always dissent. There are still people who deny that the earth is round or that it revolves around the sun and others who deny that there was a Holocaust. This led philosophers who consider consensus to be philosophically valuable to attempt to prescribe whose opinions matter for determining whether or not there is a consensus on beliefs. Reliance on professional organizations or academic institutions, affiliations, and certifications is a tempting approach. If all professional astronomers agree that the earth is round and revolves around the sun, it must be because they have knowledge of the heavens and those who honestly dissent must be either ignorant or irrational. At their best, professional and academic institutions should indeed reflect the qualities that make consensus among their members significant as a possible indicator of knowledge. Still, this appeal to authority failed too often in history. Academic and professional institutions have proved themselves to be too susceptible to political threats and manipulation, economic dependence and graft, or the common biases of a class of people who share professional interests and often social background. The corruption of the German academic system under the Nazis, the rejection of relativity in physics, the destruction of psychology, anthropology, and historiography in favor of dark racist fantasies is just the most extreme example of the ever-present temptation of academic and professional institutions, even in previously excellent academic systems, to prefer their institutional, class, and professional interests to intellectual integrity.

The alternative approach I present here does not have to rely on authority, nor does it require universal consensus. It merely requires unique noncoerced heterogeneity: It does not matter if some do not agree to a set of beliefs, as long as the people who do, are sufficiently different from each other to reject alternative hypotheses to the knowledge hypothesis, and those who dissent are sufficiently homogenous to support hypotheses that explain their dissent by particular biases. For example, the group that reached consensus on Darwinian evolution is uniquely heterogeneous, it includes people who are secular and religious, and of many different faiths. The community that upholds the alternative "creationism" is quite homogenous, composed exclusively of biblical fundamentalists, almost all of whom are American Protestants, though many American Protestants believe in Darwinian evolution. Their bias in favor of an anachronistic, historically insensitive interpretation of Genesis is the best explanation of their beliefs.

SUFFICIENTLY LARGE CONSENSUS

The heterogeneous group that reaches consensus must be sufficiently large to avoid accidental results. Small groups can never be sufficiently heterogeneous to exclude hidden biases. Accordingly, statistical samples have minimal sizes. If only four scientists work on a particular problem and they agree on a set of related beliefs, it does not imply that their agreement reflects common knowledge. The four may be a professor, her assistant, a former student, and an untenured member of faculty who needs her vote on the tenure committee. The minimal size of a significant consensus depends on local circumstances such as whether the people who develop a consensus are related socially, the nature of their relations, and whether they attempted to replicate the process that generated the beliefs or merely accepted the conclusions of others on faith or authority (Sarkar, 1997, p. 510). Usually, when the consensus involves hundreds of people who are geographically, institutionally, and professionally dispersed, it is safe to assume that it is large enough. If the consensus is on an esoteric topic, and only a handful of experts are competent or interested enough to reach the consensus, they may posses knowledge, but their consensus cannot function as an indicator of knowledge. It is necessary to follow their reasoning to evaluate the status of their beliefs.

Consensus on beliefs may be epistemically useful as an indicator of knowledge in three cases: First, it may be difficult or even impossible to examine or trace a belief-forming process because evidence for the process is missing. Following this process may be too time consuming: Understanding the process may require specialized arcane background knowledge. For example, lay patients ask for second and even third medical opinions because they are unable to evaluate by themselves the medical justifications for the opinions of any single doctor, but can evaluate that the best explanation for agreements among doctors is that they reflect common knowledge. Second, in some cases, consensus on beliefs may follow many different routes or different justifications, as when different theories reach identical conclusions. Instead of examining each of these routes to the shared beliefs, it is easier to treat the consensus on beliefs as evidence for shared knowledge, irrespective of how it was arrived at. Thirdly, as in our case of historiography, we may be interested in examining in detail the knowledge forming process in a broad epistemic area where it is not obvious where to look for such processes. An uncoerced and uniquely heterogeneous consensus on beliefs may be an indicator of knowledge, a focus for inquiry into knowledge and justification of beliefs: How do historians reach such consensus, with the help of which theories and methods? On the basis of what kind of evidence?

Standard realist philosophy of science considers knowledge to be the best explanation of the success of science (Putnam, 1975). But success is far vaguer, or at best more ambiguous, than consensus. Solomon (2001) divided scientific success into "empirical" and "theoretical."

Though she regards empirical success as necessary: "[N]o one has a good, comprehensive definition of empirical success. . . . Empirical successes can be observational, predictive, retrodictive, experimental, explanatory, or technological – to mention some of the main categories. During different historical periods, and in different fields, there has been focus on one or another kind of empirical success. . . . There is no paradigmatic or typical kind of empirical success. This is another instance of the disunity of science. Attempts to define empirical success run the risk of being too specific, and not including all empirical successes, or too vague, and not characterizing anything" (p. 21–2). "There is a variety in what counts as a theoretical success. Different historical periods, different scientific fields, and different scientists all can have different – even contrary – views about theoretical success" (p. 17). It is easier to agree on what constitutes uncoerced, uniquely heterogeneous, and sufficiently large consensus than on what constitutes success. Success is value laden; persons who hold diverse values may value the same results as successful or unsuccessful. Success may be in prediction and in the generation of technological innovation (Putnam, 1975). But some kinds of scientific knowledge, especially knowledge of the past, can neither generate predictions (Hobbs, 1993), nor have pragmatic applications that make human life more tolerable.

COGNITIVE VALUES AND CONSENSUS ON BELIEFS

It may be argued that the uncoerced sufficiently large and seemingly heterogeneous groups whose consensus on beliefs should indicate knowledge are actually homogenous because they share cognitive values. Cognitive values consider which statements are worthy of being considered knowledge, absolutely or in comparison with competing statements. An alternative reformulation of the knowledge hypothesis could suggest then that consensus on beliefs results from shared cognitive values that determine what a community considers knowledge in the first place. For example, the birth of science was accompanied by a shift from cognitive values that considered knowledge to be the result of faith, revelation or the wisdom of the ancients, to ones that consider knowledge to be the result of empirical investigations. Kuhn (1996, pp. 184–6) suggested that the scientific community is constituted by values (accuracy, consistency, scope, simplicity, and fruitfulness) that are shared more widely than theoretical models. Such values have changed more slowly than theories during the history of science. Scientists may share cognitive values, but still disagree because they dispute the evidence or have different theoretical backgrounds. If shared cognitive values are necessary but insufficient conditions for the emergence of consensus on beliefs, the knowledge hypothesis may have to be qualified as relative to particular sets of cognitive values.

It is possible to avoid this conclusion by denying that consensus on facts, methods, and theories necessitates consensus on cognitive values (Laudan, 1984, pp. 43–6; Laudan & Laudan, 1989). The logical relations between cognitive values and methods and knowledge are neither sufficient nor necessary, though shared axiomatic cognitive values "sure help," as Laudan (1984, p. 46) put it. The historical correlation between consensus on beliefs and consensus on cognitive values may suffice to warrant a discussion of cognitive values as causes of concrete consensus on beliefs.

Cognitive values emerged, became dominant and acceptable in the course of history. If cognitive values come and go for no discernable reason, it is difficult to explain why large uncoerced and heterogeneous groups of scientists and laymen come to agree on them. Some philosophers retreated into metaphysics and explained the evolution of cognitive values by reducing it to developments in the *zeitgeist* (Hegel) or the history of being (Heidegger). Yet, a part of making the often interesting observation that some aspects of culture change simultaneously (Spengler), and perhaps influence each other or are influenced by a common cause, these metaphysical entities do not say much beyond recognizing that various aspects of culture change together, while claiming that human agency can do little or nothing to affect historical changes in cognitive values. Various hypotheses may explain historical shifts in cognitive values. A particularly interesting hypothesis from an epistemic perspective would suggest that a concrete consensus on cognitive values emerges because new cognitive values are more conducive to the attainment of knowledge than those that preceded them, let's call it the *conduciveness hypothesis.* Proving the fallible plausibility of this thesis requires proving only that it is better than competing explanations of concrete uncoerced, heterogeneous, and sufficiently large consensus on cognitive values. The conduciveness hypothesis can be supported by using the strategies that supported the knowledge hypothesis: When an uncoerced, sufficiently large, and uniquely heterogeneous group agrees on a set of cognitive values, hypotheses that attempt to explain the consensus by factors that only a part of the group share are at a disadvantage in comparison with the conduciveness hypothesis.

Hypotheses that explain a uniquely heterogeneous consensus on cognitive values by any particular social, cultural, or historical variables would find it quite difficult to explain the unique appeal of these values to very different people. Sarkar (1997) criticized Kuhn for on the one hand claiming that all scientists choose theories according to five cognitive values – accuracy, consistency, scope, simplicity, and fruitfulness – while on the other hand maintaining that scientists form their opinions according to their various social, cultural, national, historical, and so forth, circumstances. In Sarkar's interpretation, Kuhn suggested that though scientists have different starting points, backgrounds,

nationalities, or upbringing, they travel different roads to reach the
same destination, the five cognitive values. Different backgrounds may
affect the value scientists put on each of the five cognitive values; for
example, some scientists may prefer scope to simplicity or vice versa.
Sarkar is quite right to describe this hypothesis as assuming an incredible accident. If various biases have resulted in exactly the same
cognitive values, this incredible accident parallels Solomon's incredible accident, the transmutation of the different biases of scientists into
consensuses on beliefs. It is possible that various biases would generate a uniquely heterogeneous consensus on cognitive values. But *ceteris
paribus,* it is less plausible than the conduciveness hypothesis because it
implies that the likelihood of a heterogeneous consensus on cognitive
values given each of the biases must be higher than its likelihood given
the conduciveness hypothesis.

For example, scientific cognitive values replaced traditionalist cognitive values that consider propositions that allegedly were handed
down along the generations as knowledge. But the rules that recognize which tradition matters and who are the legitimate bearers of
tradition differ from one homogenous community to another. A consensus on beliefs in a community that upholds a traditionalist system
of cognitive values can be achieved over time only through coercion,
otherwise natural variations and mutations fragment the tradition into
diverse traditions. Coercion can only ensure that the evolution of tradition is uniform. A crisis in traditionalist cognitive values emerges
when members of a community that share a tradition encounter other
groups that have different kinds of traditionalist cognitive values, other
rules for recognition of legitimate traditions. The realization that other
communities have different traditionalist cognitive values shakes the
confidence members of homogenous communities have in their own
traditionalist cognitive values. Some members may react to the discovery of other traditions with fanaticism; others may endorse value
skepticism or search for the kind of cognitive values that could be accepted by a heterogeneous community without coercion. The first two
solutions are unstable, fanaticism is self-destructive and skepticism un-
productive. Better cognitive values are the only stable solution for the
crisis of traditionalism. Scientific cognitive values may be introduced
either while social acceptance of traditionalism is already in decline,

or they may sneak into an entrenched set of accepted but inconsistent cognitive values and generate beliefs inconsistent with those resulting from older cognitive values. Laudan (1984, pp. 60 ff) showed how a contradiction between implicit and explicit cognitive values can cause change. Once these contradictions appear, a revolutionary or gradual process of cognitive values replacement follows.[5]

HISTORIOGRAPHIC CONSENSUS
AND EXCOMMUNICATION

Consensus in a uniquely heterogeneous, large, and uncoerced group of historians is a likely indicator of knowledge. Therefore, our inquiry in the next chapter commences with an analysis of the historical emergence of such a consensus on beliefs about history. It is also possible to prove the existence of such a heterogeneous community of historians who share cognitive values and beliefs *via negativa* by noting historiographic beliefs and cognitive values that are outside the heterogeneous consensus and are best explained by the biases of homogenous communities (Iggers, 1985, pp. 9, 11, 26). Dissenting historiographies include revisionist historiography of the Holocaust; nineteenth-century nationalist historiographies that "discovered" ancient national sagas; the changing Bolshevik historiographies of their revolution and conspiracy theories.

Following the previous discussion, the best explanation of the shared beliefs of homogenous communities that dissent from the historiographic consensus is particular biases. Jewish and Gentile, German and British, right-wing and left-wing historians agree that there was a holocaust. Revisionist historians who deny it are exclusively Nazi sympathizers. There is a wide consensus over the historiography of early medieval Europe that is agreed on by historians of all national identities and by historians who are not Europeans or do not have a national identity. The "historians" who upheld during the late eighteenth and nineteenth centuries the authenticity of various forged national sagas, from those of the Scottish "sage" Ossian to the Czech alleged medieval heroic sagas shared single national identities, and fervently so. Historians from within the consensus community distinguish themselves from illegitimate historians according to underlying cognitive values, as described in the next chapter.

Dissenting historiography usually relies on therapeutic values instead of the standard consensus generating cognitive values that historians of diverse backgrounds agree on. Therapeutic values judge historiographic propositions according to their effect on the psychological well-being of their intended audience. Frequently used therapeutic cognitive values in historiography include: Denial of historical guilt, (for example, denying the Holocaust) Promotion of self-respect through National Myths: or compensating for the sense of alienation and absurdity, by the use of conspiracy theories.

Legitimate historiographic beliefs that are within the uniquely heterogeneous consensus may have therapeutic effects on some groups. For example, a member of a racially discriminated against community such as African Americans may develop higher self-esteem if she learns during Black History Month of achievements of Africans that clearly refute dominant racial stereotypes: for example, of the ancient cultures of Africa and the contributions of African Americans to technology, industry, and letters. But the scientific cognitive values of historiography are indifferent to their therapeutic effects. For example, a member of an unsuccessful or backward community may wish to believe this situation is the result of a global conspiracy against his people directed by some group of people he considers to be better off than he is. Such faith in a conspiracy theory has a therapeutic value because it shifts responsibility for perceived misery to someone else and releases the believer from introspection and self-criticism. But scientific historiography may discover that nobody had any plan against his people or even noticed them. Their misery had no larger meaning and nobody benefited from it. The cognitive values of scientific historiography allow the therapeutic chips to fall as they may.

The distinction between the different groups that accept them is indicated by scientific and therapeutic historiography. A large, uniquely heterogeneous and uncoerced community accepts historiography founded on scientific cognitive values. Historiography founded on therapeutic values is accepted by particular homogenous groups that are clearly identifiable according to their problems and grievances: denying the Holocaust is popular among Neo-Nazis who suffer from guilt for what the Nazis did and have a political interest in dissociating the Nazis from mass murder. Particular national historical myths are promoted by nationalists who suffer from a deficit in heroic prestige. Faith in conspiracies is promoted by particular groups of people who share a sense of helplessness and meaninglessness as the world changes and passes them by. There has always been a market for therapeutic historiography because people and their institutions will always pay to promote or consume therapeutic accounts of their past. The hierarchical struggle for primacy between therapeutic and scientific cognitive values manifests itself in social conflicts. During the nineteenth century various forged ancient poetic documents surfaced in Europe but were exposed despite their therapeutic value for nationalist causes. The poems of the Scottish Homer, Ossian, were exposed in the early nineteenth century as written in the eighteenth century by James Macpherson. In the Czech lands, Tomaš G. Masaryk participated in exposing similar ancient Czech poems as forgeries. These poems were written during the Czech struggle for national self-determination to invent a heroic Czech ancient history. The universality of the cognitive values of scientific historiography is demonstrated by Masaryk's dual role as the foremost leader of the Czech national movement who became later the first president of Czechoslovakia, and as a professional philosopher who made the most significant contribution to the public exposure the forgeries.

Legitimate historians, like Masaryk, accept a hierarchy of values, according to which their scientific cognitive values take precedence over therapeutic values. We may want to believe that a group with which we identify has always been virtuous and faultless; and that whatever blemishes we find in our group are the product of the evil that was done to us unjustly by some other group(s). But if this involves overriding the critical cognitive values of the historiographic community, this is exactly what the uniquely heterogeneous historiographic community should not let us believe in. Bluntly but truly:

The final and really meaningful distinction is not between feminist and non-feminist, or Marxist and non-Marxist, but between competent historians and incompetent ones. Those who put political programmes and slogans before the much more difficult task of patient analysis of the evidence are among the incompetent ones: they may be in fashion, they may briefly provoke useful controversy, but in the slow accumulation of knowledge, their work is unlikely to have great significance. (Marwick, 1993, pp. 329–30)

Legitimate historiography is marked by the precedence of critical cognitive values over other values, not by the absence of other values that generate different historiographic interpretations. Indeed, the presence of values in historiographic interpretation is inevitable (Berlin, 1969). As long as the hierarchical precedence of cognitive to other values is preserved, legitimate historiography can accommodate myriad different and conflicting values and ensuing interpretations.

Historiographic interpretations are affected by the noncognitive values of their authors. This is the main reason for the differences between historiographic interpretations of similar topics. Yet, agreements among historiographic interpretations on their scientific cores are made possible by the identical cognitive values that they share, and a hierarchy of values that gives precedence to cognitive values over other values. Once the requirements of the cognitive values are satisfied, there is ample space for personal interpretations, value judgments, and expositions of value-laden meaning and significance. For example, legitimate Marxist historiography shares its cognitive values with the rest of the uniquely politically heterogeneous historiographic community and gives them precedence over the political values of Marxism (Iggers, 1985, pp. 123–74). When the Marxist historian David Abraham published a book supporting the Marxist thesis that the rise of the Nazis was underwritten by German big capital, but violated the cognitive values of historiography by playing fast and loose with the evidence, another Marxist historian, Henry Ashby Turner, who fully agreed with the thesis, effectively excommunicated Abraham and his book for violating the cognitive values of the historiographic community, Marxist or no Marxist (Evans, 1999, pp. 100–10). Philosophers of historiography have been debating whether historiography should or should not be value laden (Dray, 1993, pp. 46–54). Once we understand the hierarchy that gives precedence to consensus generating cognitive values over other values that divide the historiographic community, it becomes clear that value-laden historiographic interpretation is inevitable, but hierarchically inferior to its scientific core according to cognitive values.

The difference between historiographic interpretations that accept the hierarchic superiority of cognitive values and therapeutic historiography can be illustrated by comparing Holocaust denying revisionist fabrications of the past, and its "contextualization" by Ernst

Nolte's interpretation. The therapeutic-political purposes of both are similar: to eliminate Nazi or German guilt for the crimes committed by Nazis, Germans, and their allies during the Second World War, and to dissociate Nazism, or German nationalism, or radical nationalism from crimes against humanity and facilitate the resurgence of Nazism, or radical nationalism, or German nationalism. The revisionists ride roughshod over the cognitive values of scientific historiography and fantasize a Western conspiracy to forge evidence for the Holocaust as an explanation of the remains of the concentration camps, the documentation generated by German bureaucracy, and the testimonies of contemporary eyewitnesses. Nolte, by contrast, did not deny relevant evidence and the historiographic consensus concerning the events of the Holocaust. His interpretation of the Holocaust varied from that of many other historians, but without violating the basic cognitive values of the historiographic community. Nolte subsumed Nazism under a more general model of twentieth-century totalitarianism that connects it with other atrocious regimes, most notably the Soviet Union. The therapeutic effect is denial of the historical uniqueness of Nazi evil. Nolte also emphasized the benign aspects of the Third Reich, the construction of autobahns, and so on. Finally he suggested a controversial underdetermined theory that holds that one of the causes for Nazism was Bolshevism, so Nazism was a bulwark against the spread of Communism. The therapeutic effect is in shifting responsibility from the German perpetrators to their nasty neighbors in the east (Brockmann, 1990; Lorenz, 1994). Nolte's interpretation resembles the speech of a defense attorney who mitigates after the court convicts his client. He claims that the defendant grew up in a rough criminal neighborhood; he also did good deeds for the community, and was provoked by others. Nolte's causal connection between Bolshevik and Nazi totalitarianism is surely weak and controversial, but it does not violate the cognitive values of scientific historiography; it is insufficient for excommunicating Nolte. At most, his opponents can claim that he is a lousy historian, but not a fabricator. The historiographic interpretations of Nolte's opponents, such as Christian Meier and Jürgen Kocka, for the uniqueness of the Holocaust and the peculiarities of National Socialism resemble a prosecution speech highlighting the incomparable severity of the crime, the absence of extenuating circumstances, and so forth. Yet, this *Historikerstreit* demonstrates that beyond the predictable disagreements on the interpretation of recent history that have obvious implications for contemporary political debates, historians are able to agree and remain within the bounds of a united historiographic community by agreeing on cognitive values though disagreeing on political values.

Skeptical philosophy of historiography denies the exclusivity of the scientific cognitive values of the uniquely heterogeneous, uncoerced, and large historiographic community and their hierarchic primacy in relation to other values. Instead, it endorses value pluralism; it denies the precedence of cognitive values over other values. If skeptics interpret historiography as a narrative, they consider all narratives to be as good, and therefore they do not distinguish historiography from fiction. For Hayden White "historical narratives . . . are verbal fictions, the contents of which are as much invented as found and the forms of which have more in connection with their counterparts in literature than they have with those in the sciences" (White, 1978, p. 82). White concluded that the choice between competing historiographic narratives is undertaken on aesthetic grounds. White (1987) claimed that the existence of the Holocaust is dependent on political interpretation. Spitzer (1990) claimed that the guilt or innocence of Trotsky is dependent on moral values rather than on historical evidence. However, skepticism is manifestly inconsistent with the history and sociology of historiography. The existence of an uncoerced uniquely heterogeneous community of historians that reached consensus on many beliefs and cognitive values must be an incredible mystery for the skeptics. An uncoerced uniquely heterogeneous community of historians believes it can prove that there was a Holocaust and that Stalin and his minions had paranoid delusions. The skeptic would find this consensus puzzling. Had the skeptics been right, historiography should have been as sociologically fragmented as literature or art.

The skeptical interpretation of historiography is founded to a large extent on prescientific historiography and philosophy of history (White, 1973), prior to the emergence of uncoerced uniquely heterogeneous consensus in historiography. For example, Nancy Partner (1995) drew an interesting correlation between the mixing of fiction and evidence-based accounts in classical and medieval historiography and contemporary American "TV docudramas." But she brought no examples from scientific historiography that is agreed upon by a large uncoerced uniquely heterogeneous community to prove her claims.

Scientific cognitive values did not dominate historiography overnight. They emerged first in Germany at the beginning of the nineteenth century and traveled westward during that century. Prescientific historiography, written for example by Gibbon, Macaulay, and Michelet was sometimes well written and consequently had a wide reading public and a market niche during the nineteenth century even if it did not adhere to the new Rankean standards. But contemporary historians regard such historiography as prescientific, even "prehistoric," to use Elton's (1969, p. 14) phrase.

The skeptical conflation of scientific, consensus-based, historiography with prescientific historiography is joined by a confusion of scientific historiography with textbooks about the past. Literary critics may follow "New Criticism" in claiming that there is nothing outside the text, that the text is all we have to analyze. But in scientific historiography, including the historiography of literature, we certainly have far more than self-contained historiographic texts. Text refers through footnotes to evidence. The historian infers historiography from evidence, and documents it by means of the footnote.

Several philosophers argued that the demarcation of areas of historiographic beliefs where historians agree, disagree or just differ is significant for deciding issues in the philosophy of historiography. These philosophers disagreed, though, in their evaluations of the extent of agreements and disagreements in historiography and its philosophic implications. The skeptic Keith Jenkins (1991) held that historians generally disagree because evidence underdetermines historiographic inferences. McCullagh (1998, p. 22) claimed on the contrary that there are "thousands" of things historians agree on and relatively few things they disagree on. Elton (1969, pp. 80–1) thought that there is "a very large body of agreed historical knowledge." Elton assigned disagreements among historians to insufficient evidence, when extant evidence cannot determine one historiographic account as better than others. Goldstein (1976, pp. 196–216) suggested that the presence of consensus in historiography refutes the claims of the skeptics. The extent of historiographic consensus on beliefs can be assessed only empirically, through an examination of the history and social structure of historiography, over the next three chapters.

2

The History of Knowledge of History

Uniquely heterogeneous and uncoerced consensus on beliefs, following a consensus on theories and cognitive values was established among a large group of historians almost simultaneously in much of what would become Germany during the first half of the nineteenth century and spread from there to the rest of the world. The unusual (Laudan, 1984) simultaneity of the acceptance and spread of consensus on historiographic beliefs, theories, methods, and cognitive values occurred because they were imported wholesale to historiography from other disciplines – biblical criticism, classical philology, and comparative linguistics – where they had already been established earlier. The spread of these theories and cognitive values was gradual geographically across the Rhine and the disciplines, through historiography to evolutionary biology and archeology and backward, when newer disciplines exported back improved methods and theories to the disciplines from which they had imported them earlier. The expanding overlapping theoretical basis of these disciplines allowed them to achieve scientific consensuses on beliefs since the second half of the eighteenth century. In this chapter, I trace the historical development of this overlapping theoretical basis. The next chapter analyzes the results of this study in philosophical terms.

An identical set of cognitive values and theories both defines the community of historians, and must be assumed in the current inquiry into the historical emergence of this community of historians. Thus, an aspect of the philosophy of historiography is a part of historiography itself: The philosophy of historiography must rely on the cognitive values and theories of historiography to discover the historical emergence of the conditions of historiographic knowledge, the self-same cognitive values and theories. But the philosophy of historiography does not beg the historiographic question because the cognitive values and theories it shares with historiography are also assumed by other disciplines that uphold them independently. The best explanation for the heterogeneous uncoerced and amazingly wide interdisciplinary consensus on these cognitive values is their conduciveness to knowledge. The only cognitive values and theories to ever win the support of a heterogeneous and uncoerced historiographic community proved themselves to be conducive to the acquisition of knowledge on an extensive scale, across the disciplines.

It is possible to discover the cognitive values and theories of critical historiography through two comparisons: First, a comparison of the cognitive values and theories of historiography with those of the disciplines from which historiography had imported them or to which it has exported them distinguishes the overlapping theories and cognitive values from particular aspects of the various disciplines. Second, a comparison between the cognitive values and theories of the uncoerced, large, and uniquely heterogeneous community of historians that developed in the first half of the nineteenth century with the cognitive values that preceded them should clarify the nature of the scientific revolution in historiography.

At its inception, traditionalist values were the main competing cognitive values to those of critical historiography. Traditionalist historiography judges historiographic propositions according to their connection with traditional authority, in the European context the authority of the Judeo-Christian scriptures, classical Greek and Roman historiography, and various local chronologies or oral traditions. Traditionalist historiography follows oral or written interpretations of these authorities by designated authoritative interpreters. Tradition is derived etymologically from the Latin verb *tradere*, to hand over, hand down, or transfer. Similarly, the Hebrew *masorah* is derived from the verb *limsor*, to hand over or transfer. Respect of the authority of tradition as a cognitive value assumes that the information that is handed over in tradition has been preserved accurately and authentically, through continuous transmissions, as a coin maintains its shape, consistency, and value, if not its shine, through numerous transactions. The authority of tradition can be sustained only as long as faith is maintained in an unbroken, uncorrupted, and accurate informational chain that connects present authoritative information to a legitimate origin. During the Middle Ages, traditionalist cognitive values dominated all fields of knowledge. In philosophy, Halevi's (1964; Tucker, 2002) historical proof for the existence of God as well as Saul Kripke's contemporary theory of proper names (Kripke, 1981; Tucker, 2002), and Gadamer's (1989; cf. the discussion of Gadamer in chapter four) hermeneutics all assume traditionalist cognitive values.

Critical cognitive values compete with traditionalist ones; they counsel suspicion, mistrust of evidence and testimonies (Langlois & Seignobos, 1926, pp. 156–7). Whereas traditionalist cognitive values counsel trust in a tradition, critical cognitive values demand the examination of evidence for the causal chain that allegedly connected past events with present evidence. Critical cognitive values probably emerged systematically for the first time in courts of law in the presence of inconsistent testimonies that led inevitably to the conclusion that at least one is false. The rudimentary method for guarding against false witnesses, the presentation of at least two independent witnesses, also emerged first in the courts and can be found both in biblical and Roman Law, *testis unis, testis nullus.* But it was easy to compartmentalize this cognitive value. It is one thing to acknowledge the advantages of treating interested witnesses with suspicion in court. It is quite another to criticize authorities from the highest political and spiritual echelons of society who trace their tradition to God, the mythical founders of the nation or of religion, or the great scholars and nobles of antiquity. Respect for the authority of antiquity that marks traditionalist cognitive values prevents questioning the motives and interests of the authors of ancient traditions or their contemporary interpreters. Critical, scientific, historiography began when historians "put their authorities in the witness-box" (Collingwood, 1956, p. 237) and subjected them to cross examination to elicit information that they did not want to divulge or were not aware of. Authorities became sources, *sub-judice,* judged by the historian (p. 259).

Critical biblical scholars, classicists, and following them, historians were not the first to note discrepancies and contradictions among documents that were granted authority by tradition. Considerations of contextual, grammatical, and stylistic inconsistencies were raised during debates about the canonization of documents in the early Christian church: Origen questioned the Pauline authorship of "Hebrews" on the basis of stylistic criteria. Dionysius of Alexandria argued that the style and vocabulary of the author of the fourth gospel were inconsistent with those of the author of the Apocalypse of John. But these were ad hoc pragmatic considerations of which texts should be canonized. Further systematic theorizing and application did not follow. Once the codifying institution reached a decision, it linked its own authority with the authority of the canonized documents, and it had to justify this authority by claiming that the authenticity of the canonized documents is a patent absolute truth and enforce this belief by persecuting its deniers. Further discussion of the matter was prohibited among Christians, just as it had been among Jews following the canonization of the Bible and would be among Moslems following the canonization of the Koran. After a politically backed compendium of Holy Scriptures is codified, critical considerations are classified as heresies, as violating traditionalist cognitive values. Even if some people develop critical cognitive values and amend consequently their beliefs, they cannot pass on their discoveries and methods and remain isolated figures.

Inconsistencies and discrepancies between traditionally sanctioned documents have been noticed for as long as people have been reading and comparing them. But people who uphold traditionalist values interpret apparent inconsistencies as conveying a deeper consistent truth. For example, Jewish medieval biblical exegesis consisted to a large extent of explanations of discrepancies in the Bible by invoking an alleged deeper, hidden, layer of meaning. Apparent inconsistencies were considered an economic method for adding, at times mystical, layers to texts. Similarly, historians attempted in the seventeenth century to interpret the scriptures as consistent with the geographical, anthropological, and historiographic discoveries of their era. For example, much work was devoted to presenting the chronologies of Chinese historiography as consistent with the biblical chronology of world history. The attempt to present diverse texts that are patently inconsistent as consistent is based on the cognitive value of faith and trust in the authority of tradition. No document was subjected to public criticism or doubt; such a possibility was not rejected, it could not be considered in the first place. An apparent inconsistency implied therefore that the reader misunderstood at least one of the sources, perhaps because he was not privy to a secret tradition that interprets it correctly.

Lorenzo Valla (1922) proved in the fifteenth century that the *Donation of Constantine*, a document allegedly signed by the fourth-century Eastern Roman Emperor that granted Pope Silvester, and by extension the papal state, vast territory was a forgery. Valla analyzed the language of the document and proved that it was written in Carolinian, rather than fourth-century Latin. Valla assumed a theory of language that takes languages to gradually mutate in time. Each historical linguistic layer is marked by different vocabulary, grammar, and syntax. On the basis of this theory of the history of language, it is possible to date firmly some documents by comparing their language to the language of independently dated documents. Valla inferred the comparative or critical method. Valla applied this method to some of the ancient historians and even to the New Testament. Yet, he was an isolated figure. His use of the comparative-critical method to analyze documents was on behalf of the territorial interests of his patron, the Aragonese king of Naples. When he wrote a historiography of the father of his patron, he did not use critical methods because it would have been against the interests of the Aragon dynasty (Le Goff, 1992, pp. 190–1).

Since the ideology of the traditional, *ancien regime*, social order in Europe was based on uncritical reverence for ancient authorities, political and ecclesiastic powers coerced (by punishment of) and cajoled (by providing employment to) historians to achieve a local homogeneous consensus on historiographic issues, as journalists have been treated by more recent authoritarian states. When the present is the dominant time frame of humanity, journalism is the relevant medium for manipulating popular consciousness. When the dominant temporal reference for locating the place of the person in the universe is the past, historians are important in influencing popular consciousness and consequently popular behavior in the present. The cognitive values of traditionalist historiography and the local consensus on beliefs they generate come under strain initially when a group of people realizes that other groups have other traditions that are inconsistent with their own, though they are justified by similar traditionalist cognitive values. Traditionalist cognitive values were dealt a first blow in Europe with the Reformation. Jews, pagans, and Moslems were excluded from much of Europe for much of the Middle Ages. The dominant Christian tradition developed over centuries detailed explanations of these alternative traditions in Christian terms that preserved traditionalist cognitive values. Martin Luther made a successful frontal attack on the local traditional, homogenous by coercion, interpretation of the scriptures. Though Luther expected texts to speak for themselves, to have a single literal meaning, it soon became apparent that the text spoke in different voices to different readers. Once the coercive element in the Christian tradition was weakened, the tradition began to fragment and mutate, as all traditions do naturally. Consequently, several mutually inconsistent competing traditions congealed. The coexistence of inconsistent traditions weakened the authority of all traditions and of traditionalist cognitive values.

The scientific revolution of the seventeenth century dealt a second significant blow to the authority of ancient texts. If Aristotle was mistaken and corrected by Galileo and Newton, Herodotus and Tacitus may not be in a more privileged position. Facing this assault on traditionalist cognitive values, their advocates could only council *sacrificium intellectus*, not a very convincing solution once tradition has already been subjected to widespread fragmentation and mutation. During the seventeenth and eighteenth centuries, traditionalist cognitive values continuously lost ground and were replaced by skepticism of the possibility of knowledge of history. Instead of valuing all ancient texts and traditions as equally true, they were considered equally false.

The rationalists, most notably Spinoza, considered the Bible a highly unreliable historical document of questionable origins. Others suggested that it is impossible to know anything about history with the exception of recent history. For example, the Jesuit monk Hardouin maintained that the entire codex of ancient historiography was fabricated during the thirteenth century by monks.[1]

Rationalist philosophers like Descartes and Bayle doubted the possibility of any knowledge of history. Locke and Hume were skeptical of the possibility of knowledge of history due to the corruption of transmitted information over time. Their epistemology was essentially individualistic; they did not consider gaining knowledge from comparing multiple testimonies (Coady, 1992). Locke did not consider that events may initiate more than a single chain of information; the tree-like cladistic structure of the historical transmission of information was unknown to him. Laplace, a contemporary of the emergence of critical historiography, considered "the influence of time upon the probability of facts transmitted by a traditional chain of witnesses" (Laplace, 1951, p. 123). The longer the informational chain, the lower is the probability that ancient information was preserved by it. In Laplace's skeptical opinion, the passage of thousands of years renders knowledge of even simple historical facts doubtful, because even if the rate of distortion in each stage of transmission of a tradition to the next link on a chain is low, a long tradition multiplies errors incrementally with the passage of time. Since despite the invention of printing, the decay of any monument to the past will necessitate copying, Laplace predicted that in the distant future facts about our own era that are obvious to us will not be known with any certainty. This analysis led Laplace and others to doubt the possibility of knowledge of all of history but the most recent.[2]

David Hume in his famous rejection of evidence for miracles (1988, pp. 100–19) subjected testimonies for supernatural historical events to critical analysis. Such testimonies are inconsistent with countless other observations that confirmed the universality of the laws of nature. The witnesses are usually unreliable, the manner of delivering the testimonies casts further doubt on their reliability, and the witnesses stood to gain by presenting such testimonies. Testimonies for miracles may be explained by supernatural hypotheses, or by naturalistic hypotheses, such as delusion, hallucination, or deliberate fabrication. The naturalist hypotheses are more plausible than the supernatural ones because they accord with all other reliably recorded evidence. Yet, Hume had nothing interesting to say about the documents that testified to supernatural events or what they can tell us about their authors or when and why they wrote those texts. Likewise, in his *History of England*, Hume's approach to evidence was bivalent, he accepted or rejected it, but did not use it to infer knowledge beyond the intended meaning of the text. A new approach to documents beyond faith and skepticism could originate only in a cultural environment where neither enlightenment skepticism, nor traditionalist faith reigned supreme.

Scientific historiography emerged out of the crisis of historiographic cognitive values to overcome the dismal choice between blind faith in a tradition and equally blind skepticism. Critical historiography accepted from the enlightenment its critical cognitive values. Yet, to be able to say something positive about the past, to gain knowledge of history, historiography had to use theories about the transmission of information in time.

BIBLICAL CRITICISM

The first application of critical cognitive values in conjunction with new theories and methods to generate new knowledge of the past from present evidence was in biblical criticism. The new cognitive values allowed scholars to consider the scriptures as evidence rather than as knowledge *tout court* or useless noise. The foremost traditionalist documents of Western Civilization, the Judeo-Christian scriptures, were not the easiest subject matter for critical analysis due to the dearth of external evidence, especially during the eighteenth century prior to the archeological discoveries of other documents from the biblical period in Egypt, and Babylon and the unearthing of material evidence in biblical sites. But the cultural significance of the scriptures as well as the institutional basis that existed for their examination in academic theology departments made them the obvious first choice for the application of critical cognitive values.

The earliest critical editions of the scriptures, including all available textual variations were published in the early eighteenth century. In 1753 Jean Astruc analyzed Genesis as a composite of four sources, according to the four different proper names used to refer to God in the book. Astruc assumed a rudimentary theory of language: As languages change in time, some parts change more slowly than others. The proper names used to refer to the concept of God, must change more slowly because they are more important for their users than common everyday words. Astruc added the assumption that later religious editors who revere the deity would not dare revise its proper names, though they may edit the text and update the vocabulary of other parts of the text. Therefore, the use of different proper names for God in a single text indicates that the text is a composite of documents that were written at different times and/or places. Though rather crude in comparison with later biblical criticism, these basic theoretic assumptions about linguistic change sufficed to discover the composite and documentary nature of Genesis. Yet, Astruc did not found a paradigm because he did not found a community of scholars who shared his theories and methods. Two decades later, Reimarus and Johann Salamo Semler found the paradigm in biblical criticism because they were followed by a uniquely heterogeneous large community that shared a philological research program and critical cognitive values. This community was initially homogeneous, composed exclusively of German-speaking Protestant academics. But within a century, it expanded and became heterogeneous, composed of scholars of most if not all branches of Christianity, other religions, no religion, and all nationalities. No agreement on issues relating to the scriptures is even remotely as heterogeneous as that of the community of biblical critics.

As a paradigm, biblical criticism started circa 1780 (Rogerson, 1985, p. 18). The main theology centers at the universities of Halle, Jena, and Göttingen trained their students in critical methods. From the founding of the University of Berlin (1810–1819), de Wette, who institutionalized the paradigm in biblical criticism, taught at the university of the Prussian capital, where Ranke, the paradigm founder of historiography, had been based since 1825. Anticritical backlash from traditional *confessionalists*, which consequently limited the freedom to exercise critical cognitive values in theology departments appeared in Germany only in the late 1820s. By then the critical "genie" had already been out of the bottle (Rogerson, 1985, p. 139). Once scholars adopted critical cognitive values for studying the scriptures as evidence and survived it politically, the export of their critical values, theories, and methods to less politically charged fields like historiography was smooth and risk free.

A number of external factors may explain why a community united by a critical approach to the scriptures emerged in the Protestant principalities of what became Germany. By 1860 there were 21 faculties of Protestant theology in Germany. The Humboldtian research university model provided stronger incentives to faculty members to be productive than competing academic systems. German members of theology faculties could rely further on support from experts in philology departments. By comparison, England had only the two universities until 1828, and they resembled finishing schools for the upper class more than research institutions. Even after the University of Durham and London's Kings College were founded, critical research was limited by allegiance to the established Anglican Church. In the German principalities, economic resources, separation of church from state and political freedoms encouraged the development of new sciences especially in disciplines where countries like Britain and France had not already established dominance. The romantic backlash against the Enlightenment in Germany following the French Revolution further encouraged studies of the past, though the lingering influence of Enlightenment cognitive values sufficed to mandate an examination of the past through the use of new critical methods.

Eichhorn's *Einleitung in alte testament,* Introduction to the Old Testament (1780–3) (Wolf, 1985, pp. 227–31), substantiated the documentary hypothesis that the Bible is a composite of many different documents that were written by different people at different times in different places and were edited and stitched together without modern sensitivity to historical authorship after the return of the exiles from Babylon. Eichhorn supported this hypothesis by a comparison of linguistic similarities and differences in the Bible. Eichhorn assumed a theory of the historical development of language as constantly mutating. The best explanation of textual linguistic similarity and difference is the historical period and space of composition. Consequently, texts that share a similar vocabulary and grammar were written at the same time and place. Languages absorb foreign words during historical periods when its speakers interact with speakers of source languages. The presence of borrowed foreign words in a text dates it to no earlier than the historical period when speakers of the two languages came into contact.

The method that follows from this theory is the comparative philological analysis of texts. Since the language of the Pentateuch is not significantly different from that of Samuel and Kings, it could not have been written 500 years earlier, but was given its current form at the same time as Samuel and Kings. Since different parts of Genesis use different names for God, Eichhorn followed Astruc in dividing Genesis into Jehovah and Elohim sources that originated in different times or places. Since the language of various parts of Psalms is different, it must be composed of documents from various times and places. The later texts in the Bible can be dated according to their use of Aramaic words, borrowed after the Babylonian exile. Jeremiah and Ezekiel are replete with such Aramaic words.

Eichhorn concluded that Chronicles was written after the Babylonian exile on the basis of a comparison of its religious conceptual framework with that of Samuel and Kings on the one hand, and the concepts of the Zoroastrian religion of ancient Persia on the other hand. Chronicles mentions Satan often and has a developed angelology. By contrast, Samuel and Kings make no reference to Satan or a developed angelology. In Chronicles, Satan induces King David to conduct the prohibited census, whereas in Samuel it is God's wrath. The Zoroastrian religion of ancient Persia was dualistic; it had two main gods that represented good and evil. Eichhorn proposed that Persian influence is the best explanation of the similarity between the dualistic divine framework of Chronicles and the religion of ancient Persia that is not shared by Samuel and Kings. This explanation makes the evidence more likely than, for example, a spontaneous evolution of Judaism or a faction of it that invented Satan independently of the Persian religion and wrote Chronicles at the same time as Kings was written by another faction that did not recognize Satan. Eichhorn must have assumed a theory that evaluates the probability that Judaism mutated spontaneously to become dualistic as far lower than the probability that it incorporated elements of the Zoroastrian religion as a result of coming into contact with it during the Babylonian exile.

Consequently, it is possible to date Chronicles to the period that followed the contact between Jews and Persians. Further discrepancies between 2nd Samuel, 1st Kings, and Chronicles led Eichhorn to believe that the earlier books could not have been direct sources for the later book. The best explanation for the overwhelming similarities was in Eichhorn's opinion a lost common source that reached the author of Chronicles in a short and mutated form (Rogerson, 1985, p. 22).

W. M. L. de Wette in *Contributions to Old Testament Introduction* (Halle, 1806–1807) agreed with Eichhorn that Chronicles was composed long after Samuel and Kings, as well as on the reasons for believing so. Yet, de Wette argued against Eichhorn that there is insufficient evidence for claiming that Chronicles shared a lost common source with Samuel and Kings. A more parsimonious hypothesis is that Samuel and Kings were some of the sources for Chronicles (Rogerson, 1985, p. 28). The similarities between Chronicles, Samuel, and Kings cannot be coincidental. So, either they had a common source, or the earlier books affected the later book. Wette appealed to the cognitive value of parsimony to prefer the later hypothesis.

Descriptions of religious practice are more particular and meticulous in Chronicles than in Samuel or Kings. They reflect a more standardized and complicated ritual that fits late practices in the Jerusalem temple. In its description of the revolution of King Joash, Chronicles exaggerates the role of the Levites, in comparison with the description in Kings, in terms that fit their later dominance in Jerusalem (Rogerson, 1985, pp. 30–1). De Wette's best explanation of these discrepancies is that Chronicles had a Levite and Judaic (the Kingdom of Judah as opposes to Israel) bias in comparison with Samuel and Kings. The best explanation of the similarities between Chronicles and ritualistic practices in the Second Temple is a late date of composition. To justify this explanation, de Wette must have assumed a theory of the role of historiography in traditionalist cultures: When the legitimization of institutions, practices, social stratification, ritual, and so forth, is founded on their antiquity, on precedent, interest groups would try to present, even falsify historiography to fit their desirable present or future.

De Wette used Astruc and Eichhorn's theories of language and historiography in traditionalist societies to argue that the Pentateuch was composed much later than the events it describes could have taken place; some of its parts may have been composed as late as during the early period of the second temple. Had the Pentateuch been written 500 years before the monarchic period, it would have been written in an archaic form of Hebrew, not in the same language as the monarchic books of the Bible. The Pentateuch ascribes to Moses religious practices and institutionalized structures that could have been introduced only in an organized temple with a specialized priesthood during the monarchy. De Wette suggested that the discovery of the Book of Law in the temple during the reign of King Josiah, as described in II Kings, refers to a part of Deuteronomy. Much of the Pentateuch could have been written to legitimize King Josiah's late seventh-century BCE reforms and the attempt to centralize and monopolize religious worship in the Jerusalem temple. This hypothesis has been accepted for the past 200 years (Finkelstein & Silberman, 2001). The Pentateuch is not mentioned in Samuel and Kings, quite possibly because it had not been written yet. The Samaritan exclusive acceptance of the Pentateuch and the Book of Joshua was presented as evidence in favor of the antiquity of the Pentateuch. Arguably, the Samaritans adopted those parts of the Bible that had already been codified before they seceded from mainstream Judaism. Wette's alternative explanation of this evidence is that the Samaritans adopted these books later, during the era of the second temple from the returning Jewish exiles, after much of the Bible had already been assembled. Gesenius endorsed this approach suggesting that the Samaritan Pentateuch is as late as the establishment of the center on Gerizim in the late fourth century BCE that resulted in the break with mainstream Judaism, centered in Jerusalem.

In his 1815 *History of the Hebrew Language and Script*, the philologist Gesenius accepted the theory of linguistic change that his predecessors had used in combination with a more detailed comparison of the documents that compose the Bible. Chronicles is a late book that used Samuel and Kings as sources because it substitutes newer words for more archaic forms in Samuel and Kings. Chronicles also added grammatical glosses, explanations, and minor interpretations for the earlier books, proving that its author needed to explain the older materials to readers who could no longer understand them without an interpretation. Gesenius argued that Deuteronomy is later than the rest of the Pentateuch because its language resembles more that of Jeremiah than that of the rest of the Pentateuch. The language of the rest of the Pentateuch is not different from that of the monarchic books. It was written most probably just before the exile. This hypothesis has become the subject of a consensus (Rogerson, 1985, p. 52).

Gramberg attempted in *Critical History of the Religious Ideas of the Old Testament* (posthumous 1830) to date the old Testaments, assuming the theory about the function of historiography in traditionalist cultures to legitimize new practices by inventing their ancient history. The Pentateuch and Joshua were composed in connection with King Josiah's centralist political and religious revolution because these books are replete with projections on earlier periods of post-revolutionary practices. Gramberg suggested that these precedents were invented as part of the religious and political struggle of the Jerusalem religious center and priesthood against existing decentralized polytheistic practices.[3] Gramberg suggested that the best explanation of the biblical "prophecies" is that they were written after they had been "fulfilled," rather than expand our metaphysics to include the possibility of foretelling the future through divine inspiration. Assuming that biblical prophecies were written after they had been fulfilled, it is possible to know the earliest possible date for their composition. For example, Abraham is presented in Genesis as a precursor of King David, therefore it could not have been written before the establishment of the Davidian dynasty in Jerusalem. The Book of Joshua presents retroactive explanations of later monarchic realities, but does not explain the reality that the Book of Judges reflects. Therefore Joshua must have been written after the materials that compose Judges (Rogerson, 1985, pp. 57–63).

The founders of biblical criticism have been comparing parts of the Bible as units of evidence together with evidence about the Persian religion and language to infer their origins, concluding that the best explanation of the similarities and differences between the various linguistic levels, religious conceptual schemes, and descriptions of social, political, and ritualistic practices is that most of the Bible was written in conjunction with King Josiah's revolution, while the later books were written during and after the Babylonian exile. Consequently, the Bible is not a reliable source for history prior to the seventh century BCE, but can serve as evidence for later history.

CLASSICAL PHILOLOGY

Theories and methods that were developed in biblical criticism were exported next to the analysis of ancient Greek and Latin texts. A poorly paid, ill-populated, and culturally marginal field like classical philology in eighteenth-century Germany drew on the achievements of the more central and prestigious theology. Friedrich August Wolf applied in his *Prolegomena ad Homerum* (1985/1795) the new critical theories to analyze the *Iliad* and the *Odyssey*. "Wolf's main achievement... was the annexation for classical studies of a sophisticated set of methods formed by a contemporary [Eichhorn] in another field of work [biblical criticism]" (Grafton et al., 1985, p. 26). The *Prolegomena* initiated a paradigm shift in classical studies. The young scholars who filled the new Humboldtian Classical Philology departments accepted Wolf's paradigm against the older generation of philologists. For example, F. K. Heinrich followed Wolf's model in 1802 to analyze the origins of Hesiod's *Shield of Hercules*. Despite doubts about Wolf's originality, his

status as a paradigm founder has not been questioned. "Why did contemporaries – and even Wolf himself – come to see the *Prolegomena* as
the source rather than the tributary of theological research, the foun-
tainhead of Tübingen rather than an offshoot of Göttingen?" (Grafton
et al., 1985, p. 29). The answers for this question are just as relevant
for a parallel question about Ranke's status as the paradigm founder
in historiography. Wolf's English language translators mention first
some external, institutional factors: Humboldt, the Prussian Minister
of Education and the founder of the University of Berlin and his fellow academic reformers needed a reason to make classical philology
a central area of study since the French Enlightenment philosophers
scorned it. The *Prolegomena* legitimized this politically motivated decision. "If Wolf had not written such a book, it would have been necessary
to invent it – and to create much ballyhoo about it" (p. 29). Yet, these
externalist factors, political motivation, and facilitating institutional
structures do not explain why Wolf's book, of all the books in classical
philology, was successful in founding a uniquely heterogeneous consensus of beliefs, a paradigm. Grafton and coauthors suggested that
the *Prolegomena* had some internal virtues, good style, explicit formulation of the rules of criticism collected from the best biblical critics of the
eighteenth century, and above all, Wolf was able to write about philology without being boring! I think that the successful reception of the
Prolegomena owes much more to the prior acceptance of the theories
of biblical criticism. The intellectually informed public in what would
become Germany had already accepted Wolf's theories and methods
before he applied them to classical philology. As Grafton and others
(pp. 19–26) note, Wolf's *Prolegomena* (1795) was directly modeled after
J. G. Eichhorn's *Einleitung ins Alte Testament* (1780–83). Eichhorn studied in Göttingen under Heyne, who was also Wolf's teacher. Heyne
affirmed that Wolf copied the methods of biblical criticism. Wolf approached the *Iliad* as Eichhorn approached the Bible. The text of the
Bible went through many changes and a change of alphabet, word
divisions, and the introduction of vowels. Accents and marginal notes
of variant readings were introduced by the *masoretes*, Hebrew gram-
marians of the first millennium CE. The Venice *scholia* resembled the
Masorah in producing the "authorized" version of Homer. Neither preserved individual recensions or attempted to distinguish earlier from
later sources (Grafton et al., 1985, pp. 19–26).

Wolf considered the Homerian texts as evidence. He accepted from biblical criticism the principle of *recentior non deterior*; the newness of a document does not imply that it is less reliable than an older one, if it is based on an older and reliable source. Elegant and clean texts are less reliable than ones that contain mistakes because they are likely to have gone through later editing (p. 59).

Wolf assumed that no long text such as the *Iliad* can be written down before a number of necessary conditions are satisfied: Material conditions include the presence of appropriate writing materials. Stones, woods, pieces of metal, and waxed tablets are not useful for the preservation of long texts. The first appropriate material in Greece was parchment. Ancient sources testify that the discovery of the usefulness of goat or sheepskins for writing took place after the first Olympiad (776 BCE). Papyrus was adopted only in the sixth century BCE. A system of writing, appropriate for the spoken language of the text, is another necessary condition. It must have taken time to adapt the Phoenician system to the Greek language, more time for it to be used for composing long texts in a crude 15-letter alphabet, and even more time for that knowledge to be disseminated widely. The 24-letter Greek alphabet in which the Homeric sagas are written dates only to 403 BCE.

Laws are shorter and their fixed form is more important for society than the codification of heroic sagas. Therefore the Homeric poems could not have been written before the first laws in Greece. There is no evidence for written laws in Greece before 664 BCE. The first certain system of written laws is Solon's from 594 BCE. Since prose, unlike poetry, cannot be memorized, nobody would compose it without a method for preserving it. The emergence of prose must follow the widespread use of writing (p. 91). Therefore, the presence of prose is an indicator of widespread literacy. In the case of Greece, this indicates again an era no earlier than that of Solon. Book-length texts could and did appear only during the reign of the Athenian tyrant Pisistratus (560–527 BCE).

These considerations led Wolf to defend the historiographic hypothesis that the Homeric poems were composed and transmitted by illiterate rhapsodists. There is no intrinsic evidence to the contrary because the Homeric poems do not mention writing. The rhapsodists spent all their lives reciting, memorizing, and inventing poems. This led to corruptions as memory failed, poets improved on what they received with their own verses, and strung together poems of diverse sources. They were not interested in preserving authenticity, but in satisfying an audience. Wolf conjectured that the poems are too long and reflect too much knowledge for any single man to have invented or memorized, or even performed all at once.

The documentary hypothesis is further supported by inconsistencies in the narrative of the *Iliad*, for example, in its depiction of Achilles as heroic and unheroic. The *Odyssey* does not have a unified plot. At this early stage of classical philology, Wolf was still unable to express explicitly general rules for distinguishing documents on stylistic grounds, so he resorted to consistent subjective judgment: There are "a number of obvious and imperfectly fitted joints, which I have found, in the course of very frequent readings, to be both the same and in the same places" (p. 127). Wolf brought as examples several places where the poetic flow is broken or the style changes radically. Unusual words and phrases are also evidence for late imitations that were inserted into the text.

Finally, Wolf presented a general theory of the oral fragmentary sources of national poetic documents that are written hundreds of years after their initial composition in mutated forms. He supported this theory by considering the Bible, Charlemagne's collection of ancient German poetry, seventh-century CE Arab Divans collected in the Koran, and the connection between the (later proved as forged) Scottish poems of Ossian and the Druids (pp. 145–6). Once codified, such poetic collections were copied and corrected, creating variations. The critics-editors amended the texts according to what they took to be most befitting the poet, not what their sources could have sung but what they should have sung in the opinion of the editors. This independently confirmed theory can deduce Wolf's hypotheses about the origins of the Homeric poems.[4]

There is ample evidence for many recensions of the *Iliad*, unidentified by their authors or date, just their location. The task of the classical philologist is to infer a description of the history of the text from its extant versions and historiographic evidence about its editing. This task should be easier than that of biblical critics: "The orientalists would rejoice, I believe, if it were certain in even three places what Gamaliel or another Jewish teacher of the early period read in Moses and the Prophets; in Homer we know what Zenodotus read in some four hundred passages, what Aristophanes read in two hundred, and what Aristarchus read in over a thousand" (Wolf, 1985, p. 173). The Bible and the Homeric texts started as separate texts that were conjoined at a certain point. It is not clear who exactly made the collection and according to which principles. The collection is a product of chance rather than skill, it conflates texts old and new and of various types. The collection was followed by various recensions, various copying, and multiplications of variations. For a while the Bible was not considered holy enough to prevent editing and rewriting. When the Jews began to believe that God dictated the text they began to preserve every error and created the *Masorah.* "The Masorah is full of all sorts of absurdities and feeble, superstitious inventions; this mass of [Homeric] scholia has no lack of similar contents.... Greeks rave in one way, Jews in another..." (Wolf, 1985, p. 226).

Wolf assumed two theories about the transmission of information over time: The first theory explains the evidence for temporal correlation between the writing of laws, sagas, and prose by the development of material conditions such as ink and paper, and a convenient alphabet for writing long texts. The second theory explains the fragmentary and linguistically and thematically inconsistent nature of written sagas by the stitching together of poems that were developed over centuries by many illiterate professional bards. This theory received further independent confirmation over a century later by anthropologists who studied such bards in Yugoslavia and later in Finland.

COMPARATIVE LINGUISTICS

Textbooks of comparative linguistics usually list Sir William Jones's speech in Calcutta in 1786 as the first presentation of the Indo-European thesis, the first theory of scientific comparative linguistics. Jones suggested that the strong affinity in roots of verbs and forms of grammar between Sanskrit, Latin, and Greek could not be accidental. They must have sprung from a common source that may no longer exist. A weaker similarity with Gothic, Celtic, and Old Persian indicated in Jones's opinion that these languages could also belong to this family (Jones, 1967/1786, p. 15). This indeed has the ring of the familiar Indo-European thesis. However, the rest of this lecture proves that despite this conclusion, Jones cannot be considered a precursor of comparative philology. Jones went on to speculate that there was a common source for Phoenician and Indian (Nágarí) script. The similarities between Indian and Greek philosophy, and Indian, Greek, and Scandinavian mythology and religion indicated in his opinion similar influences. Similarities between the religions of the Incas and the Indians indicate in his opinion that the Incas may have been the descendants of the worshipers of Rama. Architectural similarities with Africa, the pyramids, and similarities in script with Ethiopian suggested to Jones that Hindustan and Ethiopia were settled by the same people. Jones perceived in monuments in Bengala and Bahar a depiction of racial characteristics that resemble those of Ethiopians. Obviously, Jones simply inferred from any perceived similarity that one caused the other or had a common cause. Without relevant theories, everything may appear similar to anything else. Concentrated observation of any random distribution of things results in perceptions of patterns and similarities. Similarities do not imply causal relations. Jones made one lucky guess about the common origins of the Indo-European languages among many nonsensical guesses; his guess had no scientific reason, no theoretical background.

Prescientific seventeenth-and eighteenth-century linguistics already possessed the idea of an extinct language that gave rise to the main European and Asian languages, an evolutionary model of the development of languages into dialects and separate languages, and the distinction between borrowed and ancestral languages (Metcalf, 1974). During the seventeenth and eighteenth centuries there were attempts to connect the Persian, Greek, Latin, Germanic and Slavic languages, and Celtic to an ur-language, presumably spoken in a region of the Caucasus by Scythians, who were associated with the descendants of the biblical Japheth, the son of Noah. This hypothesis could be entertained in Christian cultures consistently with traditionalist cognitive values since Genesis tells that there had been a universal language that mutated after the fall of the tower of Babel. A cladistic model of the history of language was consistent with Genesis. Initially, linguists, like Jones, attempted to infer historiographies of languages from similarities in sound. Etymologies were based on streams of wild associations without any theory of language to support them. For example, Becanus argued in the sixteenth century that his native Flemish is the original Scythian language from which all other European languages were derived. Becanus "supported" this claim by the similarity between the

name of the biblical Japheth's eldest son and the names of the mythical founders of Antwerp. . . . Grotius claimed that the native languages
of the Americans are derived from Norwegian, a historical claim useful to legitimize the territorial ambitions of his Swedish patrons in
America.[5]

Johannes de Laet's *Notae* (1643) foreshadows modern comparative
linguistics because it presented a theory that distinguishes the kinds of
linguistic similarities that are indicative of common origins. De Laet assumed that languages constantly change and expand to accommodate
new forms of society, technology, culture, and so on. Related languages
may preserve similar vocabulary only of basic words that had existed
before they differentiated from each other: Words that refer to parts
of the body, family relationships, the first few numbers, and so forth.
He also assumed that some words mutate more slowly than others, for
example, geographical terms. Therefore, the words whose sounds are
genetically indicative are those that refer to most common domestic
objects, numbers, parts of the body, family relationships, the method
of counting, and geographical terms. De Laet used his method to conclude that Norwegian and Icelandic, Welsh and Irish are clearly related
whereas Welsh, Danish, and native North American languages are not
related.

De Laet assumed that on average indicative words in separate languages mutate at a constant rate. Therefore, the degree of similarity
between the basic relevant vocabularies of related languages is commensurable with the period of time that elapsed since these languages
differentiated from an ancestor language. De Laet used this theory to
argue against Grotius's hypothesis that the North American languages
split from Norwegian after English had split from German. Since the
approximate date of the split between German and English is known
on the basis of independent evidence, and the similarity between Norwegian and Native American languages is clearly smaller than that
between English and German. De Laet is a true precursor of scientific
comparative linguists, however he did not become a paradigm founder
because no community of scholars used his theories systematically to
solve problems in comparative historical linguistics.[6]

Scientific comparative linguistics is associated usually with Rasmus
Rask's, *Investigation on the Origin of the Old Norse or Ice-landic Language,
1814*. Though Rask published in his native Danish, his book was read

by Jacob Grimm and through him influenced the community of comparative linguists, most notably in Germany. Rask was inspired by Linné's *Systema Naturae* to catalogue languages according to their similarity and genetic relations using the following hierarchic categories: (1) *race* (e.g., Indo-European), (2) *class* (e.g., Germanic), (3) *stock* (e.g., Scandinavian), (4) *branch* (e.g., Southern Westgermanic), (5) *language* (e.g., Danish), (6) *dialect* (e.g., Jutlandic). Rask proposed theoretically based criteria for genetically relevant similarities between languages and groups of languages: The oldest stock of words is that of the most essential, concrete, and indispensable primary words, in contrast to technical terms, words of politeness or commerce with others, social relations, education, and science. Additionally, Rask stipulated that to be considered theoretically relevant similar words must be connected systematically according to phonetic laws of the transition of letters from one language to another, for example, the Greek "e" and "o" turn into the Latin "a" and "u" respectively; other phonetic rules can transform Greek or Latin words into Icelandic ones.

The rate of change of grammatical structures is slower than that of vocabularies, even basic ones, partly because they are more resistant to foreign influences. Languages like English and Spanish that absorbed a great deal of foreign words and lost some of their own inflections did not absorb the inflections of languages that affected their vocabulary like, respectively, Icelandic and French, Arabic and Gothic. Grammatical agreement in inflection and structure is a more reliable indicator of a genetic relationship than vocabulary. Languages tend to mutate in the direction of losing their grammatical inflections and endings. This theory is confirmed by the greater simplicity of Danish in relation to Icelandic, English in relation to Anglo-Saxon, Italian in relation to Latin, modern in relation to ancient Greek, and contemporary in relation to old German. Therefore, newer languages have simpler grammar than their progenitors and related languages whose grammar was codified earlier (Rask, 1967, pp. 31–7).

Rask divided language into pronunciation, grammar, and lexicon. Neighboring languages affect only parts of the lexicon. Other parts of the lexicon are more immune to influence: Words for the weather, climatic phenomena, flora, fauna, kinship, pronouns, and demonstratives. Languages with common origins therefore display similarity in lexical stock and grammatical structure, the most stable parts of language. When Rask found that two languages such as Icelandic and Welsh do not share a grammatical structure, he assumed that lexical similarity must be the result of borrowing rather than common origins. Forms of pronunciation are language specific. But the inference of common origins can confirm rules of correspondence between pronunciations in different languages that share common origins, for example, "f" in Icelandic corresponds to "p" in ancient Greek (Percival, 1974).

Rask's Indo-European thesis was, actually, only a European thesis. He did not consider the Indian languages. Rask compared exclusively the grammatical structures of Greek, Latin, the Germanic languages, most notably Icelandic, and the Slavic languages and discovered that their inflections are similar: They have three noun forms (feminine, masculine, and neuter) and five cases, unlike other languages. Rask inferred from this similarity that they are all descendants of a single language that he called Thracian, after the possible homeland of the ancient speakers of that original European language. Since Icelandic inflections are simpler than Greek and Latin ones, Rask inferred that it was derived from Thracian, later than Greek and Latin.

Franz Bopp is the paradigm founder of comparative linguistics, Ranke's equal and colleague. Bopp was appointed professor at the University of Berlin in 1821. He confirmed the Indo-European hypothesis through a systematic comparison of verb structures and inflections in Sanskrit, Greek, Latin, and Persian (Bopp, 1816/1845).

Bopp brought to linguistics...a *paradigm* of historical explanation, in the sense in which Kuhn has introduced this term. A historical explanation of an inflectional form was to him a demonstration that the form was derived from a proto-form in which each of the primitive concepts into which its meaning was analyzable was expressed by a separate morpheme. This paradigm was based on the belief that the methods of comparative reconstruction, applied to what Bopp considered the greatly decayed and disorganized morphological debris of the attested Indo-European languages, would yield a proto-morphology. (Kiparsky 1974, p. 333)

Bopp was able to formulate criteria for genetically relevant similarity according to laws of morphological correspondence between languages. The Indo-European hypothesis, an extinct language from which all the Indo-European languages descended was the best explanation of these similarities. Bopp could not infer the properties of the hypothetical proto–Indo-European language and the stages of linguistic development that could mediate between it and known languages. Kiparsky claimed that since Bopp had no theory of reconstruction of proto–Indo-European, he had to resort to ad hoc hypotheses for the reconstruction of the history of the Indo-European languages. The similarity between pronouns and corresponding verb endings in the Indo-European languages led Bopp to conclude that personal endings were originally pronouns attached to the verb stem, for example the original first person ending *ma* and the second person *tva*. Bopp intuited several hypothetical intermediary links, for which there is no direct evidence, to mediate with the Greek "s" and Sanskrit "tha." Later linguistics rejected these speculative hypotheses. Kiparsky concluded that Bopp was not interested in the history of the Indo-European languages, only in their common origin.

Jacob Grimm, who discovered rules of consonant shift in his *Germanic Grammar*, (1814–1822) completed the work of Rask and Bopp. He introduced nine rules of correspondence between German, Greek, Latin, Sanskrit, and other Indo-European languages. Grimm's laws had a wide scope that allowed individual linguists to work on puzzle solving within their framework for the next half century. When Ranke founded scientific historiography, it was against the background of established, successful, and fruitful paradigmatic, theoretically founded, biblical criticism, classical philology, and comparative linguistics that enjoyed large uniquely heterogeneous consensus on beliefs and cognitive values. As we see next, the theoretical foundations and methods of all these reconstructions of the past are quite similar.

SCIENTIFIC HISTORIOGRAPHY

Krieger (1977, p. 3) expressed puzzlement at the consideration of Ranke as the "Copernicus" or "Kant" of historiography: The critical attitude to sources dates back to Thucydides. The crucial significance of original documents for historiographic reasoning had already been recognized in humanist scholarship since the fifteenth century and was defended systematically by Jean Mabillion and the Maurists in the seventeenth century. The theories and methods of philology developed in seminars in the early nineteenth century and were applied "spectacularly" to Roman historiography by Barthold Georg Niebuhr, whom Ranke acknowledged as his mentor. Peter Burke (1990) disputed the claim that Ranke was the first to turn from historiographic narrative to emphasis on the documentary record and criticism of narrative sources. Criticisms of the reliability of narrative sources had already been conducted in the sixteenth century. Ranke followed the critical model of classicists like Wolf and Niebuhr. The study of official records had begun already in the seventeenth century. Ranke returned to those methods after a new historiography, covering broader aspects of history than political and religious history, had developed during the eighteenth century. Krieger argues that Ranke's contributions lay not in any single breakthrough, but rather in the unprecedented way he put familiar notions together and in the new contexts he found for them.

Thus he applied to *modern* history the documentary and philological methods which had been specifically devised for penetration into remote ages.... Ranke's incremental historical criticism converted principles which had been the tenets of individual historians into a paradigm which could be communicated to an entire profession as its distinctive collective identification. Science in its modern connotation is characterized precisely by the collective prosecution of a singular method, and it is in this sense that Ranke initiated the modern science of history. (Krieger, 1977, p. 4)

Krieger conflated "putting together notions," converting "principles" and "tenets" into a "paradigm" and pursuing "a single method." Indeed, such confusions abound in Krieger's book on Ranke. Krieger failed to clearly characterize the critical theories, and methods that Ranke adopted and used, or what was significant about them. Instead, he concentrated in his book on those idiosyncratic contingent elements in Ranke's historiography that had hardly any effect on the values, theories, and methods of historiography. Still, Krieger was right in noting that the significance of Ranke is in the founding of a community of historians united by theory and method. Butterfield (1955) and Lefebvre (1971) concurred, though they disputed the precise time and place where a community of critical historians emerged for the first time.

Butterfield (1955) argued that a new historiography was born around 1760 by historians with backgrounds in biblical criticism, especially in Göttingen, where a philological approach to the Bible espoused by Mosheim, Semler, and Michaelis, and to classic Greek sources developed by Gesner and Heyne, had already been established. In Butterfield's opinion, modern historiography began with the nomination of Johann Christoph Gatterer to the chair of history in Göttingen in 1759. Gatterer established a historical institute that Butterfield considered a precursor to the seminar, as well as promoted auxiliary sciences such as geography, genealogy, heraldry, and numismatics and founded scholarly journals of historiography. By 1768 Gatterer proposed to produce a critical edition of the evidential sources for German historiography. The Göttingen historians mastered the critical approach to historical evidence and began to apply it to the historiographies of other nations by collecting all the relevant sources-evidence and subjecting them to criticism. For example, Schlözer devised a research program for Russian history, taking account of all the relevant evidence in various languages. Schlözer cited in his introduction precedents for his critical approach to documents exclusively from the methods and rules of critical editions of the New Testaments and the classics: "The collation of manuscripts; the recovery of a purified text; the diagnosis of interpolations and corruptions; the discovery of earlier sources which the writer has used" (Butterfield, 1955, p. 58). In his dedication to his critical edition of the *Chronicle of Nestor*, Schlözer inquired where Nestor acquired his information and how it reached the present, inferring extinct original sources of medieval chroniclers. Schlözer claimed that if the principles he used are applied consistently they will lead to a revision of historiography. Butterfield noted that Schlözer had not applied his principles consistently, and his work appears naive and uncritical by contemporary standards, but Butterfield recognized that the significance of the University of Göttingen was in its success in generating a socially significant movement, a community where a continuous development could take place, in contrast to isolated "precursors" who may have practiced some critical historiography but had no effect on their social-intellectual environment.

   Lefebvre (1971, pp. 34–5) traced the birth of a collective enterprise of critical historiography to seventeenth-century France or more strictly to nineteenth-century Germany. Lefebvre argued that historiographic scholarship requires a quantity of research and level of specialization that no single person can achieve. Institutions and schools are necessary. Critical, collective erudition emerged for the first time at the end of the seventeenth century during the reign of Louis XIV among clerical communities of Jesuit and especially Benedictine monks that were sufficiently rich and had the resources for research, libraries, and collections of documents, as well as the political influence to gain access to the archives of the state and the nobility. The Benedictine Jean Mabillion developed, in the course of defending his historiography of his order against Jesuit criticisms, an explicit formulation of methods for authenticating historical documents from their forms, the subdiscipline of "diplomatic," which he published as *De re diplomatica*. The debates between the Bollandist Jesuits and Maurist Benedictines over historical documents contributed further to the creation of systematic paleography, the study of historical handwritings, by Bernard de Montfaucon.

Lefebvre (1971, p. 106) claimed that Germans resuscitated in the nineteenth century the modern historiographic method that "we" (i.e., the French Benedictines and French-speaking Jesuits from Belgium) created without always acknowledging their debt. The French monks were the first to develop auxiliary sciences, to edit collections of documents as evidence, and to extol the cognitive value of truth above the aesthetic value of literary beauty in historiography. Lefebvre admitted though that the practice of the critical method in the seventeenth century was rudimentary. The sole criterion for preferring one document to another was its antiquity. The monks ignored the possibility that later documents may be more reliable than older ones if they are based on reliable but extinct sources. Nor did they examine whether the oldest source was forged intentionally. They identified truth with antiquity, following their traditionalist cognitive values. The seventeenth-century development of some critical methods arose in the context of a parochial debate about the history of the Benedictine order, motivated by struggle for prestige. The debating monks did not attempt to apply critical theories or methods systematically to other historiographic problems; they did not found a paradigm.

The chief precursor of Ranke was Niebuhr who was the first to examine critically the evidence for early Roman history. Niebuhr accepted Perizonius's testimony that information from the early period of Roman history reached historians who wrote hundreds of years later through three institutional information transmission chains, banquet songs *carmina*, funeral panegyrics, and annals kept by the high priest, *pontifex maximus.* No direct information about these alleged media of transmission has outlasted antiquity. Niebuhr attempted to distinguish mythical from historical events in Roman legal history by speculating whether the evidence for them is connected to the events it reports by one of the above three types of information chains. Niebuhr clearly attempted to copy the theories and methods of biblical critics and classical philologists, most notably Wolf. Niebuhr described Wolf's *Prolegomena* in 1827 as an investigation "in which the higher branch of criticism reached its perfection" (Grafton et al., 1985, p. 28). But the relative paucity of independent evidence for the information-causal chains that allegedly connected late historiographic descriptions with early Roman history prevented Niebuhr from confirming his hypotheses without adding speculative assumptions.

For a work of critical historiography to become the founding text of a successful new paradigm, in conjunction with its theories, its surprising and new hypotheses must increase dramatically the likelihood of the evidence in comparison with alternative hypotheses, as was the case with the theories of the founders of biblical criticism, classical philology, and comparative linguistics. Niebuhr's hypotheses, theories, and methods, though innovative in the context of the historiography of Rome, could not generate sufficient degrees of beliefs among his readers that would warrant a consensus, because Niebuhr's evidence for the three information delivery chains consisted of two sentences in Cicero allegedly based on Cato and an incomplete sentence by Varro that can be found in Nonius. His hypotheses were that plebeian poetry was composed of banquet songs, *carmina*, while the patricians' poetry was in the form of the annals of the pontiffs. Nitzsch criticized Niebuhr's hypothesis, noting that had the source for the Roman legends been Plebeian poetry, it would not be likely that all the heroes of those legends would be patricians (Momigliano, 1977, pp. 235–6). Though Niebuhr's Italian disciple, De Sanctis, "felt that Niebuhr's theory provided the best explanation for the legendary character of early Roman tradition" (p. 236), Niebuhr's contemporaries thought they had better explanations of the evidence. A. W. Schlegel and Mommsen considered the similarities between Greek and Roman legends and inferred that Greek legends, rather than ancient Roman oral poetry, are the best explanation for late Roman accounts of ancient Roman history. Momigliano (1977, pp. 239–41) summed up the reasons for rejecting

Niebuhr's hypotheses: The similarities between known Greek sources and the Roman legends could not be coincidental. Since the Greek sources are earlier, it is probable that they influenced the later Roman sources during the Hellenic period, possibly even earlier. The "poems hypothesis" does not make the content of Roman legends probable because heroic poetry usually does not allow its heroes to die in bed of old age nor does it blur the line between friends and enemies as Roman legends do; nor do the legends keep a strict class distinction between patricians and plebeians. An ancient, fourth-to fifth-century BCE origin does not make this feature of the legends very likely because that was the period of class strife in Rome. The legends seem to reflect in that respect a third-century BCE social reality. Women figure prominently in the legends, an unlikely feature of poetry that should have originated in male banquets. The subject of many of the legends is local: Traditions, monuments, and cult places. This feature is better explained by local traditions that attached legends to visible objects in their environment than by Niebuhr's lost poems. The annalistic Roman tradition about the early Republic is more "poetic" than the legends on the monarchy. Unlikely, given Niebuhr's hypothesis. Momigliano concluded that the extant traditions on ancient Rome most likely originated in the third century BCE. The annalists who wrote them down may have been influenced by more ancient, possibly poetic, traditions. But their highly selective editing of these sources prevents us today from knowing anything about those possible poetic sources.

Unsurprisingly, Ranke's upbringing brought him under the influence of the three disciplines that exported their cognitive values, theories, and methods to historiography. Ranke's male ancestors were Lutheran ministers except for his father who was a lawyer. At the university of Leipzig he studied theology and classical philology. He took one compulsory course in history but after his exposure to the critical methods of theology and philology, he found it disappointing. Ranke's favorite authors were Niebuhr and Thucydides. His teacher of classical philology, Gottfried Hermann introduced him to the methods of classical philology, which he then exported to historiography (von Laue, 1950). Ranke's first book, the *Histories of the Latin and Germanic Nations* (1824), already contained the main principles of the Rankean paradigm: Historiographic consensus can be built on the basis of evidence of public, documents. "Any one who steeps himself in these dry studies, and has access to all the historical documents, especially the electoral rolls of the ecclesiastical princes, will be able to discover, from Frederick II's time, a new history" (Ranke 1909, p. 103). Ranke ordered known sources according to their temporal proximity to the hypothesized events. In case an author was not an eyewitness, Ranke inquired for the source of the information. Ranke preferred primary sources written by contemporaries of the events that were not intended to record history, such as diaries, "the truth of which it is impossible to doubt" (Ranke, 1909, p. 170), and letters to narrative interpreted historiography that was designed to create an impression of the past. Ranke examined the identity of the authors of narrative historiography to identify possible biases. When considering different sources, Ranke considered whether they were independent of each other. For example, he traced a mistake common to several English historians (Hume, Rapin, and Bacon) to their common source, Polydore Virgil (Ranke, 1909, p.130, note7). Ranke concluded that Guicciardini copied other books, much of what he copied was false in the first place, much was doubtful, speeches were invented, treaties altered, and important facts were misrepresented (Gooch, 1959, p. 72–97).

The theoretical core of critical historiography overlaps with that of biblical criticism, classical philology, and comparative linguistics. These sciences attempt to infer information about a cause from relevant similarities among its putative present effects, the evidence, by inferring the information-causal chains that connected the cause, the alleged source of the information, with its effects, the alleged receptors of the information. In the case of Ranke's historiography, the similar effects are documentary evidence. Unlike in the case of comparative linguistics, it is not necessary to have a strong theoretical background to determine relevant similarities between historiographic evidence. The likelihood that independent texts would describe details of similar events without a common cause that is the source of the information is usually negligible. One obvious hypothesis is that the common cause that best explains the similarity is the event that the similar evidence describes. Alternative hypotheses would suggest other common causes such as late forgeries. Critical historians find which hypothesis better explains the evidence by discovering the history of the evidence, and examining the links on the information-causal chain that may connect the similar evidence with a common cause. Historians assume the gradual involuntary mutation of information, as do biblical critics, classical philologists, and comparative linguists about languages, oral poems, and copied documents. To minimize possible corruption of the information, Ranke introduced a methodology that usually admits as evidence only the testimony of eyewitnesses and excludes memoirs and later narrative accounts that must be at best copies of copies. Even when evidence for many of the links on the information-causal chain is missing, it is possible to infer with high probability the properties of some of the missing links and the cause. This is to a large extent the special wisdom and craft of professional historians who use rules of "conjectural emendation" (Langlois & Seignobos, 1926, pp. 76–9).[7]

A second group of historiographic theories are of common-sense psychology and social science. Unlike other philosophers who expressed this opinion (Berlin, 1960), I argue that these common-sense theories explain evidence, not events. These theories explain why evidence may misrepresent what took place. Historians must ask themselves, why do people in general misrepresent what they know to be true and whether such circumstances were present when the evidence was generated? People have interests and may wish to spread false information to gain an advantage. Other people may be in a position where they are forced to lie. Personal sympathies and antipathies cause people to misrepresent themselves and groups they identify with or resent. Vanity causes people to misrepresent their own actions as more important than they actually were. Some writers misrepresent what took place to fit the values and fashions of their intended readership. Aesthetic, literary, and rhetoric norms may cause writers to embellish their accounts to fit mythical or heroic narrative models (Langlois & Seignobos, 1926, pp. 166–72). In traditionalist's societies, fabrications of the past were designed to establish a historiographic precedence for a desired social or international state of affairs, for example, much of the Pentateuch was written to establish precedence for late monarchic policies (Finkelstein & Silberman, 2001); or to manipulate the behavior of readers by generating consciousness of alleged historical grievances that need to be redressed or avenged; or to instill suspicion or mistrust in certain groups; or to excuse by denial historical personal or group behavior that the author has an interest in concealing; or any of many other reasons that motivate people to misrepresent the past.

The simplest method for avoiding misrepresentations of the past is to avoid when possible relying on intentionally written historiographic interpretations, or if there is insufficient nonintentional evidence, rely on evidence that goes counter to the interests and vanity of its authors (Langlois & Seignobos, 1926, pp. 186–7).

Ranke's theories and methods led him to find in archives the best evidence that was not written for the historical record. Following Ranke's appointment to the University of Berlin, he discovered for the first time unpublished documents, Venetian diplomatic reports from the sixteenth and seventeenth centuries, which he used for his 1827 *Princes and Peoples of Southern Europe*, where he wrote mostly about the Ottomans and the Spanish monarchy. He found in the Venetian archives evidence for Venetian administration, trade, and finance as well as politics. During 1827 to 1831 Ranke traveled to Austria and Italy to examine the archives there. Ranke became the founder of a new paradigm not just because of the theories and methods he borrowed from biblical criticism and philology, but because these theories and methods were fruitful in directing him and his followers to the discovery of new evidence and consequently to the confirmation of many new and surprising historiographic hypotheses.

Ranke's allegiance to the conservative politics of restoration in Prussia was useful in helping him gain access to archives that had been guarded by servants of other restoration regimes in Europe prior to the 1848 revolutions. For example, in Vienna in 1828 he befriended Metternich's advisor, Friedrich Gentz, who gained access for him to the Venetian papers in the Vienna archives. Ranke's first discovery of evidence was of the Venetian *Relazioni*, three centuries of reports by Venetian ambassadors from European courts. Ranke was the first historian to examine them as well as archives in Rome and Florence. Though the archives of the Vatican remained closed to him, he was able to use the archives to which he had access to write the *History of the Popes*. His *German History in the Reformation Era* used the 96 volumes of reports of the Frankfurt deputies at the Imperial Diet 1414 to 1613. Ranke supplanted them (the records of the reports of the Frankfurt deputies) with discoveries in archives in Weimar, Dresden, and Dassau. In Brussels Ranke found the correspondence of Charles V that he compared with the Paris archives and some of the Italian materials he collected earlier. The *History of Prussia* was based on letters of the French ambassador and on the Prussian archives opened to the state historiographer. Ranke researched the archives of France, Italy, Belgium, Germany, England, and Spain for his 1853 *History of France.* On the basis of his superior theory and successful results Ranke dismissed the established authorities in French historiography: Davila's *History of the Civil Wars* was derived from De Thou:

Richelieu's Memoirs were almost wholly spurious, those of De Retz genuine but grossly misleading. On reaching Saint-Simon he emphasized the late date of composition and the violence of his prejudices, and confronts him with the contemporary authority of Dangeau and the correspondence of Charlotte of Orleans with her German relatives. The 'French History,' with its mass of new material was welcomed in France. (Gooch, 1959, pp. 87–8)

Ranke introduced scientific progress to historiography by writing historiographies that were clearly superior to those that had preceded them in discovering new information or confirming old hypotheses, not just different interpretations as before the scientific revolution in historiography. Ranke was the first to insist on constructing historiography from contemporary sources.

When he began to write, historians of high repute believed memoirs and chronicles to be primary authorities. When he laid down his pen, every scholar with a reputation to make or to lose had learned to content himself with nothing less than the papers and correspondence of the actors themselves and those with immediate contact with the events they describe.... He founded the science of evidence by the analysis of authorities, contemporary or otherwise, in the light of the author's temperament, affiliations and opportunity of knowledge and by comparison with the testimony of other writers. Henceforth every historian had to inquire where his informant obtained his facts.... (Gooch, 1959, p. 97)

Acton dated the opening of European state archives to 1830, a date that coincides with Ranke's coming to age as a scholar. The Italian revolution of 1860 accelerated this process by forcing rival states to open their archives to prevent historiography from reflecting exclusively the evidence discovered in the archives of their enemies. The Austrian archives were opened by Arneth to expose forgeries that were against the interests of the Habsburgs. The opening of the archives led to rewriting of ecclesiastic historiography but influenced mostly political historiography.

Once Ranke demonstrated the success and fruitfulness of the theories and methods of scientific historiography in conjunction with the new archival evidence, historians who worked within his paradigm were able to practice "puzzle solving" in the Kuhnian sense, search untapped archives, certain that if they were successful in discovering new evidence there, they would make historiographic discoveries that would be respected by other historians. The research program of Ranke's historiography has led to the discovery of new evidence that is the hallmark of scientific theories (Lakatos, 1978), as well as necessary for deciding among competing theories (Laudan, 1998; Thagard, 1998). The new scientific historiography became a progressive science.

The ascension of Frederick William IV to the Prussian throne in 1840 brought Ranke state patronage and an appointment in 1841 as the official Prussian state historiographer. This state appointment released him from dependence on teaching at the University of Berlin, where burgeoning nationalist therapeutic cognitive values were pushing German historiography in a nonscientific direction. The German reading public generated more demand for nationalist therapeutic historiography than for Ranke's scientific variety. Ranke's *The History of Prussia* was considered too "cold" to be popular. The nationalist reading public valued therapeutic and ideological effects above knowledge of history. But by then Ranke and scientific historiography were not dependent on the Prussian reading public or the nationalist tastes of the Berlin student body. The Bavarian king, Maximilian II, appointed Ranke to chair the Historical Commission of the Bavarian Academy of Science and choose its first members. The commission brought together the leading German scientific historians. It published major monographs and sources such as *Annals of the Medieval Empire* and *Acts of the Imperial Diet*, as well as the first German biographical dictionary. Heinrich Sybel, the secretary and a student of Ranke, edited their *Historische Zeitschrift*. These honors enabled Ranke to form institutional foundations for scientific historiography, a bulwark against its popular nationalistic rivals. Had it not been for royal patronage, it is doubtful that Ranke could have survived institutionally in Berlin. Academics whose classes are canceled for insufficient registration would be gratified to learn that Ranke's last class at the University of Berlin had to be canceled because nobody registered for it.

Although Ranke was by all accounts a bad lecturer, he founded the community of scientific historians and a paradigm through the seminars he held at his home, usually for five to ten students, mostly about the critical examination of evidence.

Most of the great German historians of the nineteenth century, among them Heinrich von Sybel, Wilhelm von Giesebrecht, Georg Waitz, and the Swiss Jacob Burckhardt, passed through Ranke's seminar in which he applied the critical method to historical writings. These students in turn trained a generation of scholars who dominated German university chairs of history well into the twentieth century. Ranke thus became in fact the father of modern historical science in Germany. (Iggers & Moltke, 1973, p. xxvi)

Iggers and Moltke's judgment of who were "the great German historians of the nineteenth century" assumes already the cognitive values that Ranke institutionalized. As scientific historiography expanded beyond the borders of Germany over the second half of the nineteenth century, Ranke's seminar model was copied in France and the United States (Iggers, 1985, pp. 47–8).

Ranke's cozy relations with the Prussian royal family are criticized often as indicators of a bias in favor of reactionary politics in his historiographic interpretations. Actually, Ranke's royal patronage protected the establishment and institutionalization of the scientific cognitive values of historiography against their two chief contemporary competitors: Lingering traditionalism and the new popular nationalist-therapeutic cognitive values that considered historiographic "knowledge" to be whatever constructs, unites, and gives a heroic sense of purpose to a German nation. Royal absolutist hostility to premodern religion on the one hand, and populist egalitarian nationalism on the other hand facilitated the institutionalization of the cognitive values of modern historiography in Prussia. But these cognitive values achieved universal acceptance by a heterogeneous community that has included historians of all nationalities and political shades because they are conducive to the acquisition of knowledge across the disciplines. The particular political constellation in the first half of the nineteenth century in Prussia was conducive to the emergence of scientific historiography, but it could not generate an uncoerced uniquely heterogeneous consensus about it. The worsening political and academic conditions for scientific historiography in the second part of the nineteenth

century in Germany did not affect the progress of scientific historiography because by then the heterogeneity of the historiographic
community released it from dependence on any local conditions. It
is trivially true that Ranke was a product of his time and place. As
many historians noted, Ranke's interpretations reflect some of the values of his sociohistorical background, such as his Protestant religious
upbringing, his adherence to older models of universal historiography, his moderate monarchism, and so forth (Iggers & Moltke, 1973;
Krieger, 1977; von Laue, 1950). It is practically impossible for any historian to avoid making such value-laden interpretations. But, had the
significance of Ranke's historiography not exceeded these interpretations, he would not have become the founder of the scientific paradigm
in historiography (Iggers, 1985, p. 10). The peculiar values of a mid-
nineteenth century Lutheran loyal subject of imperial Prussia had no
lasting effects on members of the heterogeneous historiographic community. They accepted Ranke's universal cognitive values and ignored
the irrelevant but inevitable value-laden interpretations that historians
make along the way, but are often left on the side of the road by future
generations.

The community that Ranke founded expanded during the second
half of the nineteenth century to the rest of the world and became
independent of local circumstances. The backwardness of English-
speaking universities throughout the nineteenth century, devoted as
they were to class reproduction rather than to offering institutional incentives for research, as in post-Humboldt Germany, slowed down the
gradual expansion of critical historiography (Bentley, 1999, pp. 71–
5, 78–9). Yet, intellectual sloth and institutional designs that discour-
aged or did not promote research could only mount a rearguard battle
against, rather than offer a viable alternative to, scientific historiography. Ranke's model of historiography reached England when William
Stubbs became Regius Professor of Modern History at Oxford (1866–
1884). Stubbs wrote critical historiographies of the Middle Ages and
the *Constitutional History of England* (1873–1878). He studied Ranke's
critical method by reading and described himself as a member of a
republic of workers united by method and goals. Though Stubbs expressed unmitigated admiration for Ranke, Goldstein (1990, p. 144)
noted that Stubbs betrayed no knowledge of Ranke's "philosophical"
principles, his interpretation of world history. This is not surprising

because the universal significance of Ranke was in spreading the cognitive values, theories, and methods of scientific historiography. His historiographic interpretations are of no significance for understanding paradigmatic historiography, common to Ranke and Whig historians like Stubbs and the students he trained at Oxford. Stubbs's Whig values directed him to concentrate on English constitutional history, especially episodes that expanded liberty, such as the signing of the Magna Charta. But these choices did not matter for the science that Ranke and Stubbs shared. Rigorous techniques of investigation generated respectability and a tradition of university-based scholarship and professionalism in Britain since the fourth quarter of the nineteenth century (Goldstein, 1990).

It appears that national defeats and humiliations have been conducive to the growth of academia and the development of scholarship. In France, the academic system was revitalized to compete against German academia following its 1871 defeat by Prussia. Consequently the French adopted scientific historiography and eventually eclipsed the achievements of the Germans. In the early part of the twentieth century, scientific historiography spread further in continental Europe. This expansion was halted and then reversed by the ascendance of authoritarian and totalitarian regimes that had interest in therapeutic, ideological historiographies and consequently abolished scientific historiography in territories they controlled (Bentley, 1999, pp. 76–80).

It is significant to differentiate the local from the universal, not just in what Ranke wrote but also in what later historians attributed to him. Ranke's methods were particularly appropriate for dealing with documentary evidence, which for most of history was written by the literate classes in service of the state or organized religion. Consequently, Ranke wrote more about political events and religion than about economic or social processes. But Ranke behaved rationally, given his theories, methods, and evidential constraints. For most of history, people who authored primary documents that were preserved in archives were members of political, administrative, or religious elites. Otherwise, they were not likely to be literate and have an institution with an interest in preserving information in archives. Therefore, if one adopts a set of methods designed to infer historiography from documentary evidence, the easiest hypotheses to confirm are likely to concern political and religious history. This does not imply bias in favor of the *significance* of political history in relation to other aspects of history; it merely reflects the evidential constraints on the method. Ranke's critics accused him of being in the position of a person who looks for lost keys under a street lamp because that is where the light is. But such behavior is rational: If the keys are under the lamp, they can be found, if they are hidden in the dark, looking for them there will do no good. To look for their keys elsewhere, historians had to find other lamps, other methods for inferring historiography from other types of evidence.

A later generation of so-called Neo-Rankeans since the 1880s, associated Ranke's historiography with a state-centered approach to history that considers international power systems to determine state policies irrespective of internal politics or ideology. This theory implies the insignificance of evidence for social or economic history. This political theory fitted the policy of Bismarck's German Empire, with its emphasis on the state and disregard of society and internal political differences.[8]

The Neo-Rankeans largely misinterpreted Ranke by claiming that Ranke had considered the development of states and the system of states as a sort of superior reality, which was elevated beyond the subjectivity of party opinion and party strife. . . . By concentrating on the role of the state, as the embodiment of the real forces in history, the historical account itself acquires a higher status of objectivity. Concentration upon the objective role of the state and its perennial struggle for self-assertion within the system of powers (which was, in Lenz's view, the gist of European politics since the sixteenth century) appeared to guarantee historical objectivity. (Mommsen, 1990, pp. 132–3)

The critical theories and methods that Ranke used do not imply a political theory about the causal efficacy of the state in relation to other social institutions; their content is the transmission of information from events to evidence. The contents of archival evidence determined the kind of conclusions that could be drawn from them. Butterfield suggested that the school of Neo-Rankeans emerged out of "educational routine that had taken the line of least resistance" (1955, p. 118). When Ranke began his work, diplomatic documents were becoming available and were important sources for information about internal as well as external affairs. Ranke's self-appointed followers who elevated foreign policy to the core of their historiographic research program ignored new kinds of evidence that were just as relevant to Ranke's methods as state documents in the archives (Butterfield, pp. 100–1). As long as historians believed that "no documents, no history" (Langlois & Seignobos, 1926, p. 17) they could not see other possible evidence.

The practice of methods may be based on theoretical knowledge or trial and error. For example, one may rely on a habitual method for, say, starting a car and expect it to work because so far this method has been successful, without assuming any theoretical background. A car mechanic, however, may actually know how the car works and why certain acts ignite the engine. The two foundations for use of method are not mutually exclusive: It is possible to use a method with confidence both following an understanding of the theory behind it, and because it has worked thus far. The initial acceptance of the critical method in historiography followed the success of the method in biblical criticism, classical philology, and comparative linguistics. It also followed an understanding of the theoretical basis for the methods of these sciences. But the origins of modern historiography do not imply that all historians who have practiced successfully the critical method have understood the theoretical foundations of their methods. Some acquired the methods by imitating their elders and practiced it successfully without understanding why it worked, or why it led to new discoveries and universal acceptance. Historians who deny the use of theory are unaware of the theoretical underpinning of their own practices. Such theoretically unconscious historians may accompany their methodological practices with rituals. Imagine a person who learns how to start a car by imitating another who performs a little ritual, such as humming the first bars of Mahler's Sixth Symphony while turning the ignition key. This method works of course, though humming Mahler is superfluous for its results. A person who has some rudimentary theoretical knowledge of car mechanics would be able to distinguish the functional from the ritualistic elements of the method, but a mere imitator of method would not. Historians whose methodical practices contain such ritualistic elements have no understanding of the theoretical foundations of their methods; they turned a science into a ritualistic tradition. Historians who turned Ranke's research program into a tradition indiscriminately preserved Ranke's methods alongside the temporary constraints under which he worked. During Ranke's lifetime, archives appeared like a vast untapped natural resource for scientific historiography. Before this resource began to deplete, there had been little reason for historians to attempt to discover new types of evidence and theories.

Historiography progressed after Ranke by developing theories that directed historians to find and use new types of evidence. Ranke's students, Burckhardt and Huizinga, expanded his paradigm to use art as evidence to infer cultural historiography. The Annales school did not forsake the documentary and critical research program but sought to expand it beyond politics to social and economic historiography by using material and other nonarchival evidence. Marc Bloch innovated in introducing theories to infer economic historiography from present geographical, unwritten, evidence. The rise of world historiography after WWII reflects the consideration of a wider scope of evidence. As world historiography looks for evidence across space, serial historiography looks for evidence across time, finding statistical, computer-generated, patterns over a long time, which are founded on evidence such as church registries. Social science theories with which Ranke was unfamiliar directed a search for nested information. For example, economic theory introduced the concepts of inflation and deflation and predicts their possible manifestations in various monetary systems. This led economic historians to search and interpret numismatic evidence. The best explanation of Roman coins whose rims were shaved off is a process of devaluation of the currency, inflation, expressed in decreased gold value of a currency unit. Similarly, demographic theory can direct historians to examine parish registries of baptisms and burials to draw larger conclusions about demographic trends. Further evidence may discover correlations between demographic trends and other historical changes that may support other hypotheses. The decrease in child mortality in nineteenth-century Europe may be best explained by the spread of better hygienic conditions for which there is independent material and documentary evidence.

This description of the theories and methods of scientific historiography may seem disappointing. In comparison with the grand theories of history of the likes of Marx or Weber, scientific historiography may appear pedantic. But the possibility of consensus among the uniquely heterogeneous historiographic community arose exactly because the theories that connect evidence with historiography are pedantic, habitual, and implicit in the work of historians. Yet, the achievements and success of scientific historiography are comparable in their significance to those of Darwinian biology in offering scientific knowledge of the past.

EVOLUTIONARY BIOLOGY

Scientific historiography imported its values, theories, and methods from biblical criticism, classical philology, and comparative linguistics. But historiography was not the final destination of this march of theories and methods across Europe and through the disciplines.

The reconstruction of the history of living organisms by paleontologists is a historicist enterprise, and all of systematics (the science of inferring evolutionary relationships among organisms) is an attempt to tell the story of the common ancestry of organisms *wie es eigentlich gewesen.* Evolutionary biology . . . is a historical science. It is the purpose of all these sciences to provide a correct narrative of the sequence of past events and an account of the causal forces and antecedent conditions that led to that sequence. (Lewontin, 1994a, p. 481)

Stephen Alter (1999) examined the possible influence of comparative linguistics on the emergence of evolutionary biology. German comparative philology arrived in Britain in the 1830s partly through the efforts of Darwin's cousin and brother-in-law, Hensleigh Wedgwood, who established the philological society of London and prepared the etymologies for the *New English Dictionary.* Darwin's early (1836–44) post-Beagle notebooks mention the analogy between languages and species, philology and evolutionary biology, sciences that hypothesize a historical process to explain present diversity. Like species, words and languages change slowly, but preserve information about their origins. By 1840 there is proof of Darwin's familiarity with the Indo-European hypothesis. He mentioned evolutionary change, gradualism, and common descent in relation to language. Darwin faced a diversity of species in the Galápagos Islands and explained it with a branching, cladistic, evolutionary model. Previous evolutionary theories by contrast advocated a linear, chain-of-being, evolutionary model. Alter (1999, p. 18) claimed that the only precedent for such a branching model is philological. In this chapter I argue that a cladistic model had been used previously in biblical criticism, classical philology, and historiography.[9] All these models are of the imperfect transmission of information over time.

In an unpublished 1844 outline of his theory and in *The Origins of Species* (1859), Darwin described rudiments, hereditary features, such as the wings of the ostrich, which have no adaptational function, as similar to nonphonetic spelling that preserves information useful for tracing linguistic ancestry. For example, the silent letters in "light" prove its relation to the German "Licht." Following Latham, Darwin differentiated botanic and biologic classification by descent from classification by resemblance, upholding the first and rejecting the second as superficial, supporting what will be known a century later as Cladistics. In *The Origin of Species* Darwin compared the extant fossil record to an intermittently written chronicle of human history written in a slowly changing dialect of which only the final volume covering the last couple of centuries survived. Otherwise a short chapter or a few lines here and there were preserved. In *The Descent of Man*, Darwin wrote: "The formation of different languages and of distinct species, and of the proofs that both have been developed through a gradual process, are curiously the same." Darwin observed that comparative linguistics had more evidence than biology, so it can trace better the origins of words. Species and languages have homologies due to descent, analogies due to similar processes of formation, and rudiments, adaptationally useless vestiges of earlier stages that can assist the scientist in reconstructing the historical process that led to the present state of affairs. Languages, like species can be crossed. Darwin even suggested that a kind of competition and natural selection takes place among languages over limited human memory, which leads to the extinction of some languages (Alter, 1999, pp. 99–102).

Yet, as Alter noted, Darwin's references to comparative linguistics were made after he had already formulated his evolutionary theory. There is no smoking gun that can demonstrate a causal influence of philology on Darwinian evolutionary theory. Alter demonstrated that Darwin relied rhetorically on an analogy with comparative linguistics to support his novel evolutionary ideas. If Alter is right, it implies that by the time Darwin was prepared to publish his evolutionary theory, the theories and methods of comparative linguistics, and for that matter biblical criticism, classical philology, and historiography, were sufficiently well confirmed and entrenched to rely on in presenting Darwin's more surprising and controversial theory. The substantial similarity between the theories and methods of these disciplines assured Darwin that he was preaching to a public that had already been converted. Darwin sowed a land plowed by comparative linguistics. Alter noted that William Whewell in his *History of the Inductive Sciences* (1837) discussed the "palaetiological sciences," geology, paleontology, ethnology, archeology, and comparative philology. Whewell thought that retrodiction, an attempt to ascertain a past state by examining present evidence, is common to all these sciences. Whewell, and following him Alter, thought that these sciences modeled the history of their subject matter as progressing from simple to complex. This betrays lack of familiarity with early comparative linguistics. As we noted earlier, Rask assumed that languages evolve in the direction of simplification. Whewell projected British progressive political models on early nineteenth-century (mostly German) historical sciences. Whewell noticed, correctly, that something was common to all these sciences, though he did not quite understand what it was. Alter refers to the relations between philology and Darwinian evolution as that of analogy or metaphor, missing their deeper common methodologies and theoretical basis, the inference of common causes from information preserved by their similar effects.

SECOND-STAGE EVOLUTIONARY BIOLOGY AND COMPARATIVE LINGUISTICS

Darwin inferred the existence of a common cause from similarities between species and his theory of random mutation and natural selection. Darwin avoided a detailed characterization of the common causes, nor did he draw phylogenetic trees. Darwin's tree diagram in *The Origin of Species* presented only a most abstract paleobiological pedigree. Ernst Haeckel in *Natürliche Schöpfungsgeschichte* (1868) attempted to fill in these blanks in the Darwinian model of the history of life. Darwin described Haeckel's conjectures as bold, perhaps too bold, because theory and evidence were insufficient for confirming his cladistic models. During the 1870s and 1880s others offered speculative genealogies, some of which were mutually inconsistent. Genealogic consensus, for example, about the pedigree of the horse, emerged from better fossil records and the development of genetics, only since the beginning of the twentieth century (Alter, 1999, pp. 123–5).

Comparative linguistics developed in the same direction at about the same time. The Indo-European paradigm concluded that certain similarities among languages had a common cause. But comparative linguistics of the first half of the nineteenth century had little to offer beyond ad hoc speculations about the properties of the original language and the causal chains that should have connected it with the extant Indo-European languages. During the 1860s: "The principal goal of comparative grammar . . . became the explanation of phonological features of the individual daughter languages on the basis of the reconstructed proto-language" (Kiparsky, 1974, p. 338). The reconstruction of proto-languages and cladistic models of linguistic mutations in time became possible following the discoveries of laws that govern phonetic changes during the 1860s and 1870s.

The founder of a new paradigm in comparative linguistics in the 1860's was August Schleicher: It is probable that Schleicher's early training conditioned him in the direction of seeing and cultivating the connection between sound change and the determination of descent. He was a classicist by training and had gone through the school of Friedrich Ritschl. This meant schooling in "the method" – the famous "via ac ratio" of textual criticism and archetype reconstruction governed by a set of formal rules. Principal among these is the doctrine of the shared error which serves as a criterion for the setting-up of subfamilies in a manuscript tradition. The subfamilies so recognized form a stemma, or tree. Its branches represent the origin, by copying, of manuscript from manuscript source (either extant or inferred, complete with all its readings, by the very act of reconstruction). (Hoenigswald, 1974, p. 352)

Schleicher was the first to attempt to reconstruct the missing proto-Indo-European words and mark them with *. Schleicher based his genealogies of languages on similar innovations shared by a family of languages, as classical philologists reconstruct the genealogy of documents based on mistakes shared by a family of documents. During the 1870s the Neogrammarians established linguistic kinship and classification on laws of phonetic shifts, and then modeled the histories of languages. For example, Ferdinand de Saussure (who is remembered today as the founder of structuralism) reconstructed the Indo-European vowel system in his *Mémoire sur le système primitif des voyelles dans les langues indo-européennes* (1879). These laws were used to reconstruct vernacular Latin for which there was no direct evidence. William F. Albright used phonetic laws that govern shifts in Semitic languages to infer the locations of biblical sites from their current names in the 1920s (Alter, 1999, pp. 130–4).

During the twentieth century, genealogic inferences in biology and philology have been interpreted in probabilistic terms, subject to revision if further evidence is discovered. Inferences of some properties of most extinct languages of species cannot be precise. The choice between inferences is guided by their scope, whether they unite various units of evidence, and their fruitfulness in leading to the discovery and explanation of implicit similarities, for example, between crocodiles and birds. Retrospective confirmation may take place mostly in biology when there are discoveries of missing links that were inferred previously (Alter, 1999, pp. 134–40; Sober, 1988).

Early nineteenth-century comparative linguistics inferred a cladistic, treelike model of the history of language. It assumed that new languages are created through the migration of a social or ethnic unit to a new geographical area. Consequent isolation from its ancestral group leads to a linguistic-semantic drift, much like the genetic drift that takes place when a species migrates and becomes genetically isolated. However the basic assumption of the cladistic model of language, that each language has one and only one ancestor, like branches on a tree, may not hold for many and perhaps most languages. The correct model for the histories of some or maybe most languages may look more like intertwining twigs or a net than a tree. Johannes Schmidt's 1872 wave theory of language proposed such a model: Languages are not clearly distinct from each other, but blurry around their edges through mutual contact and influence. Similarities may emerge as a result of convergence through contact without common ancestry. If languages are not independent of each other, similarities among them are insufficient for the inference of common ancestry. Perhaps there has never been a proto-Indo-European language, just continued interaction between increasingly similar languages (Renfrew, 1987, pp. 99–119).

The school of glottochronology (Swadesh, 1972) suggested to differentiate those parts of language that are more immune of convergence. Like some of the founders and precursors of comparative linguistics, Swadesh suggested that a core of essential words tends to change more slowly than other words, either because it mutates more slowly, or because it is more resistant to influences. Swadesh collected such a core vocabulary of 100 words and attempted to quantify and prove its rate of change over time by measuring its rate of change among languages that are known independently to be related, Middle and modern English, French and Latin of Pautus, and ancient and modern Mandarin. These comparisons yielded an 86% retention rate per millennium of this basic 100-word vocabulary. If similarity of over 8% between these words in different languages is more likely to result from historical relations than from coincidence, this method is useful for up to 11,700 years. Renfrew (1987, pp. 117 ff) criticized Swadesh's assumption of uniform rate of mutation. He suggested that levels of interlinguistic and social interaction, population density and mobility, social exclusionary use of language, and the use of written texts affect rates of linguistic change. It is fair to say that though all linguistics agree that the similarities among the Indo-European languages are the result of events in the past, there is no consensus on whether there was a single common cause, a proto–Indo-European language, a multiplicity of causes, or mutual linguistic influences.

THE HISTORICAL SCIENCES

It's obvious that all the sciences that have been discussed here share two stages of development:

1. A theory proves that similar evidence is not coincidental, but consists of similar effects that preserved information about their common cause or causes.
2. More evidence and theoretical background allow the probable reconstruction of intervening stages, informational causal links, between the common cause or causes and the similar

effects. Further theories allow the inference of properties of the common cause or causes from the information preserving properties of its effects.

Now it is necessary to present these conclusions in more formal probabilistic philosophic terms that will explain these historical patterns by the theoretical foundations of these historiographic sciences.

3

The Theory of Scientific Historiography

Historiographic propositions about the past come in all shapes and sizes, factual and explanatory, more abstract and general or more local and concrete, narrative-like, part of a story, or in plotless summaries of statistical data and relationships. Historiography can be written in prose or as a poem. As Aristotle (1996, p. 52b) argued in the *Poetics*, the style of historiography does not matter since it would be possible to turn the works of Herodotus into verse and their epistemic status would not change. Historiography is about what happened, whereas poetry is about what would have happened, requiring imagination. Leon Goldstein (1976, pp. 36–8) concluded that good historiography is distinguished from bad according to its relation with the evidence. The significant criteria are epistemic; the forms of the statements, their complexity or generality are epistemically insignificant. The form or style of historiography do not affect its relation with the evidence, its epistemic status. Narratives are not necessarily fictional. There are scientific stories about the evolution of life, the creation of the universe in the Big Bang, Luci the mother of mankind, etc. There are even logical and mathematical narratives, in which Lewis Carroll excelled. Narratives, like scientific theories or legal verdicts, can be determined, indetermined, and underdetermined. Determination is achieved on epistemic rather than stylistic grounds (Laudan, 1992, p. 64).[1]

Historiographic evidence as well comes in all shapes and sizes, including factual, explanatory, and general propositions found in documents, statistical records, and material objects, such as artifacts or the boundaries of fields. There are no observation sentences of history in historiography. Historians do not observe historical events. Historiography is not a study of the past as such, but of the present effects (traces, remains, etc.) of the past. Historiography is the art of reasoning from traces to facts (Langlois & Seignobos, 1926, p. 64). Historians begin with the evidence, because it is present, the past is forever inaccessible (Elton, 1969, pp. 20, 32). Even when alleged eyewitnesses write historical evidence, historians must evaluate and compare evidence written by possible observers. Historiographic evidence has no intrinsic properties that identify it as such. Goldstein (1996, pp. 9–10, 135 ff) argued that usually historiographic evidence can be recognized by virtue of its relation to historiography. Still, Goldstein found exceptions to this rule: Historians may recognize the evidential significance of the discovery of an archive before they know its contents, without knowing for what it is evidence. Yet, historiographic theories of the kind mentioned in the previous chapter can predict which kinds of information deposits are likely to be judged as evidence upon closer scrutiny. Ranke's theories directed him to look in the archives, and, since we share these theories, we know that a new archive is likely to be a treasure of new historiographic evidence. The judgments that distinguish valuable relics from useless derelicts are theory laden.

Dray asked: "Whether the historian's task is better described as accounting for present artifacts by reference to past states, or as justifying the assertion of past states by citing present evidence" (Dray, 1995, p. 256). Goldstein (1996, pp. 9–10) answered, both, the evidence confirms the hypotheses, and the hypotheses explain the evidence. Still, confirmation and explanation require more than historiography and evidence; they require theories that connect historiography with evidence and identify the evidence as such in the first place. The purpose of this chapter is to elucidate these relations between evidence and hypothetical past events.

According to Pompa (1981), competing historiographies are competing causal explanations that posit different descriptions of historical events to explain varying ranges of contemporary phenomena, the evidence. The best among such competing causal explanations can explain the widest range of present phenomena. Evidence can be identified then according to causal chains that connect it with hypothesized historical events. Goldstein (1996, pp. 214–18) argued against Pompa that it is merely trivially true that everything in the present is the effect of a process that connects it with the past. Pompa's identification of the evidence, claimed Goldstein, begs the question because the historiographic hypotheses that the evidence should support are assumed in identifying what is the evidence in the first place. Goldstein (1996, p. 180) claimed that the inference of descriptions of events from evidence requires the addition of many implicit "ghostly" assumptions. I agree with Goldstein that Pompa's account is incomplete; his causal criterion for historical evidence is insufficient. Dretske (1981, p. 31) cautioned against confusing a causal chain with an information flow. A causal process may not preserve information about its source. For example, the perfect crime is a causal process that does not preserve information about its origin. Yet Goldstein's account is incomplete in precisely the same way as Pompa's. Both Goldstein and Pompa's accounts miss the significant role of historiographic theories in mediating between the evidence and historiographic hypotheses, and both do not recognize that historians are interested only in particular types of causal chains, the ones that preserve information. I argue in this chapter that Goldstein's ghostly assumptions are the historiographic theories that unite the historiographic community and allow historiography to be determined. The subject of these theories, as Pompa's account hints, is the information preserving causal chains that connect historical events with historiographic evidence. Most research in historiography is actually neither about historical events, nor about their contemporary effects, the evidence, but about the processes that connects events with evidence.

Peter Kosso (1992, pp. 32–3) suggested that an information-bearing signal is conveyed through a series of interactions beginning with historical events and concluding with the evidence. Similar information-bearing signals connect evidence with events in the natural sciences. Historiographic information-bearing signals are considerably slower and composed often of words, rather than of light as in science, but these properties do not distinguish epistemically between historiography and science. Scientists understand the transmission of light; historians analyze the fidelity of textual information.

The point is that the data in history, the tokens of written reports of the past, play an evidential role that is similar to the data in science, the images in microscopes, tracks in particle detectors, and the like. Both bear information of less accessible objects of interest and both are amenable to an analysis of the credibility and accuracy of that information in terms of an independent account of the interactions between the object and the final medium of information, an account, that is, of the formation of the image. As long as we understand the formation process, in science or in history, we can be quite liberal in allowing many kinds of signals to carry the information. (Kosso, 1992, p. 33)

BAYESIANISM AND HISTORIOGRAPHIC CONFIRMATION

Understanding historiographic knowledge as theoretical requires explicating a sense of theory. A positivist account is alluring. The scientifically elusive clear distinction between theoretical and observational sentences may seem more obvious in historiography, which would be divided into eyewitness descriptions of events and historiographic hypotheses that would be connected with this evidence according to correspondence rules. Classical logical-positivism argued that theoretical statements deduce theoretical laws and empirical generalizations, which deduce observation sentences with the help of bridge laws or correspondence rules. In the case of historiography, the theories should come from the social sciences, the empirical generalizations from historiography, and the observation sentences would be eyewitness accounts collected by historians as evidence. Disagreements in historiography would then be ascribed to the absence of crucial experiments that should decide between competing theories or to radical variance in correspondence rules.

Seductive though it may seem, this positivist approach to the philosophy of historiography is as unfruitful and problematic as it is in the philosophy of science. Problems in differentiating observation from theoretical sentences are just as present in historiography, even more so. Historians must use theories to know where to search for relevant evidence, to recognize relevant evidence once they discover it, and to interpret nested evidence to generate the kind of evidence that is useful for them. Even the proverbial eyewitness accounts must be interpreted in theoretical terms to be useful. Historiography is not a collection of observation sentences with borrowed social science correspondence rules and theories. The social sciences do not have a deposit of theories to deduce from historiography with the help of initial conditions. The social sciences themselves are composed of feuding theories without a paradigm (Goldstein, 1996, p. 51).

In the philosophy of science, the theorem named after Bayes is used and debated often as an explication of the relationship between evidence and hypothesis: To what degree does a piece of evidence contribute or not to the confirmation of a hypothesis, given background conditions? The Bayesian theorem purports to state formally the relation between a particular piece of evidence and a hypothesis, the degree of probability the evidence confers on the hypothesis. I demonstrate in this chapter that an interpretation of Bayesian logic is the best explanation of the actual practices of historians. "The thesis that investigations into the past are epistemically unique can be dismissed because the problems of the historical sciences, like those of the nonhistorical sciences, boil down to the problems of warranting claims based on partial evidence" (Laudan, 1992, p. 65).

Before embarking on an interpretation of Bayes's theorem, which I believe best explains the actual practice of historians of society, nature, and language, I will state first the full version of Bayes's theorem and what it would mean for confirming historiographic hypotheses. This is for the benefit of those readers who may not have been exposed previously to this formal approach to confirmation in the philosophy of science:

$$Pr(H|E \& B) = [Pr(E|H \& B) \times Pr(H|B)]:Pr(E|B)$$

Pr stands for the probability of . . .

H   stands for any hypothesis, which in our case means any historiographic proposition about past events.

E   stands for evidence, which in our case means usually similarities between two or more independent sources such as documents, material remains, species, and languages.

B   stands for background knowledge of theories, methods, and other hypotheses about history. Most notably, background theories describe the transmission and mutation of various forms of information that were discussed in the previous chapter. Understanding these theories is crucial for understanding scientific historiography because they allow the generation of a socially heterogeneous consensus in historiography.

The vertical line | should be read as "given," for example, Pr(H| E & B) means the probability of a hypothesis given evidence and background information. For example, the probability of the hypothesis that George Washington was the first president of the United States, given the massive amount of documentary evidence for it and background knowledge of the causal chains that led to this evidence, is almost 1. We are almost absolutely certain that George Washington was indeed the first president.

Pr(H|B) is the *prior* probability of a particular hypothesis given background knowledge that may include established theories and historiography, prior to knowledge of the evidence whose value for confirming the hypothesis is evaluated by Bayes's theorem. For example, the probability of the hypothesis that there was a city of Troy that was destroyed in a war during the twelfth century BCE was low given the background information that had been known prior to the archeological discovery of the city in the late nineteenth century.

Pr(E|H & B) expresses the *likelihood* of the evidence given the hypothesis in question in conjunction with background knowledge. For example, given the hypothesis that George Washington was the first president of the United States, and background theories and information about the nature of paper and its preservation and use over two centuries and our knowledge of the paper trails that governments and politicians generate, it is highly likely that we can encounter today many contemporary documents that refer to Washington as the first president.

Pr(E|B) expresses the *expectancy*, the probability of the evidence given background information. Another way of putting it formally is:

$$\Pr(E|B) = [\Pr(E|H \& B) \times \Pr(H|B)] + [\Pr(E|-H \& B) \times \Pr(-H|B)]$$

For example, if our evidence is an invitation to Washington's inaugural, it is only to be expected, given all that we know. If however, we find it in the archives of King George with a personal dedication from Washington saying "hoping to see you there," it is highly surprising and would require rewriting American historiography.

The *posterior probability* of the hypothesis given new evidence and background information, $\Pr(H|E \& B)$, is the ratio of the *likelihood* of the evidence given the hypothesis and its *prior* probability, to the *expectedness* probability of the occurrence of the evidence whether or not the hypothesis is true. The reader who is not used to symbolic notation may imagine all the possible occurrences of a piece of evidence based on all that we know of the world, and then ask in what percentage of these cases a hypothesis H is the case, and then compute the ratio of such cases. For example, if our evidence is a book of prose in a given language and the hypothesis is that at the time the book was first published there was widespread literacy among speakers of that language, the posterior probability of this hypothesis is near 1, based on our background theory about the universal connection between literacy and prose since literature before literacy must be poetic to be retained and transmitted through memory. In other words, given what we know, in all the worlds where there are books of prose, there is also widespread literacy. By contrast, if the evidence is a fourteenth-century Persian text that describes Chinese printing techniques and the hypothesis is that Chinese printing caused the invention of printing in Europe, the posterior probability of the hypothesis is low because there are many possible worlds where a Persian author and his readers know about Chinese printing, but that information is not transmitted to Gutenberg or any of his predecessors in the printing business.

The most interesting evidence is crucial and surprising, it supports a hypothesis that had a low probability prior to the discovery of the evidence. For example, suppose the hypothesis asserts that Chinese printing caused the invention of printing in Europe, and the evidence consists of the discovery of Gutenberg's diary where he mentions an encounter with a Chinese merchant from whom he bought a printed Chinese book at a date prior to his own invention of printing. The likelihood of such evidence given that Chinese printing caused European printing is very high, though the prior probability of this hypothesis is quite low. If there was no Chinese influence on the introduction of printing to Europe, the likelihood of the evidence, Gutenberg's encounter with a Chinese bookseller, is negligible. Therefore, if such a Gutenberg diary were found it would have been crucial evidence for the probability of the Chinese hypothesis.

COMPARISON OF LIKELIHOODS: CONCISE BAYESIANISM

A frequent criticism of the usefulness of Bayesian logic for understanding science argues that it is difficult to quantify and compute the expectancy of the evidence. Another criticism of the classical Bayesian model emerged from the historiography of science: Scientists rarely consider the merits of a hypothesis in isolation. Usually scientists compare the relative probabilities of competing hypotheses. In response, some Bayesian philosophers of science suggest to concentrate on the ratio between the likelihoods of evidence, given competing hypotheses and shared background information. The evidence is more likely given better hypotheses than given less competitive hypotheses (Salmon, 1998). Elliot Sober (1988, p. 97) interpreted the choice of hypotheses and theories according to relative likelihoods of evidence as the choice of the best among competing explanations of the evidence. This interpretation of Bayesianism is in the tradition of Peirce (1957) who proposed that scientists do not evaluate explanations according to ideal independent criteria but compare them to each other in what he called "abduction." Following Sober, the best hypothesis among competing historiographic hypotheses would be the one that best explains the evidence by making it more likely, given background information.

There have been attempts to use the full Bayesian formula to evaluate hypotheses about the past, for example, whether miracles happened or not (Earman, 2000, pp. 53–9). Despite Earman's correct criticism of Hume (1988), both ask the same full Bayesian question: "What is the probability that a certain miracle happened, given the testimonies to that effect and our scientific background knowledge?" But this is not the kind of question biblical critics and historians ask. They ask, "What is the best explanation of this set of documents that tells of a miracle of a certain kind?" The center of research is the explanation of the evidence, not whether or not a literal interpretation of the evidence corresponds with what took place. One explanation of the evidence can be that miracles happened and were recorded. But in competition with the other explanations that biblical critics and historians have proposed to explain such documents, the miracles hypothesis has not fared well.[2] Biblical criticism and scientific historiography became possible following the introduction of theories that could do more than assess the probability of the literal truth of old texts, proceed to examine alternative hypotheses that can explain the same evidence.

THE HISTORICAL SCIENCES

The historical sciences are distinguished from other sciences by their evidence, which always includes correlations or similarities, between documents, testimonies, languages, or species. These sciences attempt to infer the causal origins of these correlations or similarities.

Some similarities among the members of a taxon [for example, a species or genus-AT] are the result of their independent exposure to similar environments. Other similarities are due to a trait being genetically transmitted from a common ancestor. In evolutionary biology, many (most?) of the similarities among the members of a taxon can be explained by those similarities being homologies [properties inherited from a common ancestors-AT]. No such explanation is available for the similarities found among the units of physics and chemistry. (Ereshefsky, 1992, p. 91)

The explanation of similarities by common ancestry distinguishes evolutionary biology from other sciences. Ereshefsky did not consider historiography, comparative linguistics, and the other sciences mentioned in the previous chapter, yet this holds true for them just as well.

Inferences of common causes can be divided between those of common types of causes and those of common cause tokens. "A token event is unique and unrepeatable; a type event may have zero, one or many instances" (Sober, 1988, p. 78). For example, if we share the same type of biological causes, the same types of sperm and egg, we most likely belong to the same species, we are human. If we share tokens of these causes, we are twins. Most parts of physics, chemistry, biology, and so forth, study common cause types: gravity, energy, atoms, molecules, cells etc. These sciences are interested in examining models, theories, or laws about such types of causes. They are not interested in a particular token of a cell or a molecule or a gluon or energy discharge. The inference of common cause types from their effects does not raise special issues in the philosophy of science. For example, Salmon (1984, pp. 220–1) analyzed the determination of the Avogadro number as the common cause type of various effects, different tokens, in different experiments. Salmon likened the various experiments that confirmed the Avogadro number to multiple witnesses to a murder whose testimonies agree on a core narrative, though each witness may provide different additional information. Even if the witnesses are unreliable by themselves, "It would be too improbable a coincidence for all of them to have fabricated their stories independently, and for all these stories to exhibit such strong agreement in precise detail" (p. 220). However, a murder is a token of a common cause of the testimonies, an event, not a type of constant like the Avogadro number. Van Fraassen criticized Salmon's presentation of the discovery of correlation between the number of molecules in one mole of gas, the Avogadro number, and the number of electron charges, one Faraday, as an inference of a common cause. This correlation "does not point to a relationship between events (in Brownian motion on specific occasions and in electrolysis on specific occasions) which is traced back via causal processes to forks connecting these processes. The explanation is rather that the number found in experiment *A* at time *t* is the same as that found in totally independent experiment *B* at *any* other time *t'*, because of the *similarity* in the physically independent causal processes observed on those two different occasions" (Van Fraassen, 1980, p. 123). In other words, Salmon discussed a common cause type, rather than a common cause token. Common cause types are essential for confirming scientific theories when the same type of cause appears in two different theories, the confirmation of one is transferable to the other by allowing the assumption of one theory to test the other, "bootstrapping." Common cause types enable separate scientific theories to connect and interwine together to construct a net of united theories that covers a domain of nature.

A different group of sciences are systematically interested in common cause tokens, in historical events and processes. Textual criticism, comparative historical linguistics, historiography, evolutionary biology, and archeology are interested in inferring tokens of common causes, original exemplars of texts, lost languages, descriptions of historical events, extinct species, and lost cities. Sober (1988) and Hausman (1998, pp. 207–8) interpreted the question of inference to a common cause in terms of token effects and token common causes.

I follow this interpretation. I would venture further to clam that it is possible to answer the old question about the distinction between the historical and other sciences which Comte and J. S. Mill referred to as dynamic versus static sciences, governed respectively by laws of succession and coexistence, by distinguishing the quest for common cause tokens from that for common cause types.

THE MEANING OF TOKEN COMMON CAUSE EXPLANATIONS

Reichenbach (1956) suggested that when the simultaneous occurrence of two events is more frequent than their separate frequencies would lead us to expect, they probably have a common cause. When:

$$Pr(A \& B) > Pr(A) \times Pr(B)$$

it is likely that A and B share a common cause, given that A and B are not causally connected to each other. Reichenbach proposed that the common cause C "screens" A and B from each other, if:

$$Pr(A \& B|C) = Pr(A|C) \times Pr(B|C).$$

If we distinguish the inference that there was *some common cause* of A and B without specifying its properties, from the inference of a *particular*, specified, common cause, of A & B, this formula is not useful in the first case. If we do not know the properties of C, it could be identical with A or with B, it could also be both A and B, or a multiplicity of many common causes that may include A and B. Reichenbach did not elaborate on how scientists can and do eliminate these possibilities when the properties of the hypothetical common cause or causes are unknown. In this respect, his principle is at least *incomplete* if not plain useless for the inference of some common cause token.

Reichenbach did not distinguish the inference of *the properties of a particular common cause*, from the inference that *there must have been some common cause* without characterizing it further. ". . . It is one thing to infer the existence of a common cause, quite another to say what that common cause was like, on the assumption that it exists." (Sober 1989, 281–2). It is one thing to say, as Darwin did, that man and apes had some common ancestor. It is quite another to infer descriptions of some of the properties of that ancestor, as contemporary evolutionary biologists do. "In applying the principle of the common cause to examples, Reichenbach (1956) and Salmon (1984) often treat postulating a common cause and inferring the state of that cause interchangeably." (Sober 1989, 282, note 3) The history of biology and comparative linguistics clearly displays two stages: First Rasmus Rask and Franz Bopp in linguistics and Darwin in biology established that sets of languages and species had some common causes. More than a generation later, other linguists and biologists, assuming that there must have been some common causes attempted to infer the properties of some of these common causes. "The methods used in phylogenetic inference *assume* that the species surveyed are genealogically related. The question is to determine which tree is best supported by the data" (Sober 1999, 267). Actually, when scientists infer some common cause token, it may be one of five general kinds:

1. A single common ancestral cause c. For example, the correlations between two exams are attributed to a common cause c, such as a textbook or the exam of a third student from which both students plagiarized.

2. Several ancestral common causes explain the correlation or similarity. For example, the students plagiarized the same common sources, different websites, class notes, etc.

3. The common cause may be a member of the class of similar correlated events. For example, one correlated exam is copied from another or a combination of others.

4. All the similar correlated events may participate in causing each other. For example, similar exams may be the result of the collective work of all who submitted them. The wave theory of language suggests that separate but similar languages may not have a single common ancestor, but may be the descendants of a group of separate languages that influenced each other in a historical period when they were geographically adjacent.

5. Combinations of 1 or 2, with 3 or 4. For example, the students consult each other (4) and several encyclopedias (2) before composing the exam together.

The inference of some common cause is of any of the above five possible causal relations without specifying necessarily which one. First Franz Bopp in linguistics and Darwin in biology established that sets of correlated and similar languages and species had some common causes, without specifying which of the five kinds they may be and certainly without specifying their hypothetical properties. More than a generation later, other linguists and biologists attempted to infer the properties of some of these "ancestral" common causes. The history of biblical criticism, classical philology, and historiography does not display such distinct stages. These sciences skipped the first stage to consider which of the five kinds of common causes explains best the evidence and then which properties the common causes probably had. It is clear that the similarities between all the present exemplars of the Bible are best explained by a common cause. Biblical criticism advanced by proving that the fifth kind of common cause, a combination of multiple ancestral causes (second kind) and mutual influences (fourth kind) best explains the evidence. It then went further to try to infer some of the properties of individual ancestral common causes of the Bible by using critical methods to distinguish its documentary sources from each other and from later editorial revisions. This apparent methodological leap resulted from the clear likelihood of the kind of textual evidence biblical critics, classical philologists, and historians usually deal with, given some common cause hypothesis. Similar texts, unlike similar species or languages, clearly had some common cause, the likelihood of their similarities given separate causes are negligible; it is self-evident that two versions of the *Iliad* had some common cause source that transmitted information that they preserve, otherwise two separate authors composed the *Iliad* independently of each other.

HOW TO INFER COMMON CAUSES?

Sober (1988, p. 100) noted that any collection of events share trivially some common cause. At the very least, any correlated or uncorrelated collection of events shares the Big Bang as its common cause. Most random collections of events would share many more common causes. The Big Bang does not explain the correlation between texts, languages, or species. Sober suggested that scientists specify explicitly or implicitly contrast classes composed of members who should not be caused by the inferred common cause. Contrast classes specify which common cause is relevant for the explanation of the similar evidence. For example, if we ask whether a common cause explains the correlations between the properties of dolphins and whales, we also imply their dissimilarity with, say, cows. We look then for a common ancestor of dolphins and whales that is not also a common ancestor of other mammals such as cows. If we formulate the question and its contrast class differently, for example, we ask for the common cause of dolphins and whales that is not the common ancestor of fish, the answer would be an older ur-mammal creature more ancient than the previous common ancestor. Likewise, when textual critics compare texts and infer their common ancestors they group them according to certain variables that other texts do not share (Greg, 1927).

Greg called sets of texts that are considered similar or correlated according to at least one property "variational groups." I adopt this useful term. Variational groups are founded on temporally "horizontal" correlations between members of a group that share certain variables that others outside the group do not.[3] According to Greg, the degree of collation is the extent to which minute variables are used to compare manuscripts. The more minute the collation, the more abnormal variables would be found. The degree of collation depends on a theory that determines which variants are significant.

Sober noted correctly that any monotonically increasing quantities such as British bread prices and sea levels in Venice are positively correlated (1988, p. 90). Similar types of economic processes may underlie both, but not a common cause *token*. Sober (2001) demonstrated that there are plenty of similarities and correlations in the world that imply nothing about the causal processes that brought them about. For example, most conspiracy theories infer from the correlation between the particular interests of a small segment of a population and the frequency in which these interests are fulfilled in comparison with the interests of less fortunate groups, or vice versa – the correlation between the interests of a social group and the higher frequency of its frustration in comparison with other groups – the presence of a hidden conspiracy. But though the frequency of assassinations, unnatural deaths, and other misfortunes among the Kennedys is higher than that in other political clans, and those mishaps may have been in the interest of some small segment of American society, *pace* Oliver Stone, it does not imply that there was a conspiracy. It is necessary therefore to distinguish properties whose correlation is indicative of common causes.

I argue that the properties that scientists look for in variational groups in order to infer some common causes are those that tend to preserve information. For example, the process of melting metals erases any information about the original form of the metal. By contrast the exclusively male Y-chromosome, and the exclusively female mitochondria are passed respectively from father to son and mother to her descendants. Thus, they preserve information respectively about their male and female ancestors, and are used by geneticists to infer genetic histories, the common causes of contemporary Y-chromosomes and mitochondria. The extent to which certain properties of events tend to preserve more information than others is not a philosophical, but an empirical question. Some processes tend to preserve in their end states information from their initial state more than others. Processes have varying levels of information preservation, varying levels of fidelity. Fidelity measures the degree to which a unit of evidence tends to preserve information about its given cause. *Fides*, fidelity, is a term used by textual critics to evaluate the reliability of texts (Maas, 1958). *Fidelity* is used in this sense as *reliability* is used in probability theory or *credibility* in jurisprudence (Friedman, 1987). In addition to general theories about the fidelities of certain processes, the evaluation of the fidelity of properties of events may involve the examination of evidence for the causal chains that purportedly transmitted information from some common cause to the evidence, for example, the fossil record. When authors who report about historical events were separated by time or space from those events, historians look for evidence for the causal chains that may or may not have connected events with evidence and estimate their reliability.

The selection of evidence according to its information-preserving qualities is theory laden. For example, comparative linguistics considers correlations between languages that use different but corresponding sounds such as the English sound "W" and the German sound "V" or the Czech "H" and the Russian "G" as information preserving. Such information is *nested*, it can be inferred only with the aid of laws that link properties explicit in the information signal with information that is nested in it (Dretske, 1981, pp. 71–80).

Biblical criticism, classical philology, and historiography leaped forward following the discovery or at least the recognition that oral transmission has a lower fidelity than written transmission, and that memorized prose has a lower fidelity than memorized verse. These theoretical assumptions are fairly uncontroversial and are used often in everyday life: We keep notes, diaries, and appointment books because they are more reliable than our memories; and verse is used often as a mnemonic aid. In common law, hearsay evidence is excluded because its fidelity is too low. Comparative linguistics leaped forward when it discovered that some words, names of places, the first few numbers, body parts, immediate family members, and proper names of fauna and flora have higher fidelity than the rest of the vocabulary, they are more likely to preserve ancient words.

Sober concluded that "I doubt that much can be said *in general* about the circumstances in which common cause explanations are to be preferred beyond general remarks about priors and likelihoods. What more there is that needs to be said must come from specific empirical theories, not from general philosophic ones. It is the separate sciences that provide the background theories that show how observations have evidential meaning. It is these that ultimately decide whether a common cause explanation is better supported than a separate cause explanation" (Sober, 1988, p. 111). Sober has proposed in a number of publications that scientists infer common causes by comparing the likelihoods of evidence given a common cause and given separate common causes (Sober, 1999, pp. 255–6):

$$\frac{\Pr(\text{variational group}|\text{some common cause})\ \Pr(\text{common cause})}{\Pr(\text{variational group}|\text{no common cause})\ \Pr(\text{no common cause})}$$

Sober (1988, p. 95) and Forster (1988) interpreted the comparison of likelihoods of a variational group given some common and separate causes as between the best particular common cause hypothesis that specified the properties of the hypothetical common cause and the best separate causes hypotheses that likewise specifies the hypothetical properties of the separate causes. If so, there must be two stages in the inference of some common cause:

1. Two "internal" comparisons, among competing particular common cause hypotheses and among particular separate causes hypotheses that explain the same evidence.
2. A final match between the respective "champions" of the above "tournaments."

Sober (1988, pp. 105–10) acknowledged that such best-case analysis generates problems of nuisance variables/parameters. However, I think this model has a more fundamental problem because it does not correspond with the historical development of scientific inferences of common causes that proceeded from the general recognition that there must have been some common cause of languages and species that share certain information-preserving variables to the later introduction of particular hypotheses that suggested what the properties of these common causes may have been. Darwin could not have compared the best particular common cause hypothesis with the best concrete separate causes hypothesis because he did not possess them any more than Rask or Bopp knew or even speculated about the exact properties of proto–Indo-European. They must have inferred somehow that various species of finches in the Galápagos Islands, man and apes, and the Indo-European languages had some common cause without surmising anything about the properties of the ur-finch or proto-Indo-European. The founders of historical linguistics and evolutionary biology must offer the paradigmatic cases for the inference of some common cause.

Later, Sober (1999, p. 259) proposed a different method for evaluating whether some common cause is the best explanation of a variational group: Instead of the best hypothesis in each category, Sober suggested to sum up all the likelihoods of a variational group given particular common cause hypotheses, multiplied by their priors. Nevertheless, this second reductive scheme is just as inconsistent with the historical development of scientific inferences of common causes. Bopp and Darwin clearly did not sum up the concrete hypotheses they did not possess. Finally, Sober (1999) suggested that it is possible to compute the ratio of likelihoods of a variational group given some common cause to it given separate causes without actually assigning numerical values to them, if it is assumed that rates of preservation of information, of fidelity, are uniform at the same time across different causal chains: "If two branches are contemporaneous, then any conditional probability that describes the one also describes the other" (p. 260). Sober argued that given uniform rates, similarity is more likely given some common cause than given separate origins, and a more recent ancestor is more probable than a more distant one. Sober has recognized, though, in his various discussions of this problem that the assumption of uniform rates is actually false. I should add that even had the assumption of uniform rates been true (as it may be for particular local historical contexts), it would have been insufficient for distinguishing common cause *tokens* from common cause *types* because variational groups would be equally likely given contemporaneous common cause token, or tokens of the same type. However, we are interested here exclusively in a common cause token.

In the history of science, it was proved first that there was some common cause rather than separate causes before it became possible to examine what the particular properties of the common cause or causes might have been. Darwin explained the similarities among species by some common causes, ancestor species, and natural selection, but he refrained from hypothesizing what the specific properties of the common causes could have been, and dissuaded others like Haeckel and Huxley from speculating on them. In comparative linguistics, the Indo-European hypothesis was established at the beginning the nineteenth century. Yet, beyond intuition and speculation, comparative linguists had been unable to agree on the properties of proto–Indo-European before the 1860s.

A Bayesian approach to the inference of some common cause would consider the variational group as evidence and a description of some common cause as a hypothesis that should increase the likelihood of the evidence more than the competing hypothesis that members of the variational group had separate causes. It is important to note that the alternative to some common cause is separate causes, not coincidence. Much of the intuitive appeal of Reichenbach's common cause principle is the assumption that unless there is a common cause, the correlation or similarity is "miraculous" or coincidental. I will demonstrate soon that in many cases, the alternative to common cause token is different tokens of the same type of cause, tokens of an environment type in biology, a market type in economic history, a token type of structual constraints in architecture etc.

Forster (1988, 539) argued against the possibility of comparison of likelihoods of variational groups given some common cause and separate causes. He argued that such comparisons of likelihoods are incomplete because they do not mention priors and because the transition probabilities from some common cause or separate causes to their effects are not precisely, quantitatively, known. Sober (1999, p. 258) acknowledged that there is insufficient evidence to assign values to the prior probabilities of common or separate origins of all life on earth, a single start or several starts of life. Sober was forced then to compare just the ratio of likelihoods. I argue next that in most cases it is actually possible to assess priors. I acknowledge that it is often difficult to discover *precise* transition probabilities, but usually it is unnecessary because scientists do not prove the high likelihood of the variational group given the hypothesis they favor, as much as prove its negligible likelihood given the alternative hypothesis.

PRIOR PROBABILITY OF THE COMMON
CAUSE HYPOTHESIS

Suppose that a variational group is composed of two units of evidence, E_1 and E_2, which share certain variables that $E_3, E_4, \ldots, E_n$ do not share. Let us call the common cause hypothesis C. Before we can compute the likelihood of both $E_1 \& E_2$ given C: $\Pr(E_1 \& E_2 | C)$, it is necessary first to evaluate the prior probability of C, of some common cause given everything else we know: $\Pr(C|B)$.

Hitchcock (1998, p. 446) suggested that a Bayesian perspective might be beneficial for the study of linguistic inferences where the conclusions of prior research in historical, archeological, and genetic sources would be factored into the priors. Scientists examine whether causal chains that extend backward from $E_1 \& E_2$ could intersect and converge before they encounter the causal chains that extend backward from the units of the comparison group. For example, if we wish to examine the hypothesis that the similarities between the English word "tea," the Czech "*caj*," and the Hebrew "*te*" that the Polish "*herbata*" does not share resulted from a common cause, relevant background information about the history of tea, would tell us that it was initially a Chinese drink that was exported westward. Given that knowledge, it is probable that the causal-etymological chains that lead backward from these words converged in China sometime during the Middle Ages, though without further research, I cannot know the properties of the original Chinese word for tea. By contrast, the hypothesis that ascribes the similarity between the Egyptian and Aztec pyramids that other structures in Greece did not share to some common cause has very low prior probability because there is no evidence for intersection between causal chains that stretch back from the Aztec and Egyptian architects. The large distance in space between these civilizations, and premodern means of transportation and information technology, make the prior probability of such intersection negligible.

LIKELIHOOD OF A VARIATIONAL GROUP GIVEN SOME COMMON CAUSE

The assessment of the likelihoods of a variational group given the common cause hypothesis also depends on background information, including auxiliary evidence and theories. Generally, the theories involved are about the preservation of information through its transmission from one causal link to another, and the relevant auxiliary evidence is about links in the causal chains that transmit information from the hypothetical common cause to the variational group. For example, a fairly rudimentary biological theory that holds that like organisms tend to bear like is at the foundation of cladistic inferences in biology because it increases the likelihood of similarities between closely related species, given a common cause (Sober, 1988, 1989, 1999). Theories about the copying of texts, and the evolution of species and languages help in assessing the likelihoods of variational groups given some common causes. The discovery of evidence for links on the causal chains that could connect the hypothetical common cause with the similar effects that are more similar to each other than do members of the variational group, increases the likelihood of the variational group given some common cause. For example, the similarities between two species, say horses and donkeys that cows do not share, becomes more likely given some common ancestor following the discovery of fossils that resemble each other more than horses and donkeys do.

Formally, the likelihood of the evidence given the common cause hypothesis is:

$$\Pr(E_1 \ \& \ E_2 \ \& \dots \& \ E_n | C)$$
$$= \Pr(E_1 | C) \times \Pr(E_2 | C) \times \dots \times \Pr(E_n | C)$$

EVALUATING THE SEPARATE CAUSES HYPOTHESIS

Formally, assessing the likelihood of similar evidence given separate causes $(S_1, S_2, \ldots, S_n)$ and their respective prior probabilities can be expressed by the following equation:

$$\Pr(E_1 \And E_2 \And \ldots \And E_n | S_1 \And S_2 \And \ldots \And S_n)$$
$$= [\Pr(S_1|B) \times \Pr(E_1|S_1)] \times [\Pr(S_2|B) \times \Pr(E_2|S_2)]$$
$$\times \ldots \times [\Pr(S_n|B) \times \Pr(E_n|S_n)]$$

It is possible to discover the likelihood of the variational group given separate causes by considering the function, the adaptational advantage, or the rationality, of the shared properties of the members of the variational group. In such cases, the separate causes hypothesis can explain variational groups by the same type of cause. For example, given a level of building technology that does not include columns and arches, and the laws of physics, the only likely shape of a big and tall building is that of a pyramid, a solid wide base that can support a lighter structure above it. This is the only type of solution that ancient Egyptian and Aztec architects could have devised for this problem. This type of cause, interest in constructing a large building without arches or columns explains pyramids on both sides of the Atlantic, makes the similarity highly likely, though the token causes are different. Similarly, various cultures independently discovered agriculture, the taming of domestic animals, and how to build boats, because these are the best functional solutions for the universal human problems of food, shelter, and transportation. Similar technological innovations and scientific discoveries usually do not require a common cause token to be likely. In evolutionary history, functional solutions may develop independently, spontaneously, following random variations and given an evolutionary process that selects only the successful solutions. Biological evolution favored through random variation and natural selection wings and fins several times, though insects, birds and bats; fish, ichthyosaurs, and dolphins, neither evolved out of each other, nor are they genetically closely related to each other, because they are the best functional solutions for the problems of organic movement through air and water. *Homoplasy*, similarity of biological traits that results from similar environments, similar types of causes, such as between fish and sea mammals, is quite likely given separate causes. Notice that as in the case of the common cause hypothesis, it is unncessary to specify here the precise properties of the separate causes. Hydrodynamic shape gives an evolutionary edge to seafaring organisms; the properties of the ancestral life forms that preceded this shape but did not have it are not necessarily known.

Background information and theories can evaluate the prior probabilities of separate causes that are tokens of a single type of cause. For example if we find organisms with fins at a given geological level, and we explain their shape by the adaptational advantage it gives to seafaring animals irrespective of the properties of their ancestors, the prior probability of this explanation depends on whether or not there was a large body of water at that place at that geological era. In the human realm, prior probabilities depend on what we know of the historical context of the separate causes, for example, whether the builders of pyramids did not know of columns and arches.

In the human realm, there is often a best solution or set of best solutions to certain problems, under constraining circumstances; any prolonged rational process of trial and error problem solving will tend toward a certain optimal solution or set of solutions. This is the basic assumption of rational choice theory in the social sciences. The many historical cases of multiple inventions indicate that this is often the case. For example, the invention of printing was made independently in China and Europe because it is the best solution to the problem of reproducing texts or images in a mass market at an affordable price by saving on labor costs. If we discover an alien technological civilization on another planet, it is likely that their mathematics would be identical to ours. If we ask for the explanation of the similarity, as distinct from the dissimilarity in vernacular and biology between humans and aliens, the best explanation of this similarity would be a separate cause hypothesis because of the high likelihood that in order to develop a technological scientific civilization, a separate civilization in the same type pf universe must develop identical mathematical models. For example, the discovery of calculus can be achieved independently and simultaneously, as Leibnitz and Newton learned to their chagrin. By contrast, if some aliens have a copy of Proust in their language or their orchestras play Mahler's Second Symphony, it is highly unlikely there are separate causes. The likelihood of Proust being written twice, independently, is vanishingly low, even lower than its likelihood given the low prior probability of some causal informational net that includes Proust and aliens. Though the prior probability of some common cause of similar human and alien literature is just as low as that of similar mathematics, the likelihood of similar literature given separate causes is lower because literature unlike mathematics does not give its readers an adaptational advantage across the universe.

Variational groups that share properties that have no conceivable functional value, or even confer a disadvantage on their bearers, such as grammatical mistakes in texts or dysfunctional or redundant properties of species, which Darwin called *rudiments* usually radically decrease the likelihood of the evidence given the separate cause hypothesis. The likelihood of any single grammatical mistake or nonadaptive trait is low; the likelihood of identical ones given separate causes is very small indeed. The likelihood of nonadaptive traits given the common cause hypothesis is significantly higher. For this reason, geneticists and textual critics alike cherish them. Imperfections and errors in transcriptions are the best evidence for copying rather than independent reinvention because the odds against two separate processes arriving at the same dysfunctional forms are vast (Dennett, 1996, pp. 135–43). Maas (1958) meant by textual *anomalies* what biologists denote by *homologies* or *rudiments*. Maas considered similar anomalies evidence for some common cause. If there were equally useful simpler ways to express what the anomaly conveys, the anomaly must be the result of a common cause, a mutation in copying.

When the likelihood of each member of the variational group given separate causes is low, the effect of multiple members, such as many independent similar testimonies, is to decrease exponentially the likelihood of the variational group. Therefore, evolutionary biologists, comparative linguistics, as well as policemen and journalists, devote great efforts to the discovery of multiple testimonies, witnesses, and units of evidence. Still, beyond a small number of independent witnesses, marginal testimonies become redundant because the marginal decrease in the likelihood of the similar evidence, given separate causes, is so small. This "economics of witnessing" is apparent in the plea bargains police and prosecutors cut with criminals who turn state witnesses to receive reduced or suspended sentences for testifying against their accomplices. After obtaining two or three independent witnesses to the same events, the state ceases to offer plea bargains to other criminals who offer the same testimonies because the likelihood of detailed testimonies given separate causes is minuscule. Two or three witnesses are sufficient to convict beyond reasonable doubt, and the interest of the prosecutor is to keep deals with criminals to the necessary minimum to achieve conviction. Coady (1992, pp. 30–2) presented a puzzle: Suppose a jury hears identical testimonies from four different witnesses. After hearing three independent witnesses who agree with each other the jury may believe the testimonies to a greater degree than that the fourth witness who is convinced of his own testimony. How could the marginal witness increase the degree of belief of the juries who are more confident than he is? Coady answered correctly that the degree of confidence of an audience in a belief may be higher than that of a witness, if taken together with the evidence of other witnesses. Coady however, did not explain, as we can, how many witnesses are necessary for proof beyond reasonable doubt. Further, Coady did not fully recognize the significance of corroboration in decreasing the likelihood of the evidence, given the separate causes hypotheses. He found it curious that in common law, the testimony of a child may be inadmissible, while the testimony of two dubious children who corroborate each other is admissible (Coady, 1992, pp. 36–7). Elsewhere (p. 214), Coady did recognize that at least in historiography, corroboration is necessary for testimony to be epistemically useful.

COMPARISON OF LIKELIHOODS

Since in many cases it is impossible to determine precisely the valued parameters of priors of common or separate causes hypotheses, and the likelihood of the evidence given these alternative hypotheses, a significant gap between the roughly estimated likelihoods of the evidential variational group given these hypotheses is required. Multiple witnesses achieve that gap. We can formally sum up the ratio of likelihoods of similar evidence given some common cause to separate causes hypotheses as follows:

$$[\Pr(E_1|C) \times \Pr(E_2|C) \times \ldots \times \Pr(E_n|C)] : [\Pr(E_1|S_1) \times \Pr(E_2|S_2) \times \ldots \times \Pr(E_n|S_n)]$$

Where $E_1, E_2, \ldots, E_n$ stand for units of evidence members of the variational group; C stands for the hypothetical common cause; and $S_1, S_2, \ldots, S_n$ stand for separate causes. The left side of this formula represents the likelihood of the evidence given some common cause hypothesis, the right side, its likelihood given separate causes. We can also add the prior probabilities of some common cause C, given background knowledge B and the prior probabilities of the various separate cause hypotheses:

$$\frac{\{[\Pr(E_1|C) \times \Pr(C|B)] \times [\Pr(E_2|C) \times \Pr(C|B)] \times \ldots \times [\Pr(E_n|C) \times \Pr(C|B)]\}}{\{[\Pr(E_1|S_1) \times \Pr(S_1|B)] \times [\Pr(E_2|S_2) \times \Pr(S_2|B)] \times \ldots \times [\Pr(E_n|S_n) \times \Pr(S_n|B)]\}}$$

The upper part represents the likelihood of the evidence, given some common cause hypothesis; the lower its likelihood, given separate causes. The ratio of the likelihoods determines the choice between common and separate causes hypotheses.

For example, some common cause hypotheses would explain the similarity in the sounds of words in different languages by the influence of one language over others, or by the effects of a lost language on all the words in the variational group, or by the mutual effects of languages on each other. The separate causes hypothesis would claim that the similar sounds evolved independently in the history of each language. Relevant background information would mention the limited capacity of human beings to produce sounds, the limited ability of the human ear and mind to distinguish sounds, and the function of all languages to communicate many different meanings by generating distinguishable combinations of sounds that humans can reproduce. Accordingly, it is extremely likely that all languages would display some phonetic similarities irrespective of origins. Some words display similarities across languages because of common types of causes, for example nursery and onomatopoeic words (Hitchcock, 1998, p. 444). Unless there is evidence for historical contact between languages, phonetic similarities between a few words are more likely given the separate causes hypothesis than given some common cause hypothesis.

In contemporary historical linguistics some propose that the best explanation of the similarity between two African click languages, *Hadzabe* and *Ju|'hoansi* is some lost common ancestor language that was also a click language. The groups who speak these languages have been geographically distant and separated from each other, genetically, for at least 50,000 years. "Unless each group independently invented click languages at some later time . . . click languages were spoken by the very ancient population from which the Hadzabe and the Ju|'hoansi descended" (Wade, 2003). This common cause hypothesis does not say anything about the specific properties of that alleged ancient ancestral click language. The alternative separate causes hypothesis suggests that click languages are likely in societies of hunters because clicking sounds resemble natural sounds more than the sounds of nonclick languages, and so are less likely to startle prey, that is click languages are a functional solution for the problem of communication among hunters.

ALTERNATIVE COMMON CAUSE HYPOTHESES

If some common cause hypothesis explains the evidence considerably better than the separate causes hypothesis by considerably increasing the likelihood of the variational group, alternative common cause hypotheses may compete to give the best explanation of the variational group, to make it more likely. There may be two stages in this comparison between common cause hypotheses. First, the five above-mentioned possible causal nets, a single or multiple ancestral common causes, mutual influences of some or all the members of the variational group, or a combination of ancestral causes and mutual influences, compete over giving the best explanation of the variational group. Second, once one of the five possible options is chosen, scientists may attempt to infer the actual properties of the common causes. The Bayesian model is again the best explanation of the actual practices of scientists.

When evidence is scarce, all five possible types of common cause hypotheses may make the evidence equally likely. For example: In comparative philology, though it is certain that the Indo-European languages had common rather than separate causes, it is impossible to find whether it was a single language, proto–Indo-European, or whether several geographically proximate languages mutually influenced each other, or both.

Still, scientists are able in many cases to infer which of the five possible common cause hypotheses is most probable. For example, textual critics were able to prove that the various exemplars of the Bible and Homer's epics had initially multiple common causes and then they influenced each other in the process of editing. There is independent evidence in many cases for links on the causal information chains that connect events with evidence for the presence of a single common cause or multiple common causes. Composite documents may preserve linguistic differences that indicate multiple common causes. Historians and textual critics look for discontinuities in style, conceptual framework, and implicit values, as well as internal contradictions, gaps in the narrative if there is one, and parts that are inconsistent with the alleged identity of the author. Excessive uniformity of documentary exemplars or testimonies is evidence for mutual influences that created uniformity. Frequently, the theories that assist in the assessment of the fidelity of evidence and the competitiveness of the common cause hypothesis also assist in proving whether there was a single common cause or multiple common causes. For example, assuming that the mutation rates of the names of God are lower than those of other words, that the fidelity of the names of God is higher than that of other parts of edited documents, it is possible to analyze parts of the Bible into its constituent parts, as the first biblical critics analyzed Genesis. Less certain and more controversial is the temporal order of conceptual frameworks and the temporal ordering of components of composite documents according to the concepts they use. Vico ([1725] 1984) was probably the first to use conceptual analysis to discover that the author of the *Iliad* could not have been the author of the *Odyssey* because the values of the *Iliad* are of a heroic culture whereas the values of the *Odyssey* are of a commercial culture.

Another way of saying that a variational group has ancestral common cause or causes (types 1 or 2), but no mutual causal influences (types 3 or 4) is by describing its members as *independent*.

Independence of evidence is the absence of intersection between the causal-information chains that connect members of a variational group with a hypothetical ancestral common cause. The judgment of evidence as independent or not is relative to an ancestral hypothetical common cause or causes. For example, collusion of witnesses eliminates their independence in relation to the hypothesis that the common cause of their testimony is an event they observed. However, if the hypothesis is that the common cause of their similar testimonies is a meeting in which they decided to frame an innocent person, their testimony is independent. If witnesses to a crime are able to talk of what they observed between the time of the observation and the time of delivering their testimony, their testimony is not independent (type 5 in the above classification). Scientists, who are interested in inferring common causes distinct from the variational group, find type 5 to be a nuisance as it interferes with the inference of common causes. Textual critics call their influence *contaminatio* (Maas, 1958). Greg (1927) used the term *convergent variations* to describe the same phenomenon.[1]

INFERRING THE PROPERTIES OF PARTICULAR COMMON CAUSES

When one of the possible five common cause hypotheses increases the likelihood of the evidence more than the others, scientists may attempt to infer the properties of the common cause and reconstruct the genealogical causal-informational net that connects the correlated units of evidence. Sometimes there is enough evidence to prefer one of the five possible types of common causes, though the evidence is still insufficient for determining that causal net. For example (Greg, 1927), suppose that a set of similar documents can be divided into three groups:

Group one has: "To you I tell."
Group two has: "To you I say."
Group three has: "I say to you."

Clearly each group is derived from a different single source. Let us denote them as sources 1, 2, and 3. The first and third groups are more similar to the second group than to each other. So, if the second group is assumed as derived from the oldest source (2), the first and third groups (1, 3) are independently derived from source 2. However, if we assume sources 1 or 3 to be the oldest, there is a successive variation through source 2. Therefore, this variational grouping is equally likely according to three different genetic histories.

The Bayesian model is still the best explanation of the actual practices of historians. When there is sufficient evidence to determine a particular common cause hypothesis, historians evaluate the prior probabilities of competing particular common cause hypotheses that characterize the common causes of a variational group differently, according to whether the hypotheses are coherent with established historiographic beliefs, the laws of nature, as well as internally coherent (Kosso, 1993, p. 5). Through the historical development of historiography the web of historiographic beliefs has expanded and the connections among its units grew complex. By now, new historiography should fit old historiography as well as new evidence (Goldstein, 1976, pp. 79–81). Since historians have no direct access to the past, historiography has no clear, distinct, and certain foundations. Knowledge of history is founded on coherence rather than foundations (Kosso, 2001, pp. 75–6). Historiography, as a science, is holistic, it presents a net of beliefs, connected to evidence at its rims (Quine, 1980, pp. 42–6). When historiographic hypotheses are inconsistent with each other, less entrenched ones are examined first (Kosso, 2001, pp. 106–8) because they have lower prior probabilities.

The prior probabilities of particular common cause hypotheses, C_1, $C_2, \ldots, C_n$ can then be multiplied by the likelihood of the evidence, $E_1, E_2, \ldots, E_n$, given particular common cause hypotheses:

$$Pr(E_1 \, \& \, E_2 \, \& \ldots \& \, E_n | C_1) = [Pr(C_1|B) \times Pr(E_1|C_1)] \times [Pr(C_1|B)$$
$$\times Pr(E_2|C_1)] \times \ldots \times [Pr(C_1|B) \times Pr(E_n|C_1)]$$

The comparison of competing common cause hypotheses is then simply

$$Pr(E_1 \, \& \, E_2 | C_1) : Pr(E_1 \, \& \, E_2 | C_2)$$

But how do historians measure the likelihoods of evidence given particular common causes?

FIDELITY AND LIKELIHOODS GIVEN COMPETING
COMMON CAUSES

Some processes preserve in their end states information from their initial state. For example, the process of electronic mail delivery usually preserves information. By contrast, the process of throwing dice does not preserve information about the results of previous rolls. Processes such as hand copying of manuscripts have varying levels of information preservation, varying levels of *fidelity*. Fidelity measures the degree to which a unit of evidence preserves information about its cause. Obviously, the degree of fidelity of the evidence depends on the hypothesis it is proposed as evidence for, as well as on the causal chain of information transmission that allegedly connected them. For example, the Donation of Constantine has no fidelity at all for any hypothesis about the era of the Emperor Constantine, it has high fidelity as evidence for Church-state politics in the early Middle Ages. The evaluation of the fidelity of a piece of evidence requires the examination of the causal chain that purportedly transmitted information from a hypothetical common cause to the evidence.

Historians do not quantify fidelities (Coady, 1992, pp. 210–11). Murphey (1973, p. 56) thought that historians assign subjective reliability to evidence such as documents intuitively. Alvin Goldman (1999, pp. 123–5) proposed that testimonies are evaluated according to the competence of the witnesses to detect the kind of information they offer and their record for honest reporting. Ranke assumed a theory of memory that implies low fidelity of memoirs and high fidelity of contemporary eyewitness accounts written immediately after the events. Instead of valuing the fidelity parameters of memories, historians since Ranke have been exluding them from the pool of evidential sources they use. Since there is no set of algorithms for evaluating fidelities, historians exclude evidence that does not achieve a threshold of fidelity for whatever reason. Historians usually exclude evidence written by authors that were separated by time or space from the events they describe, unless there is evidence for a credible causal chain that could have transmitted information from events to evidence. Historians may assess the fidelity of some types of evidence without evidence for a causal-information chain if other independent sources consistently agree or disagree with the information conveyed by particular authors, sources, or institutions. For example, though Diodorus and Pausanias are both sources for ancient Greek history who were separated by centuries from the events they described, Pausanias is valued as having a higher fidelity than Diodorus because other testimonies and material evidence confirm much of what he wrote (Kosso, 2001, p. 120). Historians recognize the high fidelity of parish registries, while they consider the official statistics of totalitarian states unreliable. Murphey (1973, pp. 140–3) suggested that historians study the preservation, recording, and transmission norms of various institutions. Which kinds of information do they preserve and which kinds do they discard? How do they record and transmit it? Sometimes, such norms are recorded formally. On other occasions, historians must find external evidence for these norms. For example, the Pennsylvania colonial ship registry never recorded ships that were in the coastal trade. Had historians not discovered this rule, they could have inferred mistakenly that there was no coastal trade in colonial Philadelphia.

Historians search assiduously for primary sources because they have higher fidelity than secondary sources. A major part of the education of historians consists of learning to distinguish primary from secondary sources. Historians usually agree on the classifications of sources. Still, the abstract definition of primary sources is more challenging. Marwick suggested first that "primary sources are sources which came into existence during the actual period of the past which the historian is studying, they are those relics and traces left by the past, while secondary sources are those accounts written later by historians looking back" (1993, p. 199). However, some primary sources come into existence long after the events the historian is studying; for example, later copies of ancient manuscripts such as the Greek classics. Conversely, some effects that come into existence at the same period as the studied event are not primary sources because they do not preserve information about the event. Marwick (1993, p. 202) added that primary sources are raw materials more meaningful for historians than for lay readers. This seems to mean that primary sources are evidence, which is true but not informative in specifying which kind of evidence. Finally, Marwick (pp. 202–3) added a list of properties of primary sources that seems superfluous: They should be handwritten and rare.

Marwick (p. 200) noted correctly that the primacy of a source is relative to the hypothesis it serves as evidence. Obviously, primary sources are a privileged type of evidence that historians prefer to use. Primary sources are evidence that possess the highest degree of fidelity by preserving more information that is relevant for a particular historiographic hypothesis than other relevant evidence. Generally, the nearer a source is to the event on an information causal chain, the more primary it is. For example, if we wish to examine primary evidence for the philosophy of Aristotle, we use copies of the Greek original as primary sources and ignore medieval Latin translations as secondary. However if the Latin translation was made from a unique Greek exemplar that is lost, it is a primary source for reconstructing the lost Greek original that can be compared with extant Greek exemplars, as the Septuagint, the Greek translation of the Bible is a valuable primary source for the state of the Bible from the third to first centuries BCE.

Historians cannot transcend the evidence to check its reliability against history. They must bootstrap their evaluations of the fidelity of particular evidence by other evidence. Historians use independent sources to evaluate each other's fidelity. Independent sources testify to the fidelity of a source or provide information on what the author could and could not have seen or known, as well as information on the information causal chain that may or may not have connected an event or a document with the evidence (Kosso, 1993, pp. 3–4). This is the fundamental practice of historians, which is taught as part of the historiographic guild's right of passage (Evans, 1999, pp. 16–17). This is also the great success story of modern historiography as its countless exposures of forgeries may attest.

If historians, philologists, and textual critics can date two members of a variational group, documents, or languages, or types of handwriting, or the forms of official documents, or layers of language or pottery, they can measure similarity to them which together with a rough fidelity rate, can date the other members of the variational group. They can distinguish ancestors from descendants, or even model all causal-informational influences. Some texts contain internal evidence for the date of their composition. At the very least we can know for sure that documents are later than events they mention. External evidence may provide relevant information about the history of the text that allows historians, biblical critics, and classical philologists to reconstruct at least a part of the genealogy of the texts they study, as biblical critics attempted in relation to the Bible and Wolf in relation to the Homeric poems.

In historiography, the specialized, sometimes called auxiliary, fields of diplomatic and paleography are in charge of developing techniques for dating and authenticating documents. It is possible to date archeological remains according to material remains found in the same layer such as coins, as well as through carbon 14 analysis. Similar dating techniques are used to give a rough estimate of the dates of fossils. At the current mature state of historiography, archaeology, evolutionary biology, and classical studies many well-confirmed hypotheses about the dates of types of evidence are codified in specialized dictionaries and lexicons that list when words or styles of pottery appear for the first time and in which regions. Historical dictionaries also list the different meanings the same words have had in different historical periods. Currently practicing historians, classicists, or archeologists date texts or material remains by relying on these well-confirmed hypotheses that represent the accumulated results of research of generations of their colleagues.

CONSTANT RATES OF FIDELITY

Comparative linguistics leaped forward when it was discovered that some words, names of places, the first few numbers, body parts, immediate family members, and names of fauna and flora maintain higher fidelity than the rest of the vocabulary; they are more likely to preserve ancient words. In comparative linguistics there have been attempts to quantify the fidelity of the basic, slowly mutating, vocabulary. Since there is sufficient evidence to establish historiographies of some languages over thousands of years, it is possible to infer an average rate of fidelity across all languages. Vocabulary retention for this slowly changing vocabulary is according to Swadesh 0.86 per thousand years. In evolutionary biology, the use of degrees of similarity between species and DNAs as evidence for their genetic distance and to date their branching on the evolutionary tree, assumes that a particular DNA mutates at a roughly constant rate, that its fidelity per unit of time remains constant. For example, Troy and others (2001) measured the similarities between the mitochondrial DNA of Asian Indian, Middle Eastern, European, and African cattle and the now extinct Bos primigenius that existed in Europe. They assumed that the greater the divergence in their DNA sequence, the more distantly related are these types of cattle. The degree of difference between DNA sequences served as evidence to estimate the time that has elapsed since the species separated from each other. This is possible because the rate of mitochondrial DNA mutation is usually constant for a particular species. Following these assumptions Troy and others concluded that Asian Indian and European cattle diverged from each other about a million years ago. Therefore, humans must have domesticated cattle independently at least twice, in India and Europe.

In general, if paired copies of a gene have stopped recombining, their sequences will diverge increasingly as time goes by. A relatively small number of differences implies recombination stopped fairly recently; a large number means it halted long ago.

By comparing DNA sequences across species, biologists can often calculate roughly when formerly matching genes...began to go their separate ways. Such comparisons revealed that the autosomal precursors of the X and Y [genes] were still alike and intact in reptiles that existed before the mammalian lineage began branching extensively. (Jegalian & Lahn, 2001, p. 59)

Sneath and Sokal (quoted in Sober, 1988, p. 75) concluded that a uniform rate of evolution accross species is a necessary background assumption for reconstructing phylogeny. For example, if a species evolves into three different species, unless the rate of evolution remains uniform across the new species, the similarity between the species would not reflect their genetic proximity. Otherwise, a species that evolves more quickly than others would diverge greatly from its close relatives, and similarity would not indicate the degree of genetic relation. Sneath and Sokal thought that uniform rates hold, generally. Constant rates of mutation could be states as a statistical rule:

All copying of information (languages, documents, genetic data, oral histories, and so forth) generates mutations, including errors in transcription, additions and substractions. Ceteris paribus *the average rate of mutation per medium per transmission is constant.*

Average constants of spontaneous variation would vary according to the type of information that is copied (DNA, written text, spoken tradition, memories, prose, poetry, etc.) and the method of transmission/copying (text to scribe versus reader to scribe versus reader and translator to translator and scribe, bard to apprentice, and so on). Divergence, the degree of variation between similar units of evidence such as documents, layers of language, DNAs, and so on, tends to increase as variations accumulate. The fidelity of evidence depends then on the number of transmissions and the average constant rate of mutation per transmission per medium. When the number of transmissions per unit of time is roughly constant, as is the case in biological reproduction per species, though not in the copying of documents, fidelity would be commensurable with the time gap between the event and the evidence. The rule of average constant rates of mutation implies that *ceteris paribus* the degree of similarity between units of copied information that share a common cause is commensurable with the proximity of their genetic relations.

If the average constant rate of mutation and the number of transmissions are sufficiently high, the level of fidelity may be low enough to conclude that it is impossible to infer with any degree of reliability information about the properties of common causes that surely existed. For example, though there is a consensus among philologists that there was an ur-language, spoken by the first humans, it is debated whether it is possible to know anything about it with any reliability from the similarities between known languages apart from the a priori generative properties of all human languages that linguists have examined since a revolution and a new nonhistorical paradigm were introduced by Noam Chomsky.

Some biologists and Sober doubt uniform (per unit of time across species) and constant (per species in different times) rates of mutation and the ensuing quantified fidelities. In linguistics the *school* of Swadesh is just that, not a paradigm. Rates of evolution did not remain constant throughout natural history. There were periods of quick evolutionary change and other periods when evolutionary change seems to have ground to a halt. The state of the evidence does not depend exclusively on the rate of mutation during transmission. Evolution of species, languages, and texts follow random mutations that generate variations and natural selection, which selects those variations that are best adjusted to their environment. Environmental conditions neither remain constant nor change gradually or cyclically. For example, a large meteor crash can radically alter environmental conditions and cause a radical acceleration of evolution and reduction in the fidelity of the evidence, post-catastrophe life forms. Life went through five revolutions when most species disappeared from the fossil record within a short period. Recent theories suggest that these revolutions resulted from catastrophic changes in the environment, such as planetary collisions with meteors that radically accelerated the process of natural selection. In linguistics, the exact, constant or not, rate of mutation of languages is disputed. For example, Renfrew suggested that the first farmers who introduced agriculture to Europe and India spoke proto–Indo-European. His critics argued that this date is too early because any parent language that would have been introduced that early would have mutated beyond recognition by now into dissimilar languages (Wylie, 1995, p. 13). The root of this dispute is the rate of linguistic evolution. This rate may be affected by many different factors. It is difficult to extrapolate a constant mutation rate for different languages on the basis of the established historiographies of particular languages that evolved in historical periods and left sufficient evidence for determining their historiographies.

If the constant rates of mutation rule holds, it is statistical and local, true only for particular segments of evolutionary history. Particular transmissions of information may be more or less reliable than the average constant rate of mutation. As Sober emphasized, mutations can be reversed by later mutations. For example, the first copying of a sentence may mutate in a certain way, and the second copying may mutate back to its original state, so the number of transmissions is no sure indicator of the difference between the base state, the common cause, and the end state, the evidence. The evolutionary geneticist Lewontin (1994a, pp. 485–6) acknowledged that systematics involves the recognition of relevant similarities between species and the inference of evolutionary relationships and a family tree. According to Lewontin two additional rules govern the inference of ancestry from similarity: First, evolutionary reversal to an earlier stage is rare and, second, repeated independent origins of new features do not occur. Still, even the most parsimonious trees must violate these rules and include reversals and repeated independent origins, separate rather than common causes. In Lewontin's opinion, evolutionary biologists react to such internal contradictions between their rules and results by revising the tradition that determined which similar traits are genetically relevant and which are not. For example, are DNA and molecular traits better indicators than morphological traits of the histories of the species? Lewontin claims that even after such revisions, the results of systematics contain contradictions because some independent origins of similar traits and reversals are inevitable on the inferred genetic tree. Lewontin concluded that the evidence underdetermines the results of systematics because there are no general rules that can connect the evidence with evolutionary historiography.

Lewontin's conclusion does not explain how scientists are able to reach consensus on many issues in evolutionary historiography. Lewontin did not explain his two "rules" either, assigning them to tradition and experience. From a Bayesian perspective, these quandaries can be easily explained. Lewontin's first rule is probabilistic, not a law of nature. It is more probable that mutation and natural selection will result in something new than in reversal to an earlier species. Still, claiming that this is absolutely impossible constitutes the "gambler fallacy," which is the assumption that the chances of a number being drawn are lower if that number had already been drawn before. Given the results of Bayesian comparison of likelihoods given common and separate causes hypotheses discussed above, it is more probable that a similarity between two DNAs results from a common cause than from independent origins. Evolutionary biologists adopted DNA as a better indicator of genetic ancestry than morphology. The ratio of likelihoods of the evidence, given common cause hypotheses to separate cause hypotheses is higher for DNA similarities than for morphological similarities that may result from similar environmental natural selective factors.

Historians of the human past have to be cautious of voluntary deception, which has no constant rate of mutation because it is intentional. If witnesses had nothing to lose if they were found to lie and much to gain by it, then the fidelity of the evidence suffers and vice versa. Until 1851, common civil law prohibited testimonies from interested parties, principally litigants. The accused continued to be excluded from testimony until 1898 (Coady, 1992, p. 203). In common law there are few exceptions to hearsay (Coady, 1992, p. 39), mostly when the reliability of the evidence is high because it is counter to the interest of the witness as in a confession, or has no affect on its bearer, for example death bed confessions (Friedman, 1987). Death bed confessions are not helpful for historians under all circumstances because though dying men do not fear punishment in this world, they may still want to determine their historiographic legacy. Murphey (1973, pp. 59–63) followed New Testament scholarship in considering the four gospels to lack sufficient fidelity as evidence for most hypotheses about the life of Jesus. A notable exception is the hypothesis about the baptism of Jesus by John the Baptist. The evidence for this event has higher fidelity because it is inconsistent with the purpose and bias of the authors of the gospels to present Jesus as divine, a messiah that does not require baptism by a lesser prophet.

Historians assign high fidelity to unintentional evidence that was not produced for the record such as records, diaries, diplomatic and other reports, state papers, lawsuits, personal correspondence whose authors had a smaller or no interest in deception, and material remains (Elton, 1969, p. 101). Deception in a personal diary can only be involuntary, a self-deception. The competence of the witness to make the observation the documents convey affects the fidelity of the evidence: Was the witness in a position to receive that information? If she or he was, was she or he competent to be as discerning as the testimony. For example, did she or he have the medical background to make medical observations or the political savvy to discern power relations? We can liken a witness to an instrument that records information. When we receive information from such an instrument we ask about its fidelity, how sensitive it is, what kinds of information it can and cannot detect. Historians ask the same question about their witnesses as information-bearing instruments. When independent evidence coheres repeatedly, it increases our confidence in the fidelity of all the independent sources. Internal coherence does not increase fidelity, but incoherence decreases it. Realistic style and attention to detail do not increase fidelity. Descriptions of private motives and ideas of historical agents that authors could not possibly know plummets the fidelity of the evidence of historians like Thucydides (Kosso, 1993). The scientific revolution in historiography consists to a large extent of developing theories and methods that are useful for the evaluation of the comparative fidelities of historical sources.

The fidelity of a testimony is low if historians can explain its discrepancy with other evidence by causes other than the events it purports to describe. Milligan (1979) presented an excellent analysis of a typical historiographic treatment of singular evidence, a letter written by a federal officer during the American Civil War, claiming to have heard Generals Ulysses S. Grant and William T. Sherman contemplating an overthrow of the government in Washington and the Federal Admiral David D. Porter replying that his sympathies are with the Southern Confederacy. There is no other evidence for either claims. What is the best explanation of the contents of this letter? An examination of auxiliary evidence proves that the letter was indeed written at the time and place it claims to, February 28, 1863, at Vicksburg, Mississippi. It was written to the author's uncle who bequeathed it along with other family papers to the University of Michigan. Independent evidence confirms that the author was at that time in Vicksburg and was indeed present at a meeting with Grant, Sherman, and Porter. Further, since the witness recorded his recollections from the meeting in a personal letter on the same night, his memory should have been of high fidelity. At that point historians search for possible personal biases that may affect the witness. In this case, the author, Ellet, was an ambitious nineteen-year-old colonel who succeeded his fallen father as the commander of a squadron of ramming boats. He returned on that day from a failed mission, exhausted, suffering from fever, and under the influence of a tincture of opium he took for migraines. Ellet had good reason to worry that he would be blamed for a military debacle and consequently be demoted and lose his command over the ramming squadron that his late father had founded. Colonel Ellet wrote to the brother of his late father whom he knew to share his anxieties, allegiances, friends, and foes. Milligan concluded that the probability of Ellet's accusations being correct is infinitely small. In effect Milligan weighed the relative likelihood of the evidence given the prior probabilities of two alternative hypotheses, that the contents of the letter are true, or that one or more of the biasing factors resulted in the contents of the letter. Milligan, reflecting the standard judgments of historians, evaluated the second hypothesis as more probable, though not absolutely true. As Milligan (1979, pp. 180–1) stressed, there is no absolute certainty in judgments of historical documents, only probabilities. Still, Ellet's letter is useful evidence for other hypotheses, for example about the command structure and the relations between amateur and professional soldiers and sailors during the Civil War, especially since there is other evidence that agrees with it.

The ultimate assessment of the fidelity of evidence has to consider all the above elements. Its complexity may account for the absence of algorithms for such computations in historiography. Historians, evolutionary biologists, and linguists must examine the causal information chains that should connect hypothetical event with evidence. The more evidence there is for causal links (fossils, documents, languages, etc.) on that chain, the more certain is the historiographic assessment of the fidelity of the evidence because there would be fewer probabilistic inferences of information-bearing properties of missing links. Therefore, paleontologists labor hard to discover missing links on the evolutionary tree and value the discovery of new fossils of missing links.

Historiographic theories about the evolution of kinds of information in time support not just particular common cause hypotheses but also each other. When two independent theories reach indentical conclusions on the basis of separate or partly overlapping evidence, our degree of belief in the theories rises (Kosso, 2001, p. 77). The independence of these theories suggests that the best explanation of the consistency of the hypotheses they confirm is that they are true and that the theories themselves are true (Wylie, 1999). Confirmation in historiography as Clark Glymour (1980; Kosso, 2001, pp. 107–8) suggested in relation to science in general, involves hypotheses, theories, and evidence. None of the hypotheses or theories is epistemically privileged, though some are better confirmed and entrenched than others. Since none of the theories is privileged, they have to use each other for confirmation.

Some historiographic theories that connect hypothetical events with evidence of high fidelity can be confirmed by evidence that is generated in the present rather than the past: "Central place theory" explains the geographical distribution of palatial archeological remains in ancient Greece by the distribution of areas of political and economic concentration in eras of early state formation. This theory is confirmed by contemporary evidence from modern Europe, Azerbaijan, and Armenia (Kosso, 2001, pp. 137–52). The hypotheses about the composite nature of the Homeric sagas and their composition by illiterate bards were supported by general anthropological theories about bards in illiterate cultures confirmed by contemporary evidence from Yugoslavia and Finland.

Much of the progress of historiography since Ranke has consisted of introducing theories that can connect demographic, geographic, and economic information nested in nondocumentary evidence with their common causes with high fidelity. Marc Bloch in his *Les Caractères originaux de l'histoire rurale* (1931) used field patterns, cropping systems, and physical evidence for historical farming techniques as evidence for the history of medieval agriculture and the feudal social structure that accompanied it. The geographic evidence had existed before Bloch recognized it as such in the form of maps and aerial photographs. Bloch added theories that connect this evidence with past events and demonstrate that the nested information in this material evidence has very high fidelity. Similarly, economic historians use business records, land registers, tax books, and state toll records to gain economic information with the aid of economic theories. Febvre analyzed texts and the language of a period to discover the conceptual limits of thought in a historical period, concluding for example that at the age of Rabelais, nobody could have been an atheist because the concept exceeded the "mental tools" of the age. Braudel combined traditional documentary with physical and material evidence to investigate new questions about everyday life and long-term environmental history. Notary registers and trial records were used as evidence for religious and cultural historiography and historiography of the family, everday life, madness, and irrationality (Iggers, 1985).

Collingwood (1956, pp. 257–61) railed against what he called "scissor and paste" historiography that relies exclusively on the intended meanings of the evidence and merely chooses which testimonies to accept or reject. Collingwood overstated his case; it is possible to achieve a level of historiographic knowledge through what he called scissor and paste methods, by comparing sources and their reliability. The limits of scissors and paste historiography are not in the quality of the knowledge it produces, but in its scope. As Coady (1992, pp. 233–48) put it, Collingwood proved that there is more to historiography than scissor and paste, but he did not prove that historiography surpassed it completely. It is possible to get only so far without theories that go beyond the literal meaning of the evidence to extract nested information. Collingwood's animus toward scissor and paste historiography appears to reflect struggles with an older rear guard of historians, weary of the new theories that a younger generation of historians introduced after the first generation of historians had already used up much of the evidence in Europe's archives. Each generation of historians that discovers new theories which use new evidence must face resistance from an older generation who find it challenging to learn how to use new methods and types of evidence (Elton, 1969, p. 39).

FORMAL FIDELITY

If we use $F_1, F_2, \ldots, F_n$ to symbolize the fidelities of various information-transmitting processes, the likelihood of the evidence given a common cause hypothesis $Pr(E|C_1)$ equals the value of the fidelity multiplied by the prior probability of a particular common cause C_1 given background information B:

$$Pr(E|C_1) = [Pr(C_1|B)F_1] \times [Pr(C_1|B)F_2] \times \ldots \times [Pr(C_1|B)F_n]$$

Note that unlike in ordinary computations of likelihoods, we do not add here the likelihood of the evidence occurring irrespective of the common cause $Pr(E|-C)$ because this stage of comparison of alternative common cause hypotheses comes after the superiority of the common cause hypothesis to the separate cause hypothesis already had been established. At this stage we assume that there was a common cause of all the similar evidence and ask how probable is the evidence given competing common cause hypotheses; which can then be explicated in terms of the likelihood of the evidence given prior probabilities of competing common cause hypotheses multiplied by the respective fidelities of the information transmitting processes that connect each hypothetical common cause with the similar units of the evidence, the variational group, as above:

$$\frac{[Pr(C_1|B)F_1] \times [Pr(C_1|B)F_2] \times \ldots [Pr(C_1|B)F_n]}{[Pr(C_2|B)F_3] \times [Pr(C_2|B)F_4] \times \ldots [Pr(C_2|B)F_n]}$$

For example, the testimonies of criminals who become state witnesses in return for reduced sentence have low fidelity: They have an interest in lying, and if they were involved in serious crimes, they would certainly have no moral compunction to bear false witness. Yet, jurors and judges do not compute just the very low likelihood of the evidence given the common cause hypothesis that they describe what actually happened and the low fidelities, but the ratio between this likelihood and the likelihood of the evidence given other common cause hypotheses. If there is no evidence for credible processes that could have connected alternative common causes with the testimonies, the best explanation of the testimonies is that they are telling the truth, despite the low fidelity.

BAYESIANISM AND HISTORIOGRAPHY

I argue that the interpretation of Bayesianism that I present here is the best explanation of the actual practices of historians. The above Bayesian formulae can even predict in most cases the professional practices of historians. One of the implications of Bayesianism is that new evidence that was unexpected before it was discovered is highly valuable for confirming hypotheses that make it likely. If philosophers misidentify historiography with its textbooks they may conclude that there is no new evidence in historiography. However, new evidence in historiography has been discovered regularly since Ranke's first expedition into the archives. Such discoveries are particularly impressive when historians conjecture missing links on the causal chain that should link evidence and hypothesized events or a documentary common cause of descendant texts and evidence for such links are discovered. For example, Ranke's student, Wilhelm von Giesebrecht (1814–89), concluded that certain German eleventh-century chronicles had a common source that he named *Annales Altahanses* and defined its properties. Twenty-six years later this manuscript was indeed found (Goldstein, 1996, p. 11).

The evolving historiography of the centuriate assembly, *comitia centuriata*, in Republican Rome exemplifies well the applicability of Bayesianism to actual historiographic research (Ross Taylor, 1966, pp. 84–106). The centuriate assembly was one of the three electing bodies in Republican Rome. It elected the consuls and praetors, high state officials with powers of military command, and voted in trials that involved capital punishment, most notably for treason. Originally, this assembly was of the men at arms. This tradition was maintained by summoning the men to assemble with a trumpet in the *Campus Martius*. There were 193 centuries, pseudomilitary units that served as fundamental voting units, irrespective of the number of voters within each century, as in majority rule democratic systems. A majority of 97 centuries decided the vote. Initially, the 193 centuries were divided into: 18 *equites*, the old established nobility whose members were entitled to receive a horse from the Roman state for war; 170 *pedites* who brought their own arms for war; and 5 centuries of unarmed adjuncts, artisans, musicians, and proletarians, whose only property was their children. Though the proletarians were the most numerous century, they had only a single voting block out of 193. The 170 *pedites* were divided into five classes, initially according to the kind of military equipment they brought with them to war, later according to their property. The first of these *pedites* classes had 80 centuries. Consequently, if the nobles with their 18 centuries agreed with the wealthiest class with its 80 centuries, they had a majority. The order of voting proceeded according to classes, so if the nobles and rich agreed, the assembly would be dissolved because an absolute majority had already been achieved.

Between 241 and 220 BCE the centuries assembly was reformed. The centuries became divisions of the 35 Roman tribes. The tribes were locally based unites, 4 urban and 31 rural that formed the basis for voting in another assembly of tribes. According to the historian Livy who wrote over two centuries after the reforms, this reform implied that the first class of *pedites* had two centuries in each of the 35 tribes, one of juniors (younger than 46-year-old warriors) and one of seniors who were not on active duty. Consequently, the numbers of its centuries was reduced to 70 from 80 and the absolute majority of the nobles and the very rich had vanished. No information about the number of centuries of the other four classes was preserved in the classical sources for Republican Roman history.

In the sixteenth century, Ottavio Pantagato presented the hypothesis that each of the five *pedites* classes had 70 centuries, in addition to the centuries of the *equites* and the noncombatants, a total of 373 centuries. If so, the upper class would have required to gain the support of the second and third classes to reach a majority. This hypothesis can explain Livy's evidence. Yet, it can explain neither Cicero's account of 44 BCE elections that were decided by the vote of the second class, without the third class, nor the evidence for the voting patterns of the centuriate assembly that indicates that it continued to vote in the interests of the nobility and the wealthy. The continued dominance of the nobility and the wealthy is likely given an hypothesis about patronage relations between the upper classes and members of lower classes who voted according to the wishes of their patrons. This hypothesis is consistent with the 373 centuries hypothesis.

In 1822 new evidence emerged from the library of the Vatican in the form of a palimpsest of a text by Cicero that claimed that the total number of centuries remained 193, though the first class had 70 centuries as Livy claimed. Despite an apparent inconsistency with Cicero's newly discovered evidence, the 373 centuries assembly hypothesis appeared the best available. Theodor Mommsen presented an alternative hypothesis in 1887 in volume III of his *Römisches Staatsrecht*. Mommsen accepted Cicero's evidence that the number of centuries remained constant at 193, and that the first class had 70 centuries. Classes two through five must have had together about 100 centuries. To explain the evidence that the reform constituted the integration of the centuries as units in the tribes, Mommsen hypothesized that the votes of each class in two or three tribes were amalgamated to constitute a single century. Without direct evidence for this hypothesis, Mommsen's hypothesis had low prior probability and most historians rejected it.

The low posterior probability of Mommsen's hypothesis leaped as a result of the 1947 archelogical discovery of surprising new evidence, a bronze tablet known as *Tabula Hebana*, in Tuscany. The relevance of this discovery to Mommsen's hypothesis was recognized only in a 1949 article by Gianfranco Tibiletti. The *Tabula Hebana* dates to 19 CE and sets regulations for how 33 tribal units of senators and knights should be reduced to 15 voting centuries, by merging together 2 or 3 units into a single century, exactly as Mommsen hypothesized. Mommsen's hypothesis made this evidence, as well as Cicero's older evidence, likely, whereas its competitors made neither likely. The posterior probability of Mommsen's hypothesis leaped, and became universally accepted because it had low prior probability and the evidence was new and unexpected.

Historians discover new evidence regularly. This is the surest way to achieve fame as an historian. As in the case of Mommsen's hypothesis, there can be a time gap between the discovery of present effects of past events, and their recognition as evidence. The discovery of evidence can, but does not have to be, something found in an archive or in a field. It can be found already deciphered in a book, and the historian may merely recognize its relevance for a hypothesis. For example, much of the fame of Carlo Ginzburg is due to his method of gaining information about subaltern illiterate classes from judicial records, such as inquisition records of the persecution of a rural fertility cult (Ginzburg, 1983).

Another advantage of the Bayesian interpretation of historiography is the elimination of apparent historiographic anomalies when compared to science. *Colligation* is the explanation of known particular historical events by relating and synthesizing them into a single entity as parts into a directing whole that is greater than the sum of its parts. Colligation explains by adding something to previous knowledge of historical events, making them parts of a conceptual framework, for example, particular events at the end of 1989 in East Europe may be explained as parts of the collapse of the Soviet Empire, a greater whole than the sum of demonstrations, changes of government and so on. The Renaissance, the Enlightenment, the Industrial Revolution, etc. are colligatory concepts. William Whewhell introduced the term in 1840, referring to the bounding together of facts by concepts to create general terms. William Dray (1989, pp. 37–53; Cebik, 1969) explicated colligation as reorganization and synthesis of events under a classifying general concept, pattern, metaphor, or analogy that explains these events. Colligation was presented as an alternative humanistic model of historiographic explanation of *what?* to the scientific explanation of *why?* Dray connected colligation with the philosophies of Hegel, W. H. Walsh, Oakshott, and Collingwood, attempting to understand historical wholes in their individuality and context, rather than in generalities as in the sciences. If the sciences try to understand an event like the French Revolution as a case of a revolution, historiography attempts to understand many events that occurred in France since 1789 in the larger context of the French Revolution. Historians allegedly turn collections of descriptions of small events into comprehensive larger concepts.

There is no epistemologically privileged class of historical events however small or obvious with which we are acquainted or are given as facts. Therefore no historiography can be based directly on historical events. Theoretical concepts such as, the Renaissance or the Enlightenment explain a great scope of similar evidence. For example, the great volume of surviving art from fourteenth-century Italy exhibits certain similarity in the new centrality of the human figure, unlike the divine in previous Gothic art. Jacob Burckhardt suggested the Renaissance hypothesis to explain it. According to Burckhardt, a mental change took place during the fourteenth century in Italy, the birth of the modern individual self. This hypothesis explains a wide scope of evidence from Italian arts, literature, and politics. Similarly the Enlightenment hypothesis explains a wide scope of evidence that displays similarity from the second half of the eighteenth century in Europe. Since the Renaissance hypotheses was introduced by an individual historian and was not used by the historical agents to which it refers, it is less ambiguous than the Enlightenment that has been used since the late eighteenth century in different senses by thinkers as diverse as Kant and Adorno.

There is no difference between the use of such theoretical concepts in historiography to explain evidence and the use scientists make of theoretical, unobservable concepts to explain a range of evidence. For example, Dalton introduced the concept of the Atom to explain a broad scope of chemical evidence. Dalton and Burckhardt's theoretical innovations have been so well confirmed that they are considered often as facts. I suspect that most people who use the term "the Renaissance" do not even know that an individual historian introduced it in the late nineteenth century. Neither the atom nor the Renaissance are directly observable; they are extremely useful and well-confirmed theoretical concepts.

Arthur Danto (1985) argued that historiography is composed of what he called narrative sentences, which are sentences that describe a historical event by relating it to later events. For example, "The Thirty Years' War began in 1618 and was the last major religious war in Europe" refers to myriad events, to 30 years of war that ended in 1648 and to the absence of major religious wars in European history ever since. In that respect, in Danto's opinion, historiography resembles literary narratives. Historiography conveys knowledge by positing descriptions of events in the context of a story and the story in the context of other stories. Obviously, different stories can be told of the same event and there is no single conclusive story that can be told of any event. Danto's argument is useful in distinguishing historiography from history and historiography from observation. But is the narrative structure distinctive of historiography? Is historiography a story? If we consider historiography to be hypothetical, we agree with Danto that historiography is not composed of observation sentences. Hypotheses can have the form of a story and can refer to several temporal zones, for example, "our universe began with the big bang." But what turns hypotheses into knowledge is not their position in a narrative, but their relation to the evidence. We know that the Thirty Years War began in 1618, lasted for thirty years and was the last major religious war in Europe because we have evidence for it. A historian writing in 1630 knew only that a major religious war began in 1618 because the evidence that we have accumulated since was not in existence nor available to him. Historiography changes, the narrative changes if you wish, because new evidence is added. If the hypotheses concern long processes that begin in the past and culminate in the recent past, for example, "the work of Turing paved the road for the digital computer," then the evidence for them has become available only recently. True, some historians tell stories and these stories change. But these stories are not distinctive of historiography nor are their narrative structure epistemically significant. Expanding evidence for historiographic hypotheses that may or may not tell stories explains the evidence that Danto brought for his thesis better than his analysis of narrative that cannot explain the full scope of historiography that includes non-narrative sentences.

Finally, we should note that though Bayesian analysis can explain most of what historians do and how they reach an uncoerced, heterogeneous, and large consensus on determined historiography, there are occasional deviations from the Bayesian ideal. Some historians, philologists and so forth, made fallacious inferences from similarity to common cause in cases where separate cause hypotheses clearly explain the evidence as good or better than the common cause hypothesis. Similarities in discoveries and inventions were explained by a common cause as the best explanation. For example, Carter (1955; Tucker, 1990) inferred from the overwhelming evidence for the invention of block printing and movable type in China and its use in East Asia long before it was invented in Europe, a causal information chain that connected somehow Gutenberg with East Asian solutions to the problem of mass production of texts. Yet, the evidence is more likely given separate economic and technical causes that may be different tokens of similar types, than a common cause hypothesis, considering that there is no shred of evidence for any information causal chain that connected East Asia with Gutenberg. Yet, though individual historians do deviate from the Bayesian analysis presented here, there is never a consensus on such deviations.

4

Historiographic Opinion

The last chapter clarified how historians of heterogeneous backgrounds agree on much of historiography. This chapter attempts to explain historiographic disagreements. I argue that the best explanation of dissent on historiographic issues within the uncoerced heterogeneous group of historians who work within the Rankean paradigm is the absence of knowledge of history and the alternative dominance of historiographic opinion. Historiographic opinions are historiographic hypotheses that are not better confirmed than inconsistent competing hypotheses. It is necessary to understand first why some historiographic hypotheses cannot use the theories and methods outlined in the previous chapter and achieve the status of probable knowledge. Then, I will outline areas of historiographic opinion and their sociological manifestation.

Historiographic skepticism predicts disagreements among historians that should reflect their varying perspectives. If historiography is indeterminate in relation to the evidence, inconsistent historiographies could result from contradictory social interests and ideological rifts. Still, it is impossible to reduce all or even most historiographic disagreements to ideological and cultural biases or economic and social interests. To do so, skeptics must prove statistical correlations between historiographies and social or ideological variables. But fairly homogenous groups of historians are nevertheless rife with historiographic disagreements. To be sure, social and political convictions may explain differences in historiographic interpretations expressed in the values that historians use to decide what was significant, good, or bad about history. But the topic of this book is historiographic knowledge and opinion, not historiographic interpretation. I present next what I take to be a much better explanation of disagreements among historians that partake in the Rankean paradigm.

Insufficient evidence does not imply that historiography is indeterminate, that anything goes, because the evidence may still be sufficient for eliminating many improbable hypotheses, while conferring equal probability on several competing underdetermined historiographic hypotheses. Even if no single winning theory emerges from a competition, there can be many losers (Laudan, 1998). Instead of the monarchy of a single theory, we find an aristocracy of several theories that are better than others, associated with parties of advocates that are called politely "schools." From an epistemic perspective, it does not matter why historians come to identify with a school and adopt its opinions. Such allegiances may result from an infinite number of contingent external factors such as personal attachments, political sympathies, academic loyalties, upbringing, or economic incentives. The important questions are: Why are there historiographic schools in the first place; Why is it impossible for historians to agree on the superiority of one among competing theories?

Historians are able to agree on much of historiography because they agree on theories and evidence. Since historiographic evidence is public, different evidence cannot explain long-term disagreements among historians. Disagreements among historians who agree on the core theories of historiography prove that at least in some cases existing shared evidence is insufficient for deciding between some competing historiographic hypotheses (Goldstein, 1976, p. 124; 1996, pp. 95–8). Goldstein (1996, pp. 95–8) noted that evidence is insufficient for inferring historiography because there are inconsistent historiographic accounts that cite the same evidence. Goldstein's proposed explanation to the puzzling multiplicity of historiographies that cite identical evidence was that historiography is logically prior to the evidence, it directs a search for relevant evidence, as scientific theories do. "The evidence must be deducible from the event as constituted" (Goldstein, 1996, p. 204). This analysis may explain the presence of inconsistent historiographies that agree on the evidence. Yet, Goldstein conceded that he had never quite understood how this could be the case. I intend to do just that in this chapter: The theories that historians use and the available evidence are incomplete, insufficient, for determining parts of historiography. To reach an opinion on such historiographic issues, historians add controversial theories to the theoretical core and the evidence they agree on. Since historians add different and inconsistent underdetermined theories to established determined theories and evidence, they reach different and conflicting historiographic hypotheses.

It is possible to confine historiographic questions to those that the available evidence in conjunctions with the theories and methods that define and unite the heterogeneous community of historians can answer decisively. Still, many historians have found such a restriction on the scope of their inquiries too exacting. A plethora of pragmatic interests affect the directions of historiographic research. The reading public expects historiography to go beyond solving puzzles by using established theories, as scientists do most of the time according to Kuhn (1996, pp. 36–9).

Questions such as: "Did cavemen have a religion and if so, of what kind?" and "Why did the Holocaust happen?" are too interesting or important for historians to just ignore because there is insufficient evidence for a conclusive determined answer.

When the evidence and established theories are insufficient for determining historiographic hypotheses, historians may try to add theories that may infer or even deduce hypotheses. If these theories are underdetermined, the hypotheses they infer would be underdetermined as well. As much as consensus on cognitive values and theories unites and defines the historiographic community, underdetermined theories that enjoy the support of only groups within the historiographic community unite and define historiographic schools and traditions. The choice of school, unlike the choice of scientific paradigm, is influenced by external social factors such as political ideology and academic institutional affiliation (Lloyd, 1993, pp. 13–14).

The extensive debate in the philosophy of science about the underdetermination of theories by evidence is relevant for understanding underdetermined historiography. Quine (1975, 1980), following Duhem (1954), challenged the belief that evidence is sufficient for choosing rationally between theories by confirming true theories or refuting false ones. Quine argued that theories are tested holistically: Each theory has parts that are linked closely with empirical observations that should confirm it, for example by having direct empirical implications, and other parts that do not have unmediated empirical implications but connect to the world through a net of connections with other parts of the theory. Duhem and Quine claimed that different and incompatible theories can have precisely the same evidential foundations.[1] If the evidence is fixed, if no new relevant evidence can be found, the evidence cannot favor one theory over another. Arguably, if historiographic evidence is fixed, Duhem-Quine underdetermination could explain the coexistence of several evidentially equivalent but incompatible underdetermined historiographic hypotheses. If a body of historical evidence is fixed, it may be equally likely given competing historiographic hypotheses. As long as there are no further discoveries that expand the relevant evidence, it is impossible to discriminate among these hypotheses on the basis of the evidence. Quine claimed that any theory that explains fixed evidence may have an alternative, logically incompatible and irreconcilable theory that derives the same evidence.

Conversely, according to Quine, evidence cannot refute a complex theory because it is impossible to know which of the many parts, or hypotheses, that compose a theory is falsified by inconsistent evidence. Nor is it possible to conclude that the theory as a whole has been falsified because it is possible to – and scientists indeed do – add ad hoc auxiliary hypotheses to any theory to explain away inconsistent evidence. Kuhn (1996) noted that during a scientific crisis, when evidence accumulates against a dominant paradigm, such as Newtonian physics, scientists do not drop their hitherto successful theory but tinker with it ad hoc until it is consistent with the evidence. If Duhem and Quine are right, historians may react to apparent inconsistencies between historiographies and evidence by developing different interpretations that drop or add hypotheses ad hoc. Different historians may mutate a shared theory or hypothesis differently to adapt it to varying evidential pressures.

The various responses in the philosophy of science to Duhem and Quine's underdetermination of theories have been based on the apparent inconsistency between the history of science and the kind of history that Duhem and Quine's analysis would have led us to expect. Scientists have been agreeing, not immediately to be sure but eventually, to forsake some theories in favor of others. For long periods scientists work within unifying theoretical frameworks, such as Kuhn's paradigms and Lakatos's research programs. Scientists do not add auxiliary ad hoc hypotheses ad infinitum to save their theories. They choose eventually a simpler theory that does not require as many ad hoc additions and substractions. The explanations of the apparent discrepancy between the history of science and the kind of theoretical heterogeneity that the underdetermination thesis would have led us to expect range from expanding the criteria for theory choice beyond the evidence to include cognitive values such as simplicity (Laudan, 1998) to the denial that scientific evidence ever comprises a closed set, so new discovered evidence can determine theoretical disputes (Laudan & Lapin, 1991; Murphey, 1994). Clark Glamour (1980) argued that it is possible to use evidence to examine scientific hypotheses individually by repeatedly testing them against different theoretical backgrounds and to isolate the mooted hypothesis from others in the background theory. Various parts of a theory can be tested separately against diverse kinds of evidence and against varying theoretical backgrounds. It is necessary to test the hypotheses that compose a theory against a variety of evidence to decide among competing theories, and to determine which of the many hypotheses that compose a theory does the evidence test: So that:

As many hypotheses as possible are tested in as many different ways as possible. What makes one way of testing relevantly different from another is that the hypotheses used in one computation are different from the hypotheses used in the other computations. Part of what makes one piece of evidence relevantly different from another piece of evidence is that some test is possible from the first that is not possible from the second. (Glymour, 1980, p. 140)

It is unnecessary in the present context to delve further into the exact details of the various replies to the underdetermination thesis. Arguably, the evidence they present from the historiography of science is sufficient to disprove Duhem-Quine's underdetermination thesis, but it underdetermines the replies in relation to one another because they all seem to explain the paucity of underdetermination in the history of science equally well.

There is a marked difference between the history of historiography and the history of science. Outside the Rankean paradigm, historiography displays the properties of theoretical heterogeneity and fragmentation that the underdetermination thesis would lead us to expect. Whatever fails in Quine's thesis as a description of science may nonetheless hold true for parts of historiography. Historiography may be underdetermined by fixed evidence. Cognitive values may not be sufficient for discriminating among some historiographic hypotheses, and inconsistent evidence may not disprove some historiographic theories because historians add different ad hoc hypotheses to save them.

There are three types of underdetermined historiographies:

First, some historiographic accounts are underdetermined by fixed evidence that is equally likely given several historiographies. Historians choose then between historiographic accounts by adding different underdetermined theories to shared background theories. This sort of underdetermination is not exclusive to historiography. Lewontin (1994a, pp. 484–5) suggested that two schools of population genetics, Selectionists who think that natural selection explains most heritable organic variations, and Naturalists who think that chance events explain much of the same, explain precisely the same evidence. The degree and location of this kind of underdetermination in historiography can be assessed only by a thorough study of historiography. There are many undecided disputes in historiography that result from the fragmentary and imperfect nature of historiographic evidence (Marwick, 1993, pp. 328–74). For example, who were the Puritans and who actually fought on both sides of the English Civil War (seventeenth-century)? Obviously, there is no statistical registry of those who fought on both sides along with their various social, cultural, or economic variables. Different historians attempted to find new evidence, nested in property registries, biographies of the members of the Long Parliament, which lasted through the Civil War for two decades (1640–1660), and family and local archives from that period, recording the allegiances of various categories of people. A century of research disproved two main hypotheses: Engles claimed that the rebels were the new bourgeois class and the royalists were the old feudal lords. Trevor-Roper's alternative hypothesis was that the war was fought between two wings of the same ruling elite. Yet, no positive determined answer has emerged. Similar underdetermination is present in assessing the immediate effects of the industrial revolution on the standard of living of the poor. Again, there is no direct evidence. Eric Hobsbaum suggested that the use of quantities of meat sold in Smithfield Market in proportion to demographic growth proved that the standard of living actually fell during the first half of the nineteenth century; poor people ate less meat. Other historians looked at growing volume of sales in other markets. But there is no determined quantified answer to this question. There are countless such unresolved historiographic questions: How distant was the behavior and character of Neanderthals from that of Homo sapiens? How popular was the Communist Party in Czechoslovakia when it took power in 1948? Were Nietzsche and Hitler gay? There is a proliferation of historiographic hypotheses around such unresolved disputes. This proliferation of incompatible hypotheses results from an identical or nearly identical fixed evidence equally likely given all the hypotheses.

Second, historiographic hypotheses and theories can increase their evidential base, scope, by becoming more vague and so apply to a broader range of historiographic evidence. But this increase in scope comes at the expense of accuracy. Two of the most significant cognitive values that discriminate among competing theories are scope and accuracy. A theory with a broad scope has consequences that range beyond the original set of phenomena that the theory set to explain and describe (Kuhn, 1977, pp. 320–39). A theory is accurate if its consequences are in agreement with the evidence. The degree of accuracy may be measured by the degree of precision of agreement between theory and evidence. If a theory becomes sufficiently vague it can have a wide evidential scope, but it becomes underdetermined because it cannot be clearly connected with anything that is brought as evidence. Such theories "are so general that it is not at all clear how they are supposed to explain particular cases. . . . These theories are . . . models or concepts . . . having very little empirical content or reference" (Lloyd, 1993, p. 29). Lloyd's examples for such vague theories are Marx's materialist theory of history, Durkheim and Parson's functionalist theories of religion and social evolution, "Rostow's stages theory of economic growth, Olson's rationalist economic theory of the rise and decline of nations, Bendix's historical sociology of nation building, Elias's theory of social figurations, Touraine's sociology of action, and Mann's theory of social and state power" (p. 29). Such inaccurate theories form the theoretical foundations of schools that exist not just in historiography, but also in psychoanalysis (Spence, 1994; Tucker, 1999a) and even in biology: "very general causal theories about large domains of phenomena may become totally impervious to evidence. The consequence is that, although observations may abound, *evidence* ceases to exist as theories become dogma" (Lewontin, 1994a, p. 483).

Third, most underdetermined historiographic hypotheses are ad hoc interpretations of the second, vague, type of underdetermined theories. Though ad hoc and mutually inconsistent, such interpretations are accurate. Ad hoc hypotheses have only a limited, fixed, evidential base that can serve equally well as the evidential basis of alternative ad hoc interpretations of the same or other vague theories.

In the underdetermined part of historiography, theories do not enjoy at the same time broad scope and accuracy. Theories are either vague, but with a broad scope, or accurate with a narrow scope. The more accurate are the theories, the narrower is their scope and vice versa. If the theories with the broad scope attempt to become more accurate they will accumulate anomalies and be forced to narrow back the scope. The accurate theories are local; they cannot be applied beyond a fairly limited evidential base because the evidence does not agree with the accurate theories beyond a fairly local context.

Thagard suggested that the best theories are selected according to their consilience, simplicity, and analogy (Thagard, 1993, pp. 75–99). Consilience expresses the number of classes a theory participates in explaining. A theory is more consilient than another if it explains more different classes of evidence. "In inferring the best explanation, what matters is not the sheer number of facts explained, but their variety and relative importance" (Thagard, 1993, p. 81). Stephen Jay Gould suggested that the sciences that study history are marked by "consilience," which he interprets as "the confidence gained when many independent sources "conspire" to indicate a particular historical pattern (Gould, 1989, p. 282). Gould considered Darwin a superb practitioner of consilience: "We know that evolution must underlie the order of life because no other explanation can coordinate the disparate data of embryology, biogeography, the fossil record, vestigial organs, taxonomic relationships, and so on" (p. 282). Gould quoted Darwin to the effect that natural selection "explains several large and independent classes of facts" (p. 282). Though Gould (p. 282) claims that consilience is specific to historiographic explanations, Thagard (1993) showed that this is one of the properties of good scientific theories in general. He suggested that degree of consilience is one of the criteria used to evaluate the relative value of theories. Yet, Thagard and Gould are consistent if we synthesize their positions: All historiography is hypothetical, unobserved, and should be the best explanation of observable evidence. The best such explanation, the best historiography, has the greatest degree of consilience, which accounts for more classes of evidence.

Simplicity is the inverse of the number of ad hoc auxiliary assumptions necessary for an explanation. Ad hoc assumptions participate in the explanation of a narrow range of evidence since assumptions shared by competing theories are not ad hoc. Simplicity is measured by the inverse of the number of assumptions, cohypotheses, that must be added to the theory/ hypotheses in order to explain it. "If a hypothesis has more cohypotheses than facts explained, its simplicity is judged to be 0, since it needs a special assumption for everything it explains" (Thagard, 1993, p. 90). Theories can become more consilient on the expense of their simplicity, if they add auxiliary assumptions to explain more cases; and vice versa, become more simple on the expense of their consilience. Thagard's basic formula for computing the values of theories is:

$$\text{Simplicity} \times \text{Consilience} = \text{Value}$$

In the underdetermined parts of historiography, simple theories cannot explain a wide scope of different kinds of evidence because they require different ad hoc interpretations and additions to explain each portion of evidence. Nonsimple consilient theories are possible at the price of precision and internal consistency. The various vague theories that are associated with historiographic schools are consilient, but if we include all their ad hoc interpretations, they would be incredibly complex and internally inconsistent because some of the ad hoc interpretations are logically inconsistent with one another. It is impossible to choose among nonsimple vague consilient theories because according to Thagard's criteria they are underdetermined; their value in Thagard's computation is 0 because they need more ad hoc assumptions than the number of cases they explain.

Laudan and Leplin (1991, p. 464) suggested that empirically equivalent hypotheses can be determined by more general theories, confirmed by other hypotheses connected with them that do have direct empirical support. A mediating theory can connect hypotheses that are directly connected with the evidence with those that would otherwise be underdetermined. However, in historiography, and for that matter psychoanalysis, the theories that should do the mediating are underdetermined and vague. Ad hoc hypotheses interpret vague theories differently, even inconsistently. Historiographic schools stretch from the grand scope vague theories that unite schools through ad hoc interpretations that lead to increasing theoretical fragmentation to precise and ad hoc historiographic hypotheses shared by few or even a single historian. Therefore, the degree of confirmation of such ad hoc hypotheses is not transitive via the mediation of a more general theory. Ad hoc hypotheses cannot be deduced from vague theories without mutually inconsistent interpretations, additions, and subtractions.

In the Bayesian terms introduced in the previous chapter, the evidence for grand scope vague theories is not likely given those vague theories. Ad hoc interpretations are necessary to make concrete evidence likely. The same or similar broad scope of evidence is equally likely given several competing theories. The same or similar narrow scope of evidence is equally likely given several mutually inconsistent ad hoc hypotheses. These hypotheses themselves have prior probabilities that are both low and controversial. Their prior probabilities are low because many different and inconsistent interpretations of vague grand scope theories are possible. These low probabilities are controversial because disputed background grand scope vague theories confer on them different probabilities.

In Murray Murphey's opinion, historiography is not underdetermined because new data and new ways to extract new data from known evidence are constantly discovered, creating new historiographic observation sentences, just like in science.

[When] there is a fixed body of observational data, it is no surprise that alternative theories can be created which are able to explain those data equally well. It may even be that many of these alternative theories are logically incompatible with each other.... But... it does not follow that they will also be equivalent when it comes to predicting new and hitherto unknown phenomena or in accounting for observations whose relevance had not been previously detected. (Murphey, 1994, pp. 232–3)

Murphey's account fits only the determined part of historiography. Murphey's own historiographic illustration of his thesis does not quite bear out his argument. Murphey gave Greene's (1988) theory of the development of British colonies in the seventeenth and eighteenth centuries as an example for how historiography should be conducted. Greene's theory is a complex model of British colonization that fits seven positive confirming historical cases, but does not fit Puritan New England. Saving the theory requires the addition of ad hoc auxiliary hypotheses to explain away the New England deviations. These auxiliary ad hoc hypotheses are underdetermined because they apply only to a single case. Further, Murphey mentioned that Fischer (1989) introduced an alternative theory to Green's that explains the same range of evidence. Murphey was confident that future observations would decide between these two theories of British colonialization. In our private correspondence Murphey used the metaphor of a pendulum to describe the movement between alternative historiographic theories that eventually settle in the middle. I think that irrespective of whether this or that historiographic issue can be resolved by discovery and exchange of evidence, and I do not dispute that some indeed do, there are historiographic disputes that are unresolved and have been so for quite a long time, enough to conclude that parts of historiography are underdetermined. The only way to decide the extent of under-determination in historiography is empirical, through an examination of historiography, especially the parts that claim to be at once accurate and of wide scope.

COMPARATIVE HISTORIOGRAPHY

Underdetermined historiography can be determined by expanding its evidential base, by discovering new relevant evidence that can settle old disputes, including the discovery of the relevance of known evidence for disputed models. Historians tend to specialize in evidence of a particular kind, written in a language or a few languages, from a certain period. This specialization may prevent them from realizing the relevance of evidence that preserves information that originated in a different time or place but may still be highly relevant for historiographic hypotheses. For example, the decisive proof for Wolf's hypotheses about the origins of the Homeric sagas came from evidence about contemporary bards in illiterate societies in Yugoslavia and Finland. A general law about the connection between the emergence of central state bureaucracy and the invention of writing confirmed by countless archeological discoveries can be applied to civilizations that left scarce material remains. The great promise of comparative historiography is to be able to determine hitherto underdetermined historiographic hypotheses by broadening the scope of the evidence and its variety, without compromising the accuracy of the hypotheses.

The frequent problem with such attempts is that as accurate historiographic theories broaden their scope, or vague large scope theories become more accurate, they also become more complex. If we evaluate equally underdetermined historiographic theories according to the three cognitive values of scope, accuracy, and simplicity, their aggregate value, the sum total of their cognitive value according to the above three values, tends to remain constant. If a vague but large scope theory attempts to increase its accuracy, it will have to add ad hoc hypotheses to account for the complexities of the evidence and become more complex, or narrow its scope to become more accurate. Vice versa, if an accurate theory of narrow scope attempts to broaden its scope it will also have to add ad hoc hypotheses to explain its incompatibility with the broader scope of evidence and become more complex, or increase its vagueness.

Graphically, we can represent this situation in Cartesian space on a graph where the horizontal line represents the cognitive values of accuracy and scope as opposite poles, and the vertical line represents the opposite poles of complexity and simplicity. Theories can move on the horizontal line and broaden their scope by becoming more vague, or they can become more accurate by narrowing their scope. They can move on a diagonal line to increase accuracy or broaden scope at the expense of simplicity.

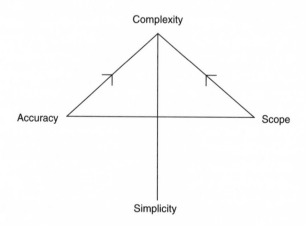

"Comparative history" is used to describe various practices of historians and social scientists (Bloch, 1967; Grew, 1980; Skocpol & Somers, 1980; Tilly, 1984). But the interesting sense that concerns us here is the development of a historiography that can determine accurate theories of a broad scope without an increase in complexity by broadening the evidential base to include information-preserving effects of similar processes that originated across historical space and time. The difficulties that some comparative historians have had in discovering sufficient evidence for determining their theories, without resorting to ad hoc auxiliary hypotheses that increase complexity or excessive theoretical vagueness, demonstrates the entrenched reasons for historiographic underdetermination.

Comparative examination of evidence could be useful in determining theories with variables that have several historical instantiations across space and time. The subdiscipline of historical sociology purports to present such theories. S. N. Eisenstadt criticized broad scope, but obviously inaccurate, social evolutionary theories that held that each society goes through exactly the same stages of development. In his opinion societies change in different directions according to concrete, local circumstances. Evolutionary theories are insensitive to these local circumstances and cannot fit specific variations between societies. Instead, Eisenstadt suggested that we compare configurations, and bounded patterns of action. Eisenstadt's theories use configurations as their main units of analysis. Eisenstadt's most famous theory concerns premodern bureaucratic empires. He argued that they depend on necessary conditions that are realized in different historical contexts. Eisenstadt's critics, for example Charles Tilly, argued that his theory is too vague and inaccurate; it does not explain detailed evidence. "The interpretation of theory and classification creates a tautological loop that is probably impossible to circumvent in configurational analysis. . . . In configurational analysis it is always tempting to make the abstraction explain historical outcomes without ever seriously confronting the historical evidence" (Hamilton, 1984, pp. 114, 117–18). Conversely, the work of Reinhard Bendix displays the alternative vice – broad scope accuracy achieved by excessive complexity that fits the evidence by adding ad hoc hypotheses. Bendix presented a theory of the relations between kings and notables in England, Japan, Russia, and Prussia/Germany, but he had to revise his theory ad hoc to explain the particularities of each of the historical cases by particular hierarchies among war leaders, their interests in profit from trade or land, types of conquest, and the power of the kings to override the historical rights of large landowners. The differences between England and Japan are ascribed to the exclusively English quasiparliamentary assembly of notables and the political and military complications that followed the mutual involvements of England and France in each other's affairs that had no parallel in insular Japan. Such explanations are ad hoc, applicable only to a single historical case (Rueschemeyer, 1984, pp. 151–3).

Theda Skocpol's celebrated *States and Social Revolutions*[2] (1979) is a good example of the difficulties in determining theories in comparative historiography. Skocpol differentiated two kinds of comparative historiography: One compares complex patterns that, due to their complexity, occurred no more than a few times in history. The second compares a single analytic feature that has a broad scope, for example what is common to all revolutions, riots, and coups, as in the theories of Ted Gurr, Chalmers Johnson, and Charles Tilly. This "historical sociology" was developed in the late sixties as a reaction against its contemporary American sociology, which generalized its findings about contemporary institutions to all societies at all times (Tilly, 1988; also Gurr, 1970; Johnson, 1966; Tilly, 1978). Historical sociology of this type presents theories of historical change that are too vague, too inaccurate. The excessive vagueness of historical sociology was noted by historians like Fredrickson who found comparative sociology inapplicable to their work: "A search for uniformities that can be described only on a very abstract plane clearly inhibits a detailed comparison involving the kind of variables that historians usually stress" (Fredrickson, 1980, p. 458).

To avoid nonhistorical vagueness, Skocpol "identifies a *complex* object of explanation, of which there are relatively few historical instances . . . rather than trying to multiply the number of cases for explanation by concentrating only upon one analytic feature . . . shared by many events of heterogeneous nature and outcome" (Skocpol, 1979, p. 5). Skocpol called the kind of comparative historiography that fits complex historical patterns "comparative historical analysis."

"Comparative historical analysis is distinctively appropriate for developing explanations of macro-historical phenomena of which there are inherently only a few cases. This is in contrast to more plentiful and manipulable kinds of phenomena suitable for experimental investigations, and in contrast to other phenomena where there are large numbers of cases required for statistical analysis. Comparative historical analysis is, in fact, the mode of multivariate analysis to which one resorts when there are too many variables and not enough cases" (Skocpol, 1979, p. 36).

Skocpol developed a theoretical historiographic model of the revolutions in France, Russia, and China. In the normal course of academic specialization, no single historian masters, or can master, the evidential sources for all three revolutions in their respective languages. Instead, Skocpol and other comparative historians rely indirectly on the evidence of primary evidence, through the work of other historians who wrote fairly determined historiographies on the basis of such evidence, as explicated in the previous chapter.

Still, the complex model of a historical process that should be confirmed does not quite fit the diverse evidence. Consequently, ad hoc auxiliary hypotheses about intervening variables must be added to account for the differences between the model and the evidence. These ad hoc hypotheses are underdetermined. Skocpol recognized these difficulties:

Often it is impossible to find exactly the historical cases that one needs for the logic of a certain comparison. And even when the cases are roughly appropriate, perfect controls for all potentially relevant variables can never be achieved. Thus, *strategic guesses* [italics added] have to be made about what causes are actually likely to be operative – that is, which one could, or could not actually affect the object of study. (Skocpol, 1979, pp. 38–9)

Skocpol's strategic guesses are underdetermined ad hoc auxiliary hypotheses. To the extent that comparative historiography must rely on such guesses, it is underdetermined.

Skocpol highlighted two groups of ad hoc hypotheses that explain the differences between the evidence and the kind of evidence the model would have led us to expect: First, hypotheses that deal with "unique processes that affect the world as a whole" (Skocpol, 1979, pp. 23–4), such as modernization. Second, hypotheses about the influence of preceding complex patterns on the development of succeeding similar complex patterns, such as that of the French Revolution on the Russian one, or of the Russian on the Chinese Revolution

(Skocpol, 1979, p. 39). These two groups of intervening variables and accompanying auxiliary ad hoc hypotheses belong to a larger class of intervening variables and auxiliary hypotheses, which should account for actual deviations from Skocpol's proposed model of succeeding historical patterns.

The classification of variables as intervening is theory relative. Modernization is certainly not an intervening variable from the perspective of modernization theory, a major large scope conglomerate of theories in comparative politics. The effects of earlier revolutions may also be studied comparatively. However, Skocpol does not study these variables and the auxiliary hypotheses she attached to them comparatively. The auxiliary hypotheses are considered ad hoc either because an attempt to increase their scope beyond a local context would result in their refutation or because any single historian lacks the resources to examine comparatively at the same time a complex model and auxiliary hypotheses beyond the local context that necessitates their introduction.

It is interesting to note Skocpol and Somers's evolving admission that they cannot achieve control of intervening variables in their "Macro-causal analysis." Initially, they claim that:

The logic involved in the use of comparative history for macro-causal analysis resembles that of statistical analysis, which manipulates groups of cases *to control sources of variation* [italics added] in order to make causal inferences. (Skocpol & Somers, 1980, p. 182)

Then, they qualify that by saying that:

The problem is that *perfectly controlled comparisons are never really feasible* [because] history *rarely, if ever,* provides exactly the cases needed for *controlled comparison.* [all italics added] (Skocpol & Somers, 1980, pp. 193–4)

The gap between the stated aim of a comparative study to determine a model by expanding a varied body of evidence and the large number of necessary ad hoc auxiliary underdetermined additions that complicates the model is manifest in Skocpol's *States and Social Revolutions* (1979).

Skocpol's main vague large scope "theoretical assumption" is about the relations between states, society, and the international state system. Skocpol (1979, pp. 23–4) assumed the "autonomy of the state": The state is a conglomerate of administrative, policing, and military organizations under a single authority that operates autonomously by extracting resources from society. The autonomous state operates in an environment composed of social classes and other competing states. States attempt to preserve their control over territories and populations, under pressure from internal social forces and external military competition. These theoretical assumptions interpret revisionist interpretations of the Marxist theoretical tradition. Marx located the state in the superstructure, under the control of the ruling class that owns the means of production. The apparent discrepancy between the theory and the anticapitalist policies of some states in the twentieth century since the 1930s led some twentieth-century social theorists within the Marxist tradition, since Gramsci, to question the theoretical reduction of the state to a tool of the dominant class, which owns the means of production. These revisionists reinterpreted Marx's theory to admit states as semiautonomous institutions, irreducible to class structure (Miliband, 1977; Poulantzas, 1973). Skocpol designated as her hypothesis an interpretation of this revisionist interpretation of Marx: The revolutions in France, Russia, and China resulted from a conflict between the need of economically backward proto-bureaucratic states to defray the costs of international military competition with more industrialized, militarily stronger states, and the interest of the agrarian upper classes in those states not to be taxed. The revolutionary crisis results from tension between the pressures of international military competition and the material interests of large land owners (Skocpol, 1979, pp. 47–51). This crisis caused peasant uprisings that transformed society thoroughly in a revolution. This model is based on the theoretical assumption that the interests and needs of the autonomous state ought to be differentiated from those of any single socioeconomic class whether it is the class of big land owners, or the revolutionary leadership that acts to consolidate its power rather than fulfill its ideological ideals and work on behalf of the workers once the revolution is won. Skocpol acknowledged that her theoretical principles are too general and vague to deduce from her specific hypothesis, or for that matter other hypotheses about other revolutions. She described in effect the interpretative relation between grand scope vague theories and clearer and more local ones in underdetermined historiography.

According to Skocpol's model, autocratic bureaucracies who maintained internal order and external security held old regimes together.

The revolutionary crisis resulted from competition over economic surplus and human capital between the state and the upper classes, forced on the state by external military threat:

> Whether, and in what form, such objectively possible conflicts of interests between monarchs and landed upper classes gave rise to actual political conflicts in old-regime France, Russia, and China depended upon historical circumstances and upon the exact institutional forms of each autocratic-imperial state. (Skocpol, 1979, p. 49)

This theory is still quite vague. The "historical circumstances" seem to be intense military competition. The "exact institutional forms" are the inability of the state to implement reforms from above against the interests of the upper classes. The central administration was then sufficiently weakened by foreign competition and the dominant classes to fall from a revolution from below. Skocpol did not define the minimal ratio of external military competition to the power of proto-bureaucratic states that should cause a revolutionary crisis. It should be possible to define this ratio numerically by comparing the resources required to meet the given external challenge and the actual resources of the state. It seems likely that the external pressures facing the Russian state in 1905 and during the 1917 revolution were considerably higher than what the French government faced in 1789. If the definition of external military pressure is vague enough, any proto-bureaucratic state that has less than friendly neighbors may be relevant for examining Skocpol's theory, depending on one's interpretation of the theory. As Tilly put it: "The parallel equates the relatively minor international difficulties of eighteenth-century France with the enormous vulnerability of Russia and China and slights the importance of divisions within France's ruling elite." Tilly retracts from his correct criticism by adding, "Nevertheless in its own broad terms Skocpol's summary does identify common properties of the three states and their revolutions" (Tilly, 1984, pp. 113–14; cf. McCullagh, 1998, 308 ff). Tilly's reference to broad terms corresponds to my claims about vagueness. Yet, this vagueness increases the scope of the theory.[3]

Skocpol, as a historian, interpreted the theory of Skocpol, as a social theorist differently when dealing with each of the three revolutions. In effect, the general theory of premodern revolutions is fragmented into three ad hoc theories that are similar, yet different. For example (Skocpol, 1979, pp. 147–54), Chinese peasants were unique in lacking the structural solidarity and autonomy of French and Russian prerevolutionary peasants. In China division of agrarian property was more equal than in France and Russia. Economic hegemony was maintained through taxes and usury that also ensured the political hegemony of the gentry. The basic social unit was the market community led by the gentry. However, as in France and Russia, the Chinese gentry were not modernized and oversaw a multitude of poor peasants. Though economically and politically strong, like English and German gentry, the Chinese gentry was dependent on the state. The peculiarities of the Chinese agrarian structure

did not afford settled Chinese peasants institutional autonomy and solidarity against landlords. But it did, in periods of political-economic crisis, generate marginaly poor peasants, outcasts, whose activities exacerbated the crisis, and whose existence provided potential support for oppositional elite-led rebellions – including in the twentieth-century context, a revolutionary movement. (Skocpol, 1979, p. 154)

The Chinese agrarian structure is depicted here as a unique combination of elements, some identical with those in prerevolutionary France and Russia, some similar to the situation in Prussia and England, and some others not compared with other historical examples. This historiographic depiction may well be right, but it is right by virtue of its relation with Chinese evidence, not because of the added evidence from France and Russia.

Another example of the vagueness of Skocpol's hypotheses is the description of the three conditions for peasant revolt that were present in France and Russia, but not in England and Prussia:

1. Degree and kind of peasant community solidarity.
2. Degree of peasant autonomy from landlord power.
3. The relaxation of coercive state sanctions against peasant revolts.
(Skocpol, 1979, pp. 47–51)

These conditions need clarification that may be quantitative if they are to be accurate and testable. Only then can it be decided whether peasant revolts in France and Russia can be grouped together and contrasted with Prussia and England. The fragmentation of the theory into accurate hypotheses of local scope continues as the model attempts to describe post-revolutionary developments.[4] The necessary ubiquitous resort to comparatively unsupported local ad hoc auxiliary hypotheses and intervening variables in Skocpol's comparative study of historical patterns undermines the chief reason for using comparative historiography, the prospect of increasing the scope of accurate theories to determine them.

COMPARISON WITH SOCIAL SCIENCE THEORIES

Some vague grand scope social science theories serve as the theoretical foundation for historiographic schools that interpret them. But most contemporary theoretical work in the social sciences is not carried out on the grand scale of Marx or Weber. The theories that most social scientists work with have a narrower scope than the grand scope of the founders of sociology, but broader than the ad hoc hypotheses historians usually develop by interpreting grand scope theories. What Merton called *middle-range theories* and Elster (1989) named *mechanisms* are not universal, they have exceptions, sometimes many exceptions. Still, instead of adding ad hoc interpretations that would increase the complexity of theories to fit the evidence as in historiography, the social sciences become inconsistent. As measured by cognitive values, branches of the social sciences may look schematically like this:

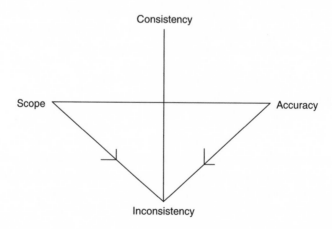

Middle-range social science theories can maintain their scope and accuracy at the cost of being inconsistent. For example, we can consider two of the main theories in international relations: balance of power theory and domino theory. Balance of power theory assumes several independent political units that wish to survive, maintain their independence, and expand. Each of the units is ready to ally itself according to their interests and is ready to go to war in service of their interests. Given these assumptions, the theory predicts that the international system will tend to achieve stability and balance irrespective of the internal calculations of the leaders of each unit. The reason for the balance is that the interest of each of the states is not to allow any single state to dominate and create an international hierarchy. Therefore, they would ally with each other against any single hegemon. Since allies and enemies are not permanent, there is no reason to break down or eliminate losing states. The maintenance of the international system is an unintended consequence of the independent decision-making processes of independent states. This theory explains a range of alliances against ascending powers, such as Napoleonic France, Imperial Germany, and Nazi Germany, as well as the absence of a single state domination of the whole system throughout history. Nevertheless, in some isolated systems, this analysis failed, as the cases of the Roman and Chinese empires may attest. Further, some wars did become total, culminating in the division and destruction of the losing state (Jervis, 1997, pp. 131–5). Similarly, domino theory can explain a large scope of evidence, yet it has many exceptions (Jervis, 1997, pp. 165–71). Domino theory makes the opposite assumption to balance of power theory: Weak states tend to join states that are reputed to be strong, instead of ally with each other to balance its power. The more strong states conquer or otherwise increase their prestige, the more likely it is that others will join them or accept their domination, and vice versa. However, as Jervis noted, there has never been a world hegemon, so in reality the domino model has never been carried to its logical conclusion, nor did Communist takeovers in Cuba, Vietnam, and Ethiopia lead to extensive Communist expansions in those areas of the world. Highly motivated insurgents would still challenge a hegemon despite its perceived superiority. The balance of power and domino theories are mutually inconsistent. According to the balance of power theory, weaker states are likely to create alliances to defeat a stronger state. According to the domino theory, weaker states are more likely to join a state they perceive as stronger. Some evidence is more likely given one theory, while other evidence is more likely given the other. For example, the coalition led by the United States during the first Gulf War in 1991 is more likely given domino theory, while the French, German, and Russian opposition to the American war with Iraq in 2003 is more likely given the balance of power theory. These two theories co-exist inconsistently within international relations. Political scientists like historians pick their theories according to problems they try to understand. But unlike historians they do not strive for consistency by increasing complexity. As Jervis put it: "I very much doubt whether balance of power theory, deterrence, or the spiral model is correct all the time; rather each generalization applies under certain conditions" (Jervis, 1997, p. 176).

UNDERDETERMINED HISTORIOGRAPHY

Van Fraassen considers theories as models:

To present a theory is to specify a family of structures, its *models*; and secondly, to specify certain parts of those models (the *empirical substructures*) as candidates for the direct representation of observable phenomena. The structures which can be described in experimental and measurement reports we can call *appearances*: the theory is empirically adequate if it has some model such that all appearances are isomorphic to empirical substructures of such model. (van Fraassen, 1980, p. 64)

A theory is an idealized class of structures, or models, a substructure of which is isomorphic to appearances. If we interpret historiography in terms of this philosophy of science, historiographic models purport to describe the evolution of historical states, in isolation and in interaction through time. The difference between scientific models, including scientific historiographic, and underdetermined models lies in their accuracy, simplicity, and scope/consilience. Underdetermined modalities in historiography can be classified between two polar types: On one pole there are grand scope vague models that may originate in philosophy or the social sciences. Unlike scientific theories, there is no substructure of vague grand scope historiographic theories that is isomorphic to observable historiographic evidence. Still, these grand

and vague models do purport to describe historical systems and states in their interrelations and changes in time though the contours of the systems are unclear, the variables are vague, and there are hardly any identifiable laws. Historians cannot simply apply some general laws or models from the social sciences to their particular problems; they must interpret the grand theories (Hay, 1980).

On the other pole there are accurate but ad hoc models that may be interpretations of some of the vague theories that are used by individual practicing historians to explain a narrow evidential base. While underdetermined minor ad hoc theories are semantically clearer than grand scope theories, they have an insufficient scope of evidence for having a clear advantage over competing ad hoc hypotheses that explain the same or similar narrow evidential scope. Between those two poles we find various theoretical models of increased scope and vagueness or vice versa, increased accuracy and locality and decreased scope. This classification was foreshadowed by Dray (1957, pp. 22–57) and Danto (1985, pp. 201–32) in their criticism of the covering law model. They argued that if every historiographic causal explanation is covered by a law that connects the explanans (what explains) with the explanandum (what is being explained), these laws are either too general and vague to deduce from concrete causal explanations or are applicable only to a single case, and therefore are not confirmable. Goldstein (1996, p. 42) similarly analyzed the various examples that proponents of the covering law model constructed to demonstrate their analysis of explanation. He concluded that they merely generalized particular historiographic causal statements that were applicable to a one and only case. If the historian wrote X caused Y, the philosopher reconstructed it as all Xs cause Ys; they replaced existential qualifiers with universal ones, as logicians would put it. But, in many cases such a replacement replaces a small truth with a large falsehood, as there are historical cases where X did not cause Y. All these so-called laws, argued Goldstein, cannot fit together to form a larger theory. These ad hoc theories have minimal scope, are mutually inconsistent, and therefore are underdetermined.

Schools consist of groups of historians who interpret the same grand scope vague theory. To fit accurately vague theories to different limited scope evidential bases, historians interpret shared grand theoretical models differently, at times inconsistently. Most practicing historians are not grand theoreticians. They confront a limited range of evidence and attempt to explain it while being inspired in their precise ad hoc modeling by their interpretation of a vague theoretical background. Interpretations generate fragmentation when different historians interpret their grand scope vague theory differently to fit different evidence. Had all the accurate ad hoc models been able to interpret the same theory identically, they would have been the isomorphic substructures of a normal scientific theory, and historiography would have been an exclusively normal science. Instead, all the inconsistent interpretations of a single vague grand scope theory form a school and a tradition but cannot amount together to a general theory of social change.

Adrian Wilson noted the mutation of historiographic concepts in the process of interaction with evidence, which he called "concept criticism":

The stimulus for this process is a perceived mismatch between concepts (or questions) and what is taken as evidence. Concept-criticism seeks to correct this perceived clash by modifying the array of concepts (questions) which the historian is deploying. (Wilson, 1993, p. 296)

Concepts are embedded in *conceptual frameworks*. When scientists communicate their results, they tend to use the shared conceptual framework of their theory or research program and communicate with people who share them, sometimes at the expense of the accuracy of their reports. Philosophers and historians of science discovered the discrepancies between some communicated reports and the actual experimental results (Cartwright, 1983). Descriptions of events are idealized to fit the model, since sciences like physics aim primarily to examine theories, rather than explain events. The process through which scientists communicate their findings exoterically by compromising on accuracy, locality, content, phenomenological truth, sensitivity, discrimination and detail is *standardization*, "the process of adapting the work of the vanguard of research into material usable in further investigation long after the vanguard has left that work behind" (Rouse, 1987, p. 117).

Wimsatt (1994, pp. 498–501) claimed that some of the theories in genetics are adhered to dogmatically despite inconsistencies with the evidence; the best scientific theories are idealizations, deliberate simplifications that are, strictly speaking, false, but are heuristically useful for organizing and structuring knowledge. Scientists study actual deviations from the ideal and attempt to understand, compare, and evaluate them. Weber construed social science theories as idealizations (Weber, 1949; Ringer, 1997, pp. 110–21). Tempting though it may seem, I do not think it is possible to construe vague grand scope historiographic theories as idealizations of the scientific variety. Ideals, since Plato through Descartes, are supposed to be clear, distinct, and timeless, for example, geometric proportions or mathematical formulae. Reality is more complex, mixed up, and transitory. The concepts of vague grand scope theories are neither clear nor distinct. They require interpretations to be useful. Vague grand scope models cannot provide an ideal standard from which historians or social scientists may explain deviations. Different interpretations of the same vague theory offer alternative standards. Historians must add ad hoc auxiliary hypotheses, adapt, change, and interpret vague theoretical backgrounds to fit their evidence because, unlike physicists, they are concerned with the evidence more than with their theories. Ad hoc versions of the grand vague theory of a school share some of their core beliefs, but they must differ to fit different subject matter. Wilson described the fitting of concepts to evidence:

> I would venture that every historian has gone through this experience – though few have recorded it, since it seems to be regarded in hindsight with some embarrassment.... [It is] inevitably, elusive to recovery.... The small-scale forms of concept-criticism are difficult to illustrate accurately because these are private and personal. (Wilson, 1993, pp. 296–9)

Scientists fit (standardize) descriptions of the evidence to the theory at the expense of accuracy in reporting concrete phenomena. Historians fit their grand scope theories to the evidence through ad hoc hypotheses on the expense of simplicity, scope/consilience, and communicability (Jordanova, 2000, pp. 69–71).

Vague grand scope historiographic theories resemble artistic styles and perspectives. Marxist or Annales historiographies are as easily identifiable as a painting is instantly recognizable as Cubist, Impressionist, or Expressionist. Ankersmit (1995) drew an analogy between the relation of picture and object and historiographic text and historical events. Like paintings, historiographic texts have a certain form or style, such as Impressionism and Expressionism in art or Marxism and Weberianism in historiography. As a painting uses a style to depict an independent object, historiography uses a theory to describe past events. For example, Canaletto and Turner painted Venice's Grand Canal; both paintings are of the same object but each is an expression of the artists' two distinctive styles. I dispute the analogy between historical events and artistic objects because the first are not directly accessible through the senses, but have to be inferred from the evidence. Still, Ankersmit is right about the stylistic aspect of underdetermined historiography, associated with partisan vague theories. Following van Fraassen's and Ankersmit's pictorial simile, scientific theories can be compared to architectural drawings, while historiographic grand scope vague theories are comparable to artistic styles. It is clear which parts of architectural drawings are designated to be isomorphic to observable parts of the actual buildings they describe, the faucets and the walls are observable, the piping that goes through them is not; flowing water in faucets is evidence for the presence of unobservable pipes. An artistic style like Cubism and the artistic school that espouses it are inspired by a certain reality and may convey an insight into that reality, but there is nothing in the real world that corresponds with it. Cubism reflected a modern technological culture and interpreted the whole of visual reality in those terms, but there is nothing in the world quite like Picasso's women, not even in Avignon.

Historically, schools evolve and mutate like species or copied documents. Literature and the plastic arts also have their schools, authority figures, and dissentions. But religious, philosophical, and artistic schools do not display the degree of theoretical proliferation and sociological fragmentation of historiographic schools or of the various schools of psychology, especially psychoanalysis, because their interpretations do not have to fit many different evidential contexts (Smith, 1997; Tucker, 1999a, 1999b). When a historian approaches a body of evidence and when a clinical psychologist faces a particular patient, their interpretations of the theories of their schools must fit the particular empirical problems they face. The mostly ad hoc revisions they introduce create a new theory that is accurate and explains a particular historiographic or psychological range of phenomena, but cannot be extrapolated beyond it. As Peter Caws observed about psychoanalysis, "clinical findings cannot reliably be extrapolated beyond the case from which they are drawn . . . the science itself, and not some boundary conditions, has to be built afresh in every new clinical encounter" (Caws, 1986, p. 230).

TRADITIONALIST SCIENCE

According to Kuhn (1996), most scientific activity is carried out as normal science, the solving of puzzles within the framework of a paradigm in which mainstream scientific work is conducted and described. By contrast, what Kuhn called pre-science has no common methods of data selection and explanation, confirmation or refutation. Pre-science is typically practiced in schools, united by some intertwined theoretic or methodological beliefs that guide selection, evaluation, and criticism of evidence. "No wonder, then, that in the early stages of the development of any science different men confronting the same range of phenomena, but not usually all the same particular phenomena, describe and interpret them in different ways" (Kuhn, 1996, p. 17).

The term "pre-science" is misleading in implying a philosophy of the history of science according to which the destiny of every pre-science is to progress and become a science. But there is no inherent scientific potential in every systematic study of a realm of evidence or nature that necessarily realizes itself in the course of historical progress. To avoid such misleading implications, I refer to a theoretically guided study of an aspect of nature that is characterized by division into competing schools, theoretical dissent, and conflicting interpretations of vague grand scope theories as *traditionalist science*. Historiography is composed of *normal science*, the Rankean paradigm, and *traditionalist science*. Each historiographic school that shares a theoretical model is also committed to a research program generated by that model in addition to the Rankean research project. The shared commitment of a group of people to a vague grand scope theoretical model and a research program constitutes a school.

The historical evolution of traditionalist science is often cladistic: A school founder that is often an authoritative parental, not to say father, figure such as Freud, Weber, Marx, and Braudel founds the school by introducing a vague new theory and research program. The founder has several intellectual descendants who are often the formal students of the founder, who mutate-interpret the theory and research program differently and even found their own schools by seceding from the school of the founder. If the founder is still present during the secession, the founder may brand some intellectual descendants as "legitimate," others as "dissenters" or even "heretics." Other descendants perish altogether, without intellectual progeny. Yet, a family of theories constitutes a tradition.

Philosophers of historiography have paid too little attention to disagreements among historians. Philosophers who investigated the textbook superstructure of historiography, narrativists and positivists alike, have ignored historiographic disputes (Goldstein, 1976, pp. 93–9). Textbooks in any discipline rarely expose disputes and disagreements. Textbooks about historiography (Carr, 1987; Elton, 1969; Jordanova, 2000) present the discipline to outsiders and neophytes without exposing its internal divisions. At most, divisions are recognized only as the result of mistakes of competing schools. Nevertheless, historians recognize each other as school members. The coexistence within the Rankean paradigm of areas of consensus and difference and the subsequent academic politics of interschool rivalry lead historians to deny, suppress, or misrepresent the social and semantic fragmentation in historiography. For example, in an introduction to an anthology on contemporary historiography, Peter Burke introduced a thesis of unified historiography. He described increasing fragmentation in new historiography due to greater division of labor among historians and the growth of new, politically motivated, subdisciplines studying the histories of previously neglected populations and subjects, women's history, colonization history, eco-history, etc. using new types of evidence. But Burke drew a picture of complementary fragmentation; each historian or group of historians works on a fragment of historiography. When joined together, the fragments fit together to create in increasing detail a jigsaw puzzle picture of the past. Burke recognized that there are semantic ambiguities in the new historiography: Historians use historiographic concepts such as popular culture, "from below," everyday life, society, and culture differently.

The discipline of historiography is now more fragmented than ever before. Economic historians are able to speak the language of economists, intellectual historians the language of philosophers, and social historians the dialects of sociologists and social anthropologists, but, these groups of historians are finding it harder and harder to talk to one another. (Burke, 1991, p. 18; cf. Jordanova, 2000, pp. 27–58)

Still, such disagreements represent more than merely a difference in semantics and research programs, as Burke recognized. There is also a difference in core beliefs and perspectives, description and explanation, a theoretical inconsistency, reflected sociologically in the presence of schools. For example, when Marxist and phenomenologically oriented historians disagree about the meaning of everyday life, they also disagree on what they consider to be significant and efficacious in history, on grand theories.

What these approaches have in common is their concern with the world of ordinary experience (rather than society in the abstract) as their point of departure, together with an attempt to view daily life as problematic. . . . However, as the sociologist Norbert Elias has pointed out in an important essay, the notion of the everyday is less accurate and more complicated than it looks. Elias distinguished eight current meanings of the term, from private life to the world of ordinary people. The everyday includes actions – Braudel defines it as the realm of routine – and also attitudes, which we might call mental habit. It may even include ritual. Ritual, a marker of special occasions in the life of individuals and communities, is often defined in opposition to the everyday. On the other hand, foreign visitors frequently notice everyday rituals in the life of every society – ways of eating, forms of greeting, and so on – which the locals fail to perceive as rituals at all. (Burke, 1991, p. 11)

The concept of everyday is embedded in various conceptual frameworks of different theories with other theoretical concepts such as daily experience, behavior, values, privacy, routine, mental habit, and ritual. The use of, and relations between these concepts change from one historiographic theory to another. Historiography is crisscrossed by divisions between vertical schools-theories and horizontal subfields. For example, the Marxist and Geertzian schools have made contributions to historiography from below as well as to cultural historiography and historiography of the family. Marxist historiography from below deals almost exclusively with economic development of politically active masses after the French Revolution. The difficulties in applying Marxist models to the study of pre-industrial societies and microhistorical subjects led historians who work on those periods or topics to follow the Annales school and to apply models borrowed from sociology and anthropology (Sharpe, 1991).

Christopher Lloyd analyzed the theoretical and sociological structure of social historiography (Lloyd, 1993, pp. 40–88). He differentiated three theoretical and social tiers in social historiography: Three theoretical models are interpreted by five traditions that are fragmented into twenty-two schools or approaches. The schools are distinguished by their theoretical assumptions about society. Individualistic theory holds that "society is an aggregate of individuals. The term 'society' is only instrumental." Accordingly, individualistic theory leads to a research program that analyses society by studying individuals and their motivation for action. Holistic theories of society consider society a closed, supra-individual system with powers of self-regulation. It dominates individuals who receive their life-courses and beliefs from the whole, which acts through them. Accordingly, the holistic research program searches for the internal determining mechanisms and/or essential meaning of structural evolution. Structurist theory holds that society is a real structure of rules, roles, relations, and meanings that has to be produced, reproduced, and transformed by individuals while causally conditioning individual actions, beliefs, and intentions. Accordingly, the structurist research program studies the structuring process over time by examining the causal interactions of individuals, groups, classes, and their structuring social conditions, beliefs, and intentions. The three theoretical models lead to five traditions: Empiricist-individualist, systematic-functionalist, interpretist, structuralist, and relational structuralist. Each of the traditions is fragmented into schools of social historiography, twenty-two in all. Lloyd's theoretical and methodological characterization of each of the schools does not always distinguish the ideology of a school, how school members like to think of their enterprise and present it to the world, from what they are really doing. But irrespective of the precise description of the theories and research programs of each school, Lloyd describes the theoretical proliferation and sociological fragmentation that is typical of historiographic schools.

Fragmentation through mutation of traditions can be detected in the history of historiographic schools such as Annales. The Annales school has been united by allegiance to the research programs of its founders – Bloch, Febvre, and later Braudel – who emphasized geographical and economic evidence and theories inspired by the social sciences, as well as the study of popular mentalities to the exclusion of the significance of short span historical processes that are referred to as *events*, the subjects of political historiography and historiography of high culture. Institutionally, Annales became associated with the Sixth Section of the *École Pratique des hautes Études* and the journal *Annales*. As Hunt (1989) noted, the Annales research program and vague theories cannot be applied to specific historical cases without revisionist interpretation. Hunt documented the division of the school of Annales between research programs of global scope, and regional scope. Still both maintained allegiance to Braudel's theoretical analysis of processes into *longue duree* – demographic, climatic, and biological factors; *conjoncture* – middle–range socioeconomic developments; and *events* – short–duration political, cultural, and intellectual changes. However, Annales historians interpreted these durations differently. *Conjoncture* can be anything from 10 to 50 years. Fluctuations in the length of *longue duree* are more extreme (Santamaria & Baily, 1984).

The Annales school split between socioeconomic historians and intellectual historians, who disagreed about the place of mentalities in Braudel's three-tier model of history. Chartier documented the further fragmentation of intellectual historiography and *histoire des mentalites*:

More important than classifications and definitions are the way or ways in which historians, at any given moment, divide this immense and vague territory and treat the units of observation thus constituted. Caught between both intellectual and institutional oppositions, *each of these diverse ways of dividing reality determines its own object of study, its conceptual tools and its methodology*. Nonetheless, explicitly or not, each one embodies a representation of the totality of the field of history and delimits both the place it claims to occupy and the places it leaves or denies to others. *The uncertainty and compartmentalization of the vocabulary of designation quite certainly relate to intra- or interdisciplinary struggles, the forms of which are peculiar to each intellectual field and the stakes in which are hegemony – above all, lexical hegemony.* (Chartier, 1988, p. 20 [italics added])

Chartier described the fragmentation of intellectual historiography as founded on institutions and research programs, followed by conceptual-semantic differences. The various institutional research programs and conceptual frameworks are not complementary but in sociological-lexical (semantic) competition.

Chartier supported his thesis by narrating the historical fragmentation of French intellectual historiography. The research program of the Annales school's founder, Febvre focused on the complex mutual influences between complex systems of thought and social reality–unlike alternative research programs that sought to fit a thinker to a familiar label and study the influences of society on thought, as in Marxism, or vice versa, as in idealism. Febvre sought to understand structures of thought in their historical context as a manifestation of a form of life. Febvre's research program used a new conceptual framework, introducing *outillage mental*, mental equipment. During the 1960s, intellectual historiography transmuted into historiography of mentalities. Le Goff characterized mentality as the impersonal content of thought that an individual shares with others in an epoch, such as everyday automatisms of behavior. This general research program into the historical limits of thought divided into intellectual and psychological research programs. The latter studies the history of collective psychology using concepts such as "idea-forces" and "collective mentality." Other Annales school intellectual historians were influenced by methods of social and economic historiography, or developed a research program of popular culture. The meaning of "popular" and its distinction from "high" culture is ambiguous, leading to different interpretations by individual historians. The fragmentation described by Chartier is concurrently social and semantic, of communities and theories. It is possible to model French intellectual historiography on a genealogical tree (Chartier, 1988, pp. 19–52). Considering this analysis, it is clear that Stoianovich's (1976) presentation of what he called the Annales "paradigm" as the last scientific level in a three-stage evolutionary scheme of the history of historiography is inconsistent with the evidence for fragmentation and absence of a unified simple and accurate paradigm in its scientific sense.

The basic vague tenet of the Marxist school of historiography is that "all history is the history of class struggle." Marx never quite defined "class" accurately. When confronting identical evidence, Marxists may observe evidence for a certain kind of "class struggle" while historians from non-Marxist schools may observe evidence for something different (Clark, 2000). Much of the initial theoretical reason for the development of economic and social historiography was Marxist.

Later, other theoretical models generated interest in evidence for economic and social history as well. For example, structuralist social historiography looks for evidence for social stability, while followers of Braudel may search for evidence for processes of long duration. Consequently Marxist and non-Marxist historians use terms such as "the French Revolution," in different senses. The non-Marxist may conceive of the French Revolution, as a protest against nascent capitalism. For the Marxists it is "a bourgeois political revolution." The pragmatic and semantic fragmentation continues below the school level. Marxist historians interpreted differently Marx's vague concepts, "class" and "class struggle", and, consequently, have different interpretations of the "French Revolution" (Amariglio & Norton, 1991).

In a historiographic context, the expression "vulgar Marxism" means the insensitive deduction of historiography from Marxist theory without attention to evidence for particular historical circumstances that do not quite fit Marxist theory. Nonvulgar Marxist historiography considers the evidence and fits the theory to its peculiarities. The examination of Marx's own historiographic writings such as *The Class Struggle in France 1848–1850* or *The Eighteenth Brumaire of Louis Bonaparte* demonstrates that he had to revise his theories facing overwhelming evidence, to explain why history did not turn out as his theories may have prepared his readers to expect. In his account of French history in the middle of the nineteenth century Marx (1978a) had to explain why the political upheavals and revolutions in the country he considered most economically advanced, except for England, did not result in a successful proletariat revolution. In his account of the February 1848 revolution, Marx had to adapt ad hoc his theory to distinguish the "finance aristocracy" that has no distinct existence in his larger theories from the "industrial bourgeoisie." More significantly, he had to add ad hoc distinctly French variables: French industry was national rather than international due to protectionist policies. Therefore, the French proletariat outside of Paris did not compose a major part of the population. This proletariat may form an alliance with other oppressed social groups outside Paris, the peasantry and the petty bourgeoisie. But their common enemy was the vaguely characterized "finance aristocracy" rather than the industrial bourgeoisie. The June 1848 proletariat revolution failed because the bourgeoisie allied itself with the feudal ruling classes. Finally, the election of Louis

Napoleon in December of 1848 is assigned to the peasant class that voted for his program of reduction in taxes and opposition to the rich and the Republic. Apart from a litany of verbal abuses against the peasants, Marx did not do much to integrate this development into his larger theory of social evolution. Marx had to multiply his units of analysis to explain actual historical developments beyond owners of, and laborers with, the means of production including: the aristocracy of finance, the industrial bourgeoisie, the middle class, the petty bourgeoisie, the army, the *lumpenproletariat*, the intellectuals, the clergy, the rural population, and the proletariat (1978b, p. 601). In explaining Napoleon III's rise to power, Marx (1978b, p. 607) claimed that he represented the interests of the class of small peasants, just as the Bourbons represented the large landed property, and the Orleans dynasty represented big finance. Yet, he also claimed that Napoleon III achieved independence for the state (which Skocpol would call autonomy) based on drunken soldiery bought with liquor and sausages. None of this quite fits the Marxian concept of the state as controlled by the class of owners of means of production. Napoleon III's power was based largely on the army and the militia, which as part of the state should serve the owners of the means of production in Marxian terms. To fit this history, Marx had to revise ad hoc his theory, add variables, and increase its complexity. Marx was not a vulgar Marxist.

Similar zero sum game of scope versus accuracy, vagueness vs. simplicity can be found in the works of Perry Anderson. Broadly speaking, Anderson worked within the Marxist school. However, he criticized the Marxist concept of feudalism for being excessively vague and corresponding with any kind of traditional landlordism. Anderson developed a more precise concept of feudalism to fit the Western European medieval model that distinguished it from a relatively similar social structure in Tokugawa Japan. When he discussed individual medieval monarchies, Anderson had to adapt ad hoc his concept of feudalism in each case except France to explain individual variations as delayed or incomplete versions of this model. For example, in explaining the Scandinavian "specificity" Anderson referred to the peculiarities of the Viking social structure. But when he attempted to fit his concept of feudalism to European absolutism, Anderson had to back off from the detailed accuracy of the concept he used earlier and make it less accurate to increase its scope (Fulbrook & Skocpol, 1984).

Similarly one could distinguish "vulgar" from nondogmatic adaptable versions of virtually all the historiographic schools, depending on whether they deduce their historiography from their theory without adjusting it to the evidence. By contrast, we cannot talk of "vulgar Newtonianism" or "vulgar genetics" because scientific theories do not have to either receive different interpretations to fit to the evidence or be dogmatic and a priori. Science can be paradigmatic while at the same time deduce standardized versions of the evidence.

The Weberian alternative to Marxism is not more accurate or sociologically united. "Weber formulated his thesis [about Protestantism as an independent variable that caused the rise of capitalism] in general terms and did not substantiate it with systematic researches of particular Protestant communities. Case studies were naturally able to reveal that Weber's overall view is apparently incompatible with the plain facts," (Weinryb, 1975, p. 48). According to Scoville, Weber's concept of Protestant psychology is that of penalized communities. This fits the history of the Huguenots that Weber was studying. Scoville's concept of Protestantism is sociopolitical rather than religious. Similarly, models from economics cannot be applied successfully to historiography without revision and interpretation. This fact led to the academic distinction of economic history from economics *simpliciter.* The "attempts at *post hoc* explanation are in fact *ad hoc* as well as radically incomplete, because of the abstraction of the economy from the wider socio-cultural and political context" (Lloyd, 1993, p. 60).

Theoretical mutation and fragmentation takes place even when historians attempt to avoid grand research programs, theoretical assumptions, and conceptual frameworks in microhistoriography. Levi noted its theoretically eclectic nature. Theoretical ideas are not created anew for each study, they are adopted in a refined form from other studies. "Concepts are ... taken from the baggage of academic science: they are useful in interpretation, but it is only in that function that they acquire concrete reality and specificity" (Levi, 1991, p. 100). Each study has a slightly different conceptual framework.

Darnton's discussion of the historiography of reading demonstrates the difficulty in avoiding an almost involuntary proliferation of meanings of basic historiographic concepts within the work of a single historian under the pressure of evidence. According to Darnton:

> Reading is not simply a skill but a way of making meaning, which must vary from culture to culture. It would be extravagant to expect to find a formula that could account for all those variations. But it should be possible to develop a way to study the changes in reading within our own culture. (Darnton, 1991, p. 152)

Reading means "a way of making meaning," presumably with the help of texts. Textual information must be sifted, sorted, and interpreted (p. 161). Still, the precise meaning of reading changes from one period to another. Had Darnton been speaking in ordinary language, we would have said that there is a family relationship between the various meanings of reading. But as Darnton makes clear in the following paragraph and his discussion of the history of French reading, he is not speaking in ordinary language.

> The most important institution of popular reading under the Old Regime was a fireside gathering known as the *veillée* in France and the *Spinnstube* in Germany. While children played, women sewed, and men repaired tools, one of the company who could decipher a text would regale them. . . . In the nineteenth century groups of artisans, especially cigar makers and tailors, took turns reading or hired a reader to keep themselves entertained while they worked. Even today many people get their news by being read to by a telecaster. Television may be less of a break with the past than is generally assumed. . . . For most people throughout most of history, books had audiences rather than readers. They were better heard than seen. . . . The reading public may have included many people who could not sign their names. But *"reading" for such people probably meant something different from what it means today.* (Darnton, 1991, pp. 150, 154 [italics added])

Darnton means that in contemporary ordinary English usage, an illiterate person is not considered a reader, subject of the historiography of reading, though this was not the case in the Old Regime.

But then we are told that many French boys under the Old Regime passed from learning the alphabet to simple syllables and then to Latin prayers, before leaving school at age seven to work. Learning to recognize prayers that had already been known by heart is called by Darnton "acquired mastery of the printed word." The boys who remained in school to learn *to read* French often acquired only the ability to recognize texts they had already known, rather than acquire new knowledge.

The use of "read" here is inconsistent with the previous uses. It accepts that reading in France of the Old Regime may mean the recognition of meanings rather than their reconstruction. Boys who recognize a text they have already known did not sift, sort, and interpret the text. Darnton began his article with a general introduction to his branch of intellectual historiography, the historiography of reading, its theories, concepts, and methods. Then, he presented a detailed example from his own particular specialty, the historiography of French reading. He had to fit a general conceptual framework to the practice of recognition of known texts in one's mother tongue, so he mutated his concept of reading as he proceeded. According to the early characterization, this was not reading. Still, Darnton fitted his concept of reading to the subject matter by broadening its meaning. To use Wittgensteinian terminology, Darnton changed a rule in his language game, as the game proceeded, without making it explicit.

THE SEMANTICS OF TRADITIONALIST HISTORIOGRAPHY

The properties of theories are syntactic, semantic, and pragmatic. Syntactic properties are determined by the relations between parts of theories irrespective of their meaning. Semantic properties concern the relation of theory to the world, its meaning. Pragmatics concerns the relation of theories to their users, such as the historiographic community or particular historiographic schools: Who uses theories and in what sense? The semantics of theories may be construed as abstraction from their pragmatics; if we learn how a community uses theoretical concepts, we learn their meanings (van Fraassen, 1980, p. 89).

The syntactic properties of some historiographic theoretical concepts such as "The Middle Ages" or "the Roman Empire" are far clearer than their semantics. The syntactic temporal position of "The Middle Ages" is clear: "The Middle Ages" preceded "the modern age" and followed "the Ancient World." But, semantically even its most tangible space-time observable characteristics are ambiguous and theory laden. Initially, the tertiary periodization of universal history referred to the history of the Christian Church. "The Middle Ages" referred then to the period from Jesus to the Reformation. Philologists, following Christopher Cellarius (1685), used "The Middle Ages" to refer to the period when New Latin replaced Classical Roman Latin (Butterfield,

1955, pp. 45–6). Other historians identified "the Middle Ages" with a mode of production, the development of the latifundium agricultural production unit in the second century AD that disappeared gradually, finally only with the demise of European feudalism in the nineteenth century. The school of Pirenne holds that "The Middle Ages" began with the destruction of trade routes from Europe to the Orient as a result of the rise of Islam and ended with the opening of new trade routes from Europe to the Orient through central Asia and later by sea. Pirenne held that the transition to "The Middle Ages" happened in Europe between 650 and 750 AD. Merovingian society displayed what Pirenne regarded as the characteristics of "Roman antiquity," in terms of trade and ensuing sociopolitical structure, while Carolingian society displayed essentially "medieval" characteristics, decline in commerce and dominance of agricultural land-based production in society. Pirenne's critics assumed different conceptualizations of "The Middle Ages." For example, Bark's religious characterization of "the Roman Empire" implies that the similarity between it and Merovingian society is superficial. Bark's essential characteristics of "The Middle Ages" are religious. Accordingly he accused Pirenne of failing to recognize the significance of Christianity. Pirenne and his critics discussed different Middle Ages (Weinryb, 1975; Pirenne, 1939).

The syntactic properties of historiographic theories are misleading because while the structural relations between concepts may be similar or identical, the semantic properties of the theories, the meanings of their concepts, are different. It is necessary to follow a semantic program to understand how historiographic theories differ from each other and ordinary language. There are no simple pure facts in historiography in their naive empiricist sense, nor is historiography written in ordinary language, as Berlin (1969) and others have claimed. Historiographic hypotheses are as theory laden as those in the physical sciences (Goldstein, 1996, pp. 238–42; Murphey, 1973, pp. 58–9, 101, 110–12). Out of their theoretical context, historiographic concepts may be ambiguous. If their underlying theory is part of the historiographic Rankean paradigm, they are clear and have determined meanings. If the concepts are ad hoc interpretations of vague underdetermined historiographic theories, their meanings may be underdetermined as well. The semantics of historiographic theories are abstracted from their pragmatics, the practice of historians as members of schools. So, understanding traditionalist historiography must be done in the context of the tradition of the school from which it emerges. A noncontextual reading of historiography may be misleading. When an historian assumes that other historians use concepts as he does and ignores alternative traditions, he risks misunderstandings.

Philosophers of science agree that within the discourse of a scientific community, there is undistorted communication. Various schools of philosophy of science disagree about the exact properties of these communities of discourse and what allow undistorted communication, for example, Kuhn's shared paradigm, or Lakatos's shared research programs and core beliefs. They further disagree whether several scientific communities usually coexist. Kuhn claimed that except for periods of transitory anomaly and pre-science, there is only a single paradigm and scientific community of discourse in each of the normal sciences. Feyerabend and Lakatos held that there are several co-existing communities of scientists at each period. But all agreed that within a sociohistorical community of discourse, a fairly undistorted and meaningful communication frequently takes place (Feyerabend, 1981; Kuhn, 1996; Lakatos, 1978).

Traditionalist historiographies use different theoretical languages to communicate their findings. The semantic fragmentation of historiographic concepts creates serious problems in communication not just between historians who work within different research programs of different schools, but even more so within each school between historians who interpret differently the grand scope vague theory of their school but are not quite aware of the small variations in the meanings they assign to the identical words they mention. If historians are unaware of the different conceptual framework of their colleagues, confusions follow (Lloyd, 1993, p. 1).[5]

Philosophical discussions of difficulties in communication among persons who hold different theories or conceptual frameworks have an unfortunate tendency to slide into extreme claims about incommensurability (Kuhn), indeterminacy of translation (Quine), or the impossibility of communication due to absence of determined meaning in the first place (structuralism and deconstruction). I do not think that such radical claims are relevant for the problems of intrahistoriographic communication. Historians are quite capable of understanding each other in principle. Philosophers of historiography can understand the theoretically laden languages of historians and convey it to their readers if they read historiography sensitively and contextually. It is possible to understand sufficiently well those historians who work within different conceptual frameworks and show that they do not understand each other. Historians who use the same words to convey different meanings sometimes misunderstand each other because they assume that other historians use words as they do. But this does not imply that historians cannot understand each other in principle, only that in some cases they do not. Another common philosophical mistake is the assumption of assured communication, too common among followers of Apel and Habermas. Rescher (1993, p. 142) is quite right to argue that communication requires understanding of meaning and not agreement on meaning. That is, we do not have to agree on the meanings of words in order to understand each other; we just have to understand how we use the same words to convey different meanings. Rescher (1993, p. 148) suggested that communication is not based on communality of belief, but on the recipient's capacity to interpret, "to make good inferential sense of the meanings that the declarer is able to send." Agreement on principles will make communication easier, but is not a requisite. Historians do not have to agree on the correct meaning of words as long as they can understand the meaning of each others' words.

Since the problems of communication in historiography are not related to philosophical incommensurability, effective arguments against Quine's (1960) indeterminacy of translation or Kuhn's incommensurability do not imply easy communication among historians. Murphey (1994, pp. 84–93) debated Quine's argument for indeterminacy of translation. He followed recent studies in cognitive psychology, concluding that natural languages can be translated into one another. But Murphey assumed that historiography is written in ordinary language and then deduced that indeterminacy of translation is not a problem in historiography. Murphey did not consider that historiography may not be written only in ordinary language but also in theoretically laden language and that a good rebuttal of Quine's argument for the indeterminacy of translation does not save historiography from communication problems. Martin Bunzl argued convincingly for the crucial importance of making sense of the notion of disagreement among historians. He concluded correctly: "Merely by allowing that disagreement is possible, you thereby commit yourself to the notion that disagreeing historians are talking about the same thing. Disagreement assumes some area of overlap about which the disagreement takes place" (1997, p. 23). Yet, Bunzl did not distinguish genuine agreements and disagreements that are founded on understanding of the various identical and different uses of words from apparent agreements and disagreements that are founded on semantic confusions. Bunzl argued against poststructuralism, that its local theory of meaning implies that historians cannot understand each other. For him, it is "a glaring fact" that historians do understand each other. Unfortunately, since he considers it a glaring fact, Bunzl did not bother to prove it empirically. There is quite a lot of communication in historiography, enough to refute radical theories of local meaning as Bunzl argues. But there is enough miscommunication that results from failure to comprehend local meanings for it to be less than glaringly obvious.

Historians who share some theoretical background may not be aware of the differences between their individual interpretations of their school's vague theory, and, consequently, they fail to understand each other. Failure to understand manifests itself in futile arguments between historians that are based on mutual misunderstandings. To take a vivid example, on July, 27, 1995, a meeting took place in Münster under the title: Round Table: Manners of Reading in the 18th Century within the 9th International Congress on the Enlightenment. It is warranted to call this round table a meeting of the Chartier School because Roger Chartier is designated on the program as the President of Honour. Chartier delivered the first lecture and summed up the discussion at the end. Most of the observers left the overcrowded room after Chartier had delivered his opening lecture; Chartier's work was the most cited in the papers. Most significantly, Chartier set the research program, discussed in greater detail by the other speakers: Was there a revolution in reading practices in the eighteenth century, specifically after 1750? What kinds of reading were practiced then? The other speakers discussed "smaller" issues within the research program, limited by space, time, or subject. Only James Smith Allen delivered a more fundamental paper questioning the periodization of the history of reading in the eighteenth century, in a polemic directed at the thesis of Robert Darnton. Darnton, who was present, denied the polemic because in his opinion Allen distorted what he meant by "revolution" and "reading." It was obvious from their exchange that they use "revolution of reading" and "continuity in reading" differently.

I noticed about five different uses of "book" in the papers and ensuing discussion. Approximately, the meanings of "book" were:

1. Functional Book: means an efficient mean (transportable, broadly distributed, and with broad circulation) for the transmission of a codex.
2. Material: a bounded collection of pages containing symbolic representation of language on both sides of each page.
3. Same as 2, but without the stipulation of binding.
4. A common term for the products of several (unspecified) technologies in various shapes including 3 but broader.
5. Hermeneutic: A book participates in the creation of meaning through the dialectics of reading and text.

I presented the participants with these radical variations of their use of the term "book" and the ensuing distortions in communication in the discussion stage by asking Uta Janssens to elucidate what she means by "book." She claimed in her lecture that the book was introduced following the appearance of Christianity, though according to 2 and 3, the book was introduced only in the third and fourth centuries AD, replacing the scroll. Janssens also discussed artistic representations of journal reading in her lecture, which did not seem to fit definitions 1 and 2. Chartier intervened to answer instead of Janssens because it is a basic question of method and discussed at some length definition 1, as fitting Janssens's claim that the book followed Christianity.[6] Still, despite this intervention by the school founder, Allen and a French-speaking observer (whose name I did not catch) suggested alternative uses of "book" (5 and 4 respectively) that in their opinions offered greater advantages for discussing the research program, whether there was a revolution in reading around 1750. Each of these initially unarticulated uses of "book" must be related to a different theory of reading in the eighteenth century that was not made fully explicit. They were not arguing about the same "book" or the same "reading."

THE FABLE OF THE "CARD GAME"

Imagine a group of people who share background, education, class, status, etc., who meet regularly to play a game of cards, each according to slightly different rules that may change as the game proceeds. Before, during, and after the game there is meaningful communication. The players share jokes, tell gossip and anecdotes, give each other career advice, offer and ask for personal practical assistance, and argue about politics. The card game serves as a social framework for all the meaningful communication that goes on during the regular meetings. There are certain game norms: Everybody sits around the table, every player receives an identical number of cards, and the game consists of exchanging cards. The players share much of the rules by which they play. However, each player plays by slightly different rules, interpretations of the vague general rules that they all acknowledge. The game goes well as long as people either do not notice or do not care that they are playing according to slightly different rules. The game goes wrong if some players decide that they play to win. When it comes to declaring a winner, the differences in the rules are likely to become manifest, when no agreed winner emerges. But this happens rarely among friends who enjoy playing more than winning. If we substitute, following the later Wittgenstein, "language game" for "card game," and words for cards, this fable explains what happens in some underdetermined historiographic discourses.

HISTORIOGRAPHIC TRADITIONS ARE NOT HISTORICAL

Some philosophers in the Hegelian phenomenological tradition sought to bypass problems of historiographic epistemology and methodology by suggesting that historiography provides us with a kind of knowledge that resembles self-knowledge, different from, yet more certain than scientific knowledge. If historiography is united with history as its self-consciousness, it is possible to know history as directly and surely as we know ourselves. Various philosophies in this tradition differ in respect to how historiography is united with history as its self-consciousness. Gadamer criticized previous philosophical attempts to construct historical intersubjectivity, for example, by Husserl and Dilthey, for failing to explain the connection between historical agents and historians. In Gadamer's opinion, the unity of historiographic subject and historical object can be achieved only within a tradition (Gadamer, 1989). Gadamer claimed that there is no objective historical knowledge divorced of perspectives or "horizons." Gadamer's horizons are traditions that transcend the present and connect the historian with the past. Historiography, historical consciousness, is an aspect and an effect of a living tradition. Understanding is the transmission of tradition through language and text. Each text is interpreted differently in different ages according to its concerns and the fusion of horizons-perspectives. Gadamer thought that his account of knowledge of history explains the difference between the history of the "human" sciences and the history of the "natural" sciences. The history of the human sciences is not "progressive." It is characterized by the handing down of traditions. Historical-historiographic traditions, unlike scientific theories, never become outdated but are constantly reinterpreted.

Historical-historiographic traditions are not mutually exclusive and can account for multiplicity of historiographies of the same events. For example, if one were to write a historiography of the French Revolution, it can only be done by joining a connecting tradition that could be Monarchist or Jacobinic for example.

Our examination of historiography discovered that indeed there are traditions in historiography, but these traditions are not connected with the part of history that they purport to study. Considering the rate of mutation of such traditions, they would have mutated beyond recognition even if they had existed in the first place. The Jacobinic and Monarchist French traditions have mercifully petered out. Older historical traditions have vanished long before the birth of scientific historiography. The traditions that do exist in historiography are historiographic, not historical. Different historians interpreted them inconsistently. Since historiographic traditions are not causally connected with the historical events they purport to write about, traditions cannot be construed as the self-consciousnesses of historical processes. Quite the opposite, the presence of traditions indicates that the evidence and paradigmatic background information are insufficient for the generation of consensus. Gadamer seems oblivious of the discoveries in the eighteenth century of the mutations of traditions. His interpretation of our knowledge of the past is essentially traditionalist and premodern.

5

Historiographic Explanation

Unfortunately, historiographic explanation had probably been the main reason for philosophical interest in historiography within the analytic tradition from the Second World War to about 1970. However, this extensive discussion and debate (Murphey 1973, pp. 67–100) had been largely misguided. Practically all the participants in the philosophic debates about explanation have been asking two questions about explanations of descriptions of events:

1. What are the defining properties of such explanatory propositions?
2. What justifies explanations of descriptions of events?

Usually, philosophers have considered the second question to be an aspect of the first question. The answer to the second question was considered a part of the answer to the first question: Philosophers analyzed the structure of the explanation of descriptions of events as composed of three parts:

1. A description of an event that is explained, the *explanandum* in Latin. Events are explained only as described or conceptualized since "any token event has an infinitely large number of descriptions true of it" (Ruben, 1990, p. 105).
2. A description of an event or events that purport to explain (1), the *explanans* in Latin.

3. An extra something that connects (2) with (1), justifies their association and thereby answers the second question.

The philosophical debate centered on the nature of (3) that extra something, whether it is a law of nature, a rule, a statistical correlation, a causal mechanism, a narrative, as so on. The logical structure that characterizes explanation appeared to hinge on the exact nature of (3). If (3) is a universal law, explanation is a deductive argument. If (3) is a statistical probability, explanation is an inductive argument. Singular causal explanations, irrelevant statistical correlations and other complications, and difficulties in applying the inductive and deductive models of explanation to actual cases led to their modifications and the introduction of "causal mechanism," "unificationist," and "counterfactual" models. Still, the differences between these models concern only the correct characterization of (3). Otherwise, they agree on the triform structure of explanation and that justification is an integral part of the structure of explanation.

The only significant exception to this philosophical unanimity of approach is the model of *inference to the best explanation*, since it distinguishes justification from explication of the structure of explanation. According to *inference to the best explanation*, explanations are chosen through mutual comparisons. It is unnecessary to examine the exact structure of a favored explanation to justify it, if it can be proved that competing explanations are not as good, according to certain external criteria. Debates within this camp range over the exact list of criteria that allow the comparison of competing explanations.

Chapters two and three in this book demonstrated that historiographic explananda (1) are usually historiographic evidence rather than events or descriptions of events. Murphey (1973, pp. 95–8) accepted that historiographic theories explain descriptions of events but "viewed as a whole" and "in an ultimate sense" they explain "present observations," or "data" that correspond with what I call evidence. However, Murphey believed that the theory (3) that justifies the connection between (1) and (2) also connects the whole explanation to the evidence. As we have seen earlier, many of the theories that connect historiography with evidence have to do with the preservation of information in time rather than with historical social or economic changes. Murphey concluded that "the whole structure of law and 'fact' is a single hypothetical construction the purpose of which is to make sense of the observational data, and the explanations of the facts are fully as constrained by the data as are the factual hypotheses themselves" (Murphey, 1973, p. 98). If so, why analyze "the whole structure"? Since its justification comes from the evidence and the theories that connect the explanatory structure with the evidence, a distinct deductive, inductive, or other (3) justification is redundant.

I suggest distinguishing *atomic explanations* of descriptions of events from their justifications, the evidence and the theories that connect explanations of descriptions of events with the evidence. There is no epistemic distinction between descriptive and explanatory historiographic propositions; both are the best explanations of the evidence. The best explanation for the absence of covering laws from historiography is that they are just not there. For example, the best explanation for the independent diaries of soldiers of the same unit that state that on a certain date their unit came under heavy bombardment and therefore panicked and retreated is that indeed they came under heavy bombardment and therefore panicked and retreated. There is no need for further knowledge of psychology or human nature under fire. Had this explanation of the retreat depended on psychological theories, it would have been indeterminate, since under fire soldiers are known to retreat out of fear, become paralyzed with fear and stay put, or become emboldened with rage and charge forward. The mere description of the stimulus together with background conditions and contemporary psychology is insufficient for explaining the actual retreat. But psychology is redundant here. The preservation of information on panic and retreat is the best explanation of the independent evidence for it in personal diaries. The relevant background theory is not psychological, but informational, the reliability of independent witnesses who witnessed and participated in the events, as analyzed in chapter three.

Take another example from historiography: It is quite uncontroversial among historians to explain the rise of Nazism by several events that preceded it, including a high rise in unemployment in Germany. Old philosophy of historiography would analyze this explanation into three components: unemployment, Nazism, and something that connects the two, for example a general law or a theory that connects high unemployment or a more general "economic insecurity" with the rise of totalitarian regimes. The debate would then rage on whether there are such laws etc., and whether historians consider unemployment a sufficient cause, a necessary cause, both a sufficient and a necessary cause, or a cause neither sufficient nor necessary for the rise of Nazism. But if we consider this explanation of the rise of Nazism as a single atomic logical unit and not analyze it further, this atomic explanatory unit is the best explanation of a range of evidence, including Nazi propaganda focused on the unemployed, evidence for local statistical correlations between unemployment and pro-Nazi voting patterns, and so on. Social scientists may attempt to develop and test a general theory about the relation between economic insecurity and the rise of totalitarianism and explain why despite high unemployment, the crisis of the 1930s resulted in the "New Deal" in the United States rather than in totalitarianism. But from the perspective of historians this would be redundant as a justification of the economic explanation for the rise of Nazism, if there is sufficient evidence that preserves relevant information about the rise of Nazism.

Explanations of descriptions of events in paradigmatic historiography are atomic explanatory units that are the best explanation of a range of evidence, given background information and theories. Further analysis of explanation of descriptions of events is redundant. Therefore, the debate on the covering law of explanation is irrelevant for historiography.

According to the covering law model, every explanation must assume a law that asserts and justifies a causal connection between the explanans (what explains) and the explanandum (what is being explained). Historiography seemed to pose the greatest challenge to the logical positivist thesis of the unity of science because there are no obvious historiographic laws that can cover explanations. Gustav Hempel originally articulated the covering law model of historiographic explanation in his 1942 article "On The Function of General Laws in History," published in *The Journal of Philosophy*. Hempel claimed that every explanation, including historiographic explanation assumes a covering law:

All scientific explanation involves, explicitly or by implication, a subsumption of its subject matter under general regularities. . . . It seeks to provide a systematic understanding of empirical phenomena by showing that they fit into a nomic nexus. This construal . . . does not claim simply to be descriptive of the explanations actually offered in empirical science. . . . The construal here set forth is, rather, in the nature of an *explication*, which is intended to replace a familiar but vague and ambiguous notion by a more precisely characterized and systematically fruitful and illuminating one. (Hempel, 1965, pp. 488–9)

It was argued against Hempel that an empirical examination of historiographic explanations does not discover any covering laws, nor do historians know of any such laws. Hempel replied that explicated historiographic explanations are sketches of explications of scientific explanations. Hempel thought that historians applied his model, though in a fairly sloppy and haphazard way. In his opinion, historians were more likely to explain by proposing necessary or neither necessary nor sufficient conditions than sufficient conditions. The elusive covering laws may also be trivial, commonsensical, or probabilistic.

Yet, as Goldstein (1996, pp. 36–44) demonstrated, actual examples for covering laws provided by advocates of this model did not provide more information than the actual historiographic explanations they sought to cover, because they merely replaced proper names or concrete terms with generalized abstract terms. If historians write that Augustus wanted to become emperor because he was ambitious, we are not better informed if we say that there is a vague general law that says that ambitious people seek power. The exchange of general for concrete terms cannot explain why historians take some explanations to be better than others. Such reconstructed laws are often either vague and often trivial and noninformative, or ad hoc, disjoined from a wider theoretical net.

The Hempelian defense even more than his original argument convinced historians that his model was actually prescriptive (Iggers, 1985, p. 34). They interpreted the covering law model as implying that historians practice bad science. If so, the covering law model is useful as a vantage point to criticize historiographic practice. Hempel's logical positivism appeared from this perspective to continue the tradition of the nineteenth-century positivist philosophy of the social sciences of August Comte and J. S. Mill (1976), who suggested what they took to be an explication of physics as a prescriptive model for the social sciences, where laws of human nature should occupy an analogical position to Newton's laws of motion in physics (Roth, 1987, pp. 116–19). I suspect that, consequently, historians such as Lawrence Stone decided that philosophers of historiography are an annoying lot who spread rumors about the professional incompetence of historians and expect them to study calculus and look for the laws of history (Iggers, 1985, p. 181). As Elton put it: "What troubles the logician and the philosopher seems least to worry those even amongst them who have had some experience of what working among the relics of the past means. From the point of view of understanding the past, the many learned discussions concerning the sense in which historians explain it are quite remarkably barren and irrelevant" (Elton 1969, p. 129).

Within the philosophy of historiography, some claimed that the covering law model of explanation is inapplicable to historiography because of this or that property of history, for example, uniqueness of events that prohibits generalizations. Others claimed that a revised covering law model could still work. The most striking aspect of this debate is the almost total disregard, not to say ignorance, of actual historiography. The discussion is of the language used by historians, of the ultimate textbook product of research, not of the process of research itself that results in adopting an explanation (Goldstein, 1996, p. 36). One could have expected Hempel to specify some empirical, historiographic, conditions that would confirm or refute his model. Instead, no matter how large are the discrepancies between historiography and the covering law model, the model is unaffected because it is of the logical structure of explanation not of historiography. Discrepancies can only show that historians are poor scientists. Hempel revised his model in response to other philosophic criticisms, not as a result of interaction with historiography. The most telling sign of the irrelevance of historiography for this debate is the exclusive discussion of the explanation of events, though historiography explains first and foremost evidence.

This account of atomic explanations of descriptions of events solves the so-called "paradox of *ex post facto* explanations," explanations that can be known only after the fact (Hobbs, 1993): If the structure of explanation is symmetric to that of prediction, as verificationists, advocates of the covering law model and others claimed, the theories that cover *ex post facto* explanations are not confirmed, since they could not predict the explananda before its instantiation, and so the explanation is unjustified. If, conversely, the covering theory is predictive, the explanation could not be *ex post facto*. The solution to this paradox is that the predictive theories are not predicting the explananda but the transmission of information. The theories do not predict explananda but evidence. This account of atomic explanations of descriptions of events also solves the problem of singular causal explanations that generated extensive philosophical discussions and complex solutions (Cartwright, 1989; Ruben, 1990). Singular causal explanations can be confirmed by the evidence and require no covering laws that connect the explaining cause with the explained effect, just like nonsingular explanations of descriptions of events.

If explanations are analyzed as atomic, their defining properties cannot be in their structure, but in their external contexts. The same proposition may be considered explanatory in one context and descriptive in another. In other words, the atomic analysis of explanations of descriptions of events is pragmatist. There are quite a number of pragmatist accounts of explanation (Achinstein, 1983; Smart, 1990; van Fraassen, 1980). A commitment to an atomic analysis of explanations of descriptions of events does not imply a commitment to any particular pragmatist theory of explanation.

It takes something like a philosophical gestalt shift to begin considering explanations of descriptions of events as justified by evidence and background information theories, and cease searching for nonexisting covering laws that should connect explanans with explananda. Still, the advantages of an atomic analysis of explanations of descriptions of events are overwhelming. It avoids the numerous known drawbacks of the covering law model, while fitting the actual practices of scientists, historians, and ordinary folks who explain descriptions of events. Those philosophers who found reading chapter two of this book a drag, may be comforted now in understanding the crucial significance of founding the philosophy of historiography on actual historiographic practice.

BEST AMONG COMPETING EXPLANATIONS

There are two possible interpretations of the *inference to the best among competing explanations* model in relation to explanations of descriptions of events. First, the competition may be between different atomic explanations that explain the same or a similar scope of evidence. The epistemic status of atomic explanations of descriptions of events would resemble then the status of scientific hypotheses that compete over being the best explanation of the evidence in the philosophy of science

(Lipton, 1991, 1998; Resnik, 1989; Thagard, 1988). Various cognitive values determine which of the competing explanations of similar evidence, that are themselves atomic explanations of descriptions of events, is the best. Second, it may be argued that various historiographic explanations compete over offering the best explanation of the same event (Martin, 1989; Scriven, 1966). For this interpretation to be applicable to historiography, historians must frequently attempt to explain the same events. Otherwise, their explanations cannot compete against each other in the sense Scriven and Martin prescribed. Goldstein (1996, pp. 83–5) argued persuasively that one of the shared mistakes of the partisans in the covering law model dispute was the assumption that historical facts are given and historians merely debate how to explain them. Ruben (1990) and others noted correctly that we do not explain events, but their descriptions, and the descriptions of the same event may differ. Still, it may be argued that historiographic explanations compete to prove that they are the best explanation of a *description* of an event.

Following van Fraassen's analysis of explanation (1980, pp. 141–57) as an answer to a why question, we can distinguished three components that should remain identical across distinct explanations of descriptions of events for them to compete: First, the *topic* of the question, the description of the event, must be identical. Second, the *contrast class*, a set of alternatives to the topic, must be identical. As van Fraassen and Lipton (1991) emphasized, explanations differ not just because they may describe differently the same event, but because they often refer to a counterfactual contrastive situation, the explanation explains not just the explanandum but also why an alternative class of events did not take place. For example, why was printing invented in Europe north of the Alps rather than south of them, or why did the Soviet Empire collapse in 1989 rather than in 1980, meaning the explanation should highlight factors that were uniquely northern European or that were added after 1980. Different counterfactual contrast classes would require different explanations. Thirdly, implicit in every explanation is its *relevance conditions*, the respect in which the explanation is sought. For example, in some historiographic contexts the explanation of the collapse of Communism is expected to analyze the drawbacks of a centrally planned economic system, in others the effects of the arms race.

Instead of conducting a careful analysis of historiographic explanations of descriptions of events to test whether they indeed compete, Scriven and Martin took historiographic textbooks at face value. They assumed that if historians think and act as if they argue against each other's explanations in support of their own, they really do participate in some kind of competition over which explanation is the best. However, Scriven and Martin's thesis confused historiographic phenomenology and ideology; what historians may think of their enterprise and how they like to present their enterprise, with actual historiographic practice. Martin suggested that:

The best historians almost always attempt to show, and often succeed in showing, that their explanations are better than the best competing explanations.... Historians are rarely able to do more in defense of their controversial explanations of historical events than to show that they are better than the best competing explanations. But that is enough....

It would be ... surprising if the ways in which explanations are actually defended in the best historical work are not fairly close to the ways in which they should be defended. The best historical work, after all, is done by the best historians. And the best historians are those who are most competent to write history. (Martin, 1989, pp. 27–8)

Philosophers of science agree often on scientific "success stories," Galileo, Newton, Darwin, Einstein, and so on, and then analyze them to understand scientific rationality. In historiography as well, we can find such indisputable success stories: Wolf's analysis of Homer, Ranke's discoveries in the archives and his inference of historiography from this evidence, Mommsen's hypothesis of Roman elections, Burckhardt's discovery of the Renaissance, and so on. All these historiographic success stories involve explanations of evidence and in some cases its discovery as well. Martin has not discussed any of them. To the extent that explanations of descriptions of events (historians can never explain the events directly, as Martin put it), are involved in these success stories, they are atomic parts of the explanation of the evidence. Martin decided arbitrarily what is "the best historical work that is available" and then attempted circularly to explicate what the best historians do, in Martin's opinion, to choose the best among competing explanations of events.

Phenomenologically, it may appear to historians that their explanations compete with each other. But this consciousness of competition does not imply that there is such a competition. Dray (1993, pp. 67, 76) noted that differing historiographic perspectives may lead to historiographic arguments at cross purposes, when historians do not realize that their opponents explain a different topic and use different comparison situations. Marwick (1993, pp. 269–78) noted the shifting meanings of historiographic proper names, classificatory generalizations, and other theoretical concepts in different historiographies, for example: revolution, liberty, democracy, the welfare state, feudalism, the Middle Ages, Europe and other geographical designations, class, ideology, capitalism, imperialism, etc.

> Only the stupid and the bigoted insist that each word must have one meaning and one meaning only, that is the meaning defined by them. What we have to do in a serious study is to understand how words shift in meaning, and always be clear which particular meaning is being used at which particular time. (Marwick, 1993, p. 276)

Martin recognized that when historians appear to argue about explanations of descriptions of events, they often argue about different topics. In relation to the collapse of Maya civilization he wrote:

> Archaeologists naturally disagree about how to explain the collapse. But they also disagree about what constitutes "the collapse." Disagreement about what needs to be explained is typical of explanatory disagreement in historical studies. While it is not an extra source of philosophical problems, it can greatly complicate an exposition of how historians argue that one explanation is better than its competitors. To simplify, I shall ignore for the time being disagreement over what constitutes "the collapse" and assume that there is some sentence, or conjunction of sentences, which all archaeologists would agree adequately characterizes what it is they are trying to explain. . . . This simplifying assumption is innocuous. . . .
>
> The reason is that the strategies historians employ to determine whether an explanans is true are exactly the same as those they employ to determine whether an explanandum is true. (Martin, 1989, pp. 32, 42)

Martin begged the question. His simplifying assumption is anything but innocuous. He assumed that historiographic explanations compete, and that historians argue with each other and then "proved" that these competitions and arguments are the justification for historiographic explanations as "the best among competing explanations." Martin should have proved first that there are competitions among explanations of descriptions of events in historiography, and that historians argue with each other. Instead, Martin confused the repeated mentioning of words such as "the collapse of the Maya Empire" by different historians with their use to convey different hypothetical descriptions of events. If explanations of descriptions of events differ rather than compete, disproving one explanation does not demonstrate the superiority of another.

For example, consider the explanations of the invention of printing, a seemingly trivial topic, free of ideological or theoretical considerations. Yet, the following four explanations differ rather than compete, even though the historians themselves did not always understand that. Miller used "printing" to denote "a process of evolving techniques and concepts," emerging in the form of seals, stamps, and rubbings, developing as block printing and culminating with modern typography. "Chinese . . . block printing developed quite naturally from the techniques of making and using seals and stamps, of taking rubbings from stone inscriptions, and of engraving on bronze and stone" (Miller, 1983, p. 1). Miller used "printing" to refer to a continuous process of conceptual and technological development that has taken thousands of years. Miller then asked why did printing develop in China rather than in the contrast class of pre-Gutenberg Europe. A relevant explanation must trace the evolution of the technique and concept back to its earliest beginnings (Miller, 1983, p. 4). According to Carter, "For any land, the invention of printing . . . transforms the education and culture of the nation" (Carter, 1955, p. 31). Chinese historiography and popular culture consider the invention of printing as that of block printing because the Confucian codex was printed using this technology, while Western historiography and popular culture regard the invention of printing as that of movable type because Gutenberg used it to print the Bible. Carter offered two explanations to each invention by deploying two contrast classes to each. In the case of China, the first contrast class consists of the situation immediately before the invention of block print; the second is the situation prior to the spread of Buddhism there. In Europe, the first contrast class is the situation immediately before Gutenberg; the second is Europe at the turn of the fourteenth century. The first set of contrast classes defines searches for *immediate* causes; the second set directs research to discover *deeper* causes.

For Butler (1940), "printing" is functional, "a mechanical aid in the scribal process." Unlike Miller, Butler would not accept mechanical reproduction of pictures in seals or textiles as early "print." He contrasted late medieval Europe and medieval Europe, asking for the causes present at the first and absent at the second. Scholderer (1963, p. 7) defined the invention of printing as "some method of superseding the pen by mechanical means of reproduction." For Scholderer, print is functionally identical to the pen. Its sole distinctions are speed and accuracy. Fourteenth-century European block printing has nothing to do with the invention of printing because it replaced the painter's brush, rather than the scholar's pen. Scholderer contrasted Europe north of the Alps with southern Europe, asking why printing was invented in the north.

Historians suggested several arguments against each other's explanations for the invention of printing. However, since they assumed their own use of "the invention of printing" rather than note that other historians used it to mean different things, they argued at cross purposes: Carter claimed that printed textiles do not explain the invention of printing in Europe because of the dissimilarity between textile prints and the earliest European prints. "If block printing had been a natural development from textile printing without outside influence we might expect a certain continuity in design" (Carter, 1955, p. 206). If textile printing is characterized according to its designs, it is not similar to printing of the written word. However, if "printing" is a technological term, there may be continuity from textile printing to text printing. Scholderer objected to Carter's claim that movable type developed in Europe out of block print. Scholderer offered three arguments against this explanation: First, the earliest surviving block prints date from the mid-fifteenth century, when movable type was invented. Second, block printing has an advantage over movable type only for printing short and popular texts designed for mass circulation, not much longer than commentaries on printed pictures. Third, the alphabet system in the West is not conducive to block print (Scholderer, 1963, p. 8). Still, these claims are based on Scholderer's own use of "printing" as a mechanical substitute to the pen. Other historians used "block print" to refer to a wider class of evidence, including prints of pictures of saints from the second half of the fourteenth century. Scholderer's second and third arguments rely on the economic and technical advantages of movable type over block print. However, Scholderer assumed here again that printing is a more efficient substitute for the pen. According to this meaning of "print," since block "print" was not economic in Europe, it was not, in effect, a kind of printing. Again, these arguments are ineffective against other uses of "print." The critical arguments we encountered are faulty because they do not recognize the differences between the theoretically laden languages of different historians who used the same words to convey different meanings.

TRADITIONALIST EXPLANATIONS

The best explanations of descriptions of events are determined by being the best explanations of evidence. Yet, other atomic historiographic explanations are underdetermined by the evidence and rely on underdetermined theoretical backgrounds. The following contrived comic example should clarify the distinction between determined and underdetermined explanations:

Suppose two independent witnesses, Mr. Kramer, who lives opposite the apartment of the Pecheur family, and Mr. Newman, a mailman, testify that they have seen Mr. Pecheur drown his son by immersing his head in the family aquarium until the son ceased moving, while shouting, "You love my goldfish, so now you can have her, forever! We could have had a future together, but you had to keep staring at the aquarium until she noticed you. I saw you, how she swam in your direction, skirting the glass walls of the aquarium. Now you are going to pay for this. You will die together with my goldfish! No one else will have my goldfish!" Further interviews by the police of co-workers, family, and neighbors corroborate the special attachment that Mr. Pecheur, Sr., had developed to the family goldfish. A diary kept by Mr. Pecheur divulges increasing infatuation with the family goldfish, which turned in the weeks before the murder into jealous rage directed at his son. Based on this evidence, the police would have to conclude that Mr. Pecheur, Jr., is dead because his father killed him and that the motive for the crime was jealousy for a goldfish. These two explanations of the evidence require no psychological covering laws because they make the evidence more likely than any alterative hypothesis, bearing in mind the independent witnesses. Any sane judge and juror would convict Mr. Pecheur of killing his son.

Suppose psychiatrists are asked to analyze this case, perhaps to determine whether the murderer was insane. It is rather unusual for a father to kill his son out of jealousy for a goldfish. It is inconsistent with much of what we are familiar with. So, the psychiatrist is likely to come with some ad hoc theory about Mr. Pecheur's personality, perhaps he transferred some conflict from his early childhood to his relations with his son and his goldfish. Perhaps the goldfish came to symbolize his elusive mother and his son merged with his abusive father? Psychologists of different schools who interpret different vague theoretical traditions could dispute such explanations and the theories behind them. The psychiatrist for the defense will say one thing and the psychiatrist for the prosecution another. A proliferation of explanations would emerge because the evidence underdetermines the hypotheses about the personality of the murderer and the reasons for his developing a bizarre jealous attachment to a goldfish and murderous rage at his own son. Nevertheless, any police report would certainly mention the murder and jealousy for the goldfish as its explanation because the evidence determines them. Since the probability that two independent eyewitnesses would decide independently to deceive the police by presenting love for a goldfish as a motive for murder is vanishing. Psychiatric hypotheses can be determined only if there is more evidence. For example, if a hundred more such murders are committed, the American Psychiatric Association would probably suggest "the goldfish jealousy syndrome" (GJS) and psychiatrists could discriminate between hypotheses according to their scope, whether or not they make all 100 cases likely.

Determined explanatory propositions do not require a particular philosophic analysis, distinct of any other determined historiographic proposition, as discussed in chapter three. Historiographic explanations of descriptions of events that are underdetermined by the evidence have the same epistemic status as any other underdetermined historiographic proposition as analyzed in chapter four. Explanations of descriptions of events that are underdetermined by the evidence rely then on a mostly ad hoc interpretation of vague theories and therefore tend to differ rather than compete. Even if the descriptions of events – the topics, comparison situations, and relevance criteria are similar – and the explanations of descriptions of events do compete, different theoretical backgrounds in traditionalist historiography preclude agreements on which competing explanation is best.

COMMON CAUSE EXPLANATIONS OF DESCRIPTIONS OF EVENTS

Some atomic explanations of descriptions of events propose a description of a common cause as the best explanation of similarity between descriptions of events that are themselves common causes for similar evidence. For example, descriptions of the Communist regimes that dominated East Europe from after the end of the Second World War to 1989 are the best common cause explanation for the mass of evidence that these regimes have left behind. But further, the best explanation of the overwhelming similarities between the regimes, irrespective of local variables of tradition or geography, is that they had a common cause, the Soviet state model that was reproduced by coercion and emulation. Like all common cause hypotheses, they must compete first with the alternative separate causes hypothesis and then against each other, as analyzed in chapter three. For example, either Poland, Czechoslovakia, etc., developed independently show trials during the early fifties, or these show trials had a common cause. There is plenty of evidence both for the intersection of backward causal chains in Moscow, and for the presence of Soviet experts in show trials in these countries, who taught the locals how to reproduce the Soviet model. Only a particular type of description of events can qualify for a common cause explanation, one that describes information, ideas that can be transmitted from a common cause to historical effects, for example, inventions, social and political models, artistic styles, and so on.

Unsurprisingly, considering the history of the historical sciences, the historiographic common cause model of explanations of descriptions of events dates back to nineteenth-century historiography. To mention again my favorite historical events, the inventions of printing in China and Europe, according to Davis (1857), stone rubbings are the precursors of print. Humphrys (1868) claimed that the use of seals accidentally stimulated the idea of inventing print. Chatto (1861) argued that block printing is an enlarged application of the principle expressed in stamps and seals, and DeVinne (1876) traced the evolution

of print back to the use of seals and stamps in ancient Egypt and
Babylon. "Printing of an *embryonic* type was practiced long ago by means
of seals made of clay or metal" (Laufer, 1973, p. 21). Miller (1983,
pp. 33–7) too suggested a continuity between the use of stencils and
wax molds in Rome and Europe and wood block printing because
they "embody the principles of the reproduction of the same pattern
many times from one original mode, exactly the principle put into effect with carved wooden block." Note the biological-genetic analogy:
"Early Chinese seals . . . contained *seeds* of the technique which later
was to *germinate* into the block printing process" (Miller 1983, p. 17).
"In China, engraving on bronze and rubbing from stone inscriptions
acted as *precursors* ushering in the technical processes later used in
block printing" (Miller 1983, p. 29).

HISTORIOGRAPHIC UNDERSTANDING (*VERSTEHEN*)

Some philosophers of historiography would argue that the foregoing
discussion is irrelevant because historians and people who read historiography are not interested in explanation but in "understanding"
(Rickert, 1962, p. 73). Collingwood (1956) is probably the best known
proponent in the Anglophone world of the view that historiography
of the human past has a different purpose and method from those of
the natural sciences and natural historiography:

History . . . is not . . . a story of successive events or an account of change. . . .
The historian is not concerned with events at all. He is only concerned with
those events which are the outward expression of thoughts. . . . At bottom, he
is concerned with thoughts alone. (Collingwood, 1956, p. 217)

Bunzl (1997) claimed that historians are committed to understanding how historical agents perceived their lives and understood their
experiences and alternative choices. Still, a brief examination of historiography shows that historians who engage in a project of such understanding compose only some of the schools that make up historiography. Writing of recent European historiography, Iggers observed that
"a broad agreement has appeared, shared by historians of very different ideological perspectives, that a history centering on the conscious
actions of men does not suffice, but that human behavior must be

understood within the framework of the structures within which they occur" (Iggers, 1985, p. 11). Braudel thought that the deepest, most significant level of historiography, should examine environmental-climactic, economic, and biological processes of long duration and slow change, which historical agents would not be conscious of due to their short life span in comparison with the length of the process. Marxist historians such as Guy Bois, Perry Anderson, and Immanuel Wallerstein wrote historiographies of impersonal economic processes (Iggers, 1985, p. 179). Demographic historiography obviously cares little for historical consciousness. McCullagh noted that historiographic explanations are not confined to the reasons by which the agents would have explained their own actions to themselves. Since Marx, Freud, and Nietzsche, it has been accepted that people are often unaware of their socio economic motives, unconscious desires, and will to power. The claim that the application of modern theories, which use new conceptual frameworks for the understanding of history, is anachronistic amounts in McCullagh's opinion to denying the influence of unconscious motives, culture, and society on human behavior. It gives a false impression of human autonomy because historical agents are conscious of their reasons for action only occasionally (1998, p. 210). McCullagh noted correctly that historians explain descriptions of actions not just by suggesting reasons, but also by descriptions of habits, events that produced new beliefs or effective emotions, traits of character, biological needs, personal needs or interests, events that created unconscious dispositions or new cultural norms, and social sanctions (p. 214).

The limitation of relevant evidence to indications of the consciousnesses of historical agents leads to strange conclusions. For example, that there was no Industrial Revolution in England during the late eighteenth and early nineteenth centuries. Clark (2000, pp. 447–70) noted that the term "Industrial Revolution" appeared for the first time in French in the 1820s and in English in 1884. The Industrial Revolution is a "term of historical art," a hypothesis in my terms. If a historian limits the relevant evidence for this hypothesis to evidence for what historical agents were conscious of, there was no Industrial Revolution because during most slow but accumulating historical changes the agents who participate in, or undergo, them cannot notice them. Clark (2000, p. 448) claimed that since Englishmen of what he called "the old society" knew their society better than we do, and they were aware only of a commercial revolution there was no industrial one. If there was no Industrial Revolution, it could not be causally related with secularization or democracy, as modernization theory proposes. Therefore, Clark argued that economic changes did not affect the reform acts of 1832 and 1867 in England. Since there is plenty of evidence for Englishmen debating the legal-political position of Catholics and dissenting Protestants, Clark proposed that these religious debates resulted in the reform bills. Clark conceded that demographic and geographic shifts and frictions within rural society over the tithe to the Church of England, the enclosure of land, and the poor law are associated with growth of Protestant dissent. Clark did not examine in detail the reasons for these demographic and geographical shifts. Of course, historical actors do not leave diaries where they consciously connect economic, technological, and demographic changes with religious reform and democratic aspirations. People who change their religious affiliations think they discovered the truth and the meaning of life, not that they react to social or economic trends. Yet, understanding historical agents in their own terms, ignoring the vast evidence for the factors that change their consciousnesses, can offer only a shallow and superficial knowledge of history.

Like Hegel, Collingwood interpreted "history" as the unfolding of reason in time. Like Hegel, he thought that as a part of this process, historical reason can understand it from within as its self-consciousness. "It is only in the historical process, the process of thoughts, that thought exists at all; and it is only in so far as this process is known for a process of thoughts that it is one. The self-knowledge of reason is not an accident; it belongs to its essence" (1956, p. 227). For historical knowledge to be a kind of self-knowledge, Collingwood had to construct a metaphysical entity where the past and the present collapse into a unity: "Since the historical present includes in itself its own past, the real ground on which the whole rests, namely the past out of which it has grown, is not outside it but is included within it" (pp. 229–30). Collingwood (1956, pp. 218–19) suggested that the re-enacting mind of the historian knows itself in the process of re-enactment because all self-consciousness of the mind is historical. Collingwood (1956, p. 231) acknowledged the existence of irrational behavior. However, he claimed that irrational behavior is the subject of psychology and not historiography because it is not part of what he took the historical process to be.[1]

Collingwood's concept of historical understanding is in the epistemic tradition that considers knowledge of history a type of self-consciousness. Idealists such as Vico assumed that since men made history, the thought structures of historical agents are contained in the eternal "modifications of the mind" (Vico. 1984, paragraph 349; Tucker, 1993). Understanding the thoughts of ancient others requires only introspection of our own minds. Vico's genius was in noting that historical agents from different eras had different modalities of thought, languages, symbolic forms, systems of values, and so forth. Vico claimed to have demonstrated that since these different modifications of historical minds are innate, we can understand the thoughts of historical agents, even those whose thought processes are very different from our own. Vico undoubtedly had flashes of intuitive genius, for example in being the first to claim that the author of the *Iliad* could not have been the author of the *Odyssey* because the culture, values, and symbolic expressions of the two texts could not have emerged from the same kind of mentality. But whether or not the historical modifications of the mind are synthetic a priori, there are conflicting accounts of them and we cannot decide between them a priori. Scientific historiography discovered that Vico was right on some things and wrong on others. When his views became the subject of a heterogeneous consensus, it was on scientific epistemic foundations, Wolf's linguistic analysis (1985) of the Homeric texts. Philosophers in the phenomenological tradition, from Hegel to Gadamer, have claimed that historians can understand the historical process because they are part and product of it. Phenomenology likes to eliminate philosophical problems by demonstrating that they are based on false distinctions such as the world as it is/the world for us; subject/object; and the historian/history. As I mentioned in the introduction, the philosophy of history is based on this alleged faculty of self-consciousness that grants us the potential to understand history as we understand ourselves. To do so, it is necessary to construct a metaphysical entity where the synthetic a priori historian can play the role of self-consciousness. Such a system can be found in its pure form in the Hegelian philosophy of history. A similar scheme operates also in Winch's (1958) philosophy of the social sciences. Winch's constructed metaphysical entity is an interpretation of Wittgenstein's life form. For social scientists to understand a foreign society according to Winch, they must merge their language with its life form and become conscious of its rules of meaning attached to behavior. Roth (1987, pp. 130–51) criticized Winch correctly for making too many metaphysical assumptions about the existence of rules that compose the alleged life form.

There are radically different and conflicting alleged synthetic a priori accounts of history. Idealist and phenomenological self-consciousnesses cannot form the foundation for historiographic consensus. Gadamer (1989) recognized it when he proposed that there are several historiographic traditions but no independent criteria to judge between them beyond biases in favor of one's own tradition. This interpretation of historiography cannot explain why there is consensus in some areas of historiography on the mental states of historical agents, for example, that Hitler was paranoid or that Caesar was ambitious. The idealist vision of understanding history or historical agents as surely and as intimately as we can understand ourselves proved to be the alchemist stone of the philosophy of history. This or that hypothetical mental state may ring familiar, it may resemble an emotional state we may have experienced ourselves. But such similarities do not amount to anything that approaches intersubjective self-consciousness of the historical process. Further, the much-touted model of self-understanding does not provide higher quality knowledge than scientific knowledge. People can deceive and misunderstand themselves. Sometimes strangers can understand people better than they can understand themselves; this is a necessary condition for the psychiatric profession.

Collingwood's most famous claim is that historians of human affairs aim to reenact the experience of historical agents from within. Understanding from within is possible only in the disciplines that study conscious beings. Scientists study events, whereas historians study acts. Behind events there are other events, behind acts there are thoughts (Collingwood, 1956, p. 214). Dray (1995) criticized Collingwood for using "reenactment" inconsistently and vaguely and failing to explicate the philosophy of mind it presupposes. "Within/without" cannot be equated with mental versus physical because historians attempt to understand through reenactment mental acts as well as physical. Dray called an interpretation of *reenactment* as what the historian would have thought had he been in the situation of the historical agent (a caricature). Dray rejected an idealist interpretation of reenactment as somehow recapturing ideal individual thoughts that exist outside time as "spooky." According to Dray, actions, including mental acts, express thoughts. Reenactment is thinking the thoughts, for example, beliefs, motives (conscious and unconscious) and rational calculations that historical actions expressed. Actions express thought in a "quasi-normative" way. Given the mental conditions of the agent, he should have acted in a certain way; if he did not, the historian should criticize the agent. Reenacting a thought means to be critically engaged in it, not necessarily to agree with its reasoning. Reenacting the thoughts of historical agents presents their actions as reasonable or permissible rather than necessary, given the thoughts and circumstances (Dray, 1995).

Private historical thoughts are inaccessible directly. They have to be reenacted through the acts that express them. Dray suggested that unlike scientists who go beyond the events to previous events to subsume them under generalizations, historians penetrate the events to discover the reasons behind them.

Dray is exceedingly vague about how historians can infer thought from action, or mental states from behavior to use the terminology of the problem of other minds. Dray is clearer on what this relationship of expression is not than on what it means. Dray rejected Donagan's position that follows Wittgenstein's *Philosophical Investigations* in taking the relation between thought and action to be analytic (Donogan, 1966; Wittgenstein, 1953, pp. 143–242). Dray argued that since thoughts are placed in holistic networks, it is necessary to have information on beliefs, motives, and so on, to make the connection between an individual thought and action sufficient. In most cases the thought makes the action just probable or permissible. Dray's reenactment is reducible to the problem of other minds: How can we attribute mental states to others if the meaning of mental terms is subjective? We seem to attribute mental states with which we are acquainted in the first person to others on the basis of their observable behavior. For example, when we observe another person being pricked by a pin and cry "Ouch!" we deduce that that person sensed pain. But, how can we know that others are in pain similar to our own sensation of pain? Following Wittgenstein, many philosophers connect the meaning of mental terms to third person public behavior. Wittgenstein thought that behavior is conceptually connected to mental states as criteria. Wright added that these criteria are defeasible, that is, the criteria may be fulfilled but the mental state false (Wright, 1984). Reenactment as a philosophical problem is composed then of two stages, two applications of the problem of other minds:

1. How can historians attribute thoughts or mental states to (historical) agents?
2. How can first-person mental states of historical agents be attributed to historians?

Still, I do not think that Dray's concept of reenactment, original or reduced to the problem of other minds can explain the practices of historians. The relation of behavior to mental states is an issue when the behavior is patent and the mental state cannot be observed and should be inferred. In historiography, by contrast, historical actions are just as unobserved as mental states are in intersubjective interactions. The attribution of mental states to historical agents in historiography is just as hypothetical as attributing them to actions. Historiographic propositions explain (or not) the evidence. Propositions about historical mental states can be the best explanation of a scope of evidence. Then they can be determined. As hypotheses, they are not better or worse than ordinary historiography. For example, contemporary witnesses may record independent testimonies to the mental states of their contemporaries. Historians can also reconstruct the peculiar psychology of different cultures from various evidential sources such as literature and art reaching generalizations such as that the ancient Romans found physical deformity funny and an appropriate object for derision and the sexual act to be an expression of male aggression. When historians study a culture, when they know all the wide diversity of relevant evidence, they are able to determine general statements about the relations between evidence and mental states in cultures that left sufficient evidence for that purpose. Then they are able to use these determined generalities and evidence to determine particular propositions about the mental states of historical agents. For example, Caesar's last words addressed to Brutus were probably "*et tu filii,*" "you too my son." Additional evidence indicates that both Brutus and Brutus's mother were lovers of Caesar. "Son" in contemporary Latin referred both to a biological offspring and to the younger passive half of a homosexual couple. In that context, Caesar could have referred to the possibility that Brutus was his biological son and Brutus was killing his own father. Or considering that the Romans interpreted the sexual act as an aggressive act, Caesar's last words probably did not express disappointment from betrayal as readers of Shakespeare may recall, but a rather aggressive comment to Brutus about what Caesar did to him and his mother.

Though there are quite a number of determined historiographic propositions about historical mental states, I guess it is somewhat more difficult to determine them in comparison with other historiographic propositions because of the paucity of relevant evidence and determined auxiliary theories about the psychology of cultures that did not generate diverse literary and artistic evidence. Yet, the difference is of degree rather than kind; there is no special procedure for gaining knowledge of historical mental states distinct of other historiographic topics. Historians offer historiographic hypotheses that postulate certain types of mental events or thoughts as unobservable hypotheses, just as theories in physics postulate a host of directly unobservable particles. As Kincaid (1996, p. 90) noted, ethologists who study animal behavior attribute mental states to the animals they study. Theories that attribute mental structures to past or present social actors may be determined at least as well, without special mind reading skills.

6

The Limits of Historiographic Knowledge

Historiography is composed of scientific-determined and tradition-alist-underdetermined parts. The historiography of science records several revolutionary transitions of traditionalist sciences into paradigmatic sciences. Is such a transition from tradition to science possible or even likely in historiography as well?

Philosophers have lost interest in the question concerning the possibility and limits of scientific historiography because it was raised originally within the context of two intellectual debates that petered out a generation ago, the epistemic foundations of Marxism and the viability of the positivist unified model of science and knowledge. Popper (1964) and Berlin (1960) attacked the idea of scientific historiography as a proxy for Marxism-Leninism. Some strands of Marxism, especially of the Soviet variety, claimed to be scientific and predict scientifically the downfall of capitalism. Liberal philosophers attempted to pull the epistemic rug from under this claim by proving that scientific historiography is impossible. During the sixties, science lost its prestigious status as the exclusive paradigm of knowledge, at least among left-leaning intellectual elites. Most Western Marxists of the no-no-nonsense variety, following the Frankfurt School, ceased to present themselves as scientists and to take seriously the Bolshevik presentation of dogma as dialectic science. Instead, Western Marxists have criticized "late" capitalism or argued for egalitarianism. Accordingly, anti-Marxist philosophers lost interest in proving that the Marxist vision of a science of society and history is an impossible fantasy, especially after the collapse of late Communism in 1989 and the ensuing ascendancy of right-wing eschatological philosophy of history (Fukuyama, 1992; Huntington, 1996).

The positivist model of knowledge was debated around the same period. In historiography, this debate focused on Hempel's covering law model of explanation, discussed in the previous chapter. Some philosophers and historians claimed that scientific historiography is impossible for epistemic or metaphysical reasons and hence the positivist analysis of historiography is misleading in elevating a chimerical fantasy to the level of a prescriptive ideal. During the sixties, the received positivist model of science crashed. Consequently, Idealist and other philosophers lost interest in proving that historiography cannot be a science at least in its positivist sense, and analytic philosophers gradually lost interest in proving that the positivist model is applicable to historiography.

Reconsidering the question concerning scientific historiography today raises two immediate objections: First, it may be argued that the question is meaningless because it is based on a false distinction. Perhaps the post-positivist analysis of science has shifted, blurred, or erased the borderlines between the sciences and historiography to the extent that the question "Can historiography be a science?" has become meaningless because "the methods of history are no more different from the methods of geology than the latter are from the methods of theoretical physics – and the difference is very great" (Miller, 1987, p. 127). Rouse claimed that there is no essential, as distinct from de facto, difference between the natural and human sciences, rejecting the claims of Dilthey, Habermas, Taylor, and Hacking (Rouse, 1987, pp. 166–208). I argued in the first three chapters of this book that much of historiography is indeed scientific and has been for almost two hundred years. I also claimed in chapter four that other parts of historiography are less than scientific because they are too vague or too ad hoc or too complex. The question concerning scientific historiography is then whether traditionalist, underdetermined, historiography may be replaced by determined paradigmatic historiography. The dissolution of historiographic schools and undistorted communication should follow.

Second, if the question is meaningful, it may be boring. The tradition that doubts the significance of scientific historiography or social sciences extends from the Neo-Kantians (Rickert, 1962; Windelband, 1980), Dilthey (1988) and Collingwood to Isaiah Berlin, Dray, Gadamer (1989), Apel (1984), and Habermas (1971, 1990). This tradition holds that historiography as a human science offers a superior kind of knowledge or understanding to scientific knowledge. If scientific historiography were possible, it would have scarcely anything interesting to say about history.

> To say of history that it should approximate to the condition of a science is to ask it to contradict its essence.... The attempt to construct a discipline, which would stand to concrete history as pure to applied, is not a vain hope for something beyond human powers, but a chimera, born of a profound incapacity to grasp the nature of natural science, or of history, or of both. (Berlin, 1960, p. 31)

I am not acquainted with the essences of historiography or history and I doubt there are any. I agree with Rorty (1979, p. 350 ff) that fields of inquiry do not have essences that determine appropriate methods of inquiry. But it is possible to discuss, empirically, contemporary historiography: The question of scientific historiography is interesting because the scientific part of historiography has been successful and progressive (Thagard, 1998) in making discoveries that expanded our knowledge of the past. It also achieved a consensus among a heterogeneous and uncoerced community of historians on determined historiography. By contrast, traditionalist historiography interprets its traditions rather than generates knowledge of the past; even the communication of its conclusions is difficult.

DISCARDING THE OLD ARGUMENTS

Many of the friends and foes of scientific historiography accepted implicitly the nineteenth-century model of science, which Lloyd (1993, p. 21) called appropriately "vulgar empiricism." This led to confusions between the rejection of scientific historiography, and the rejection of an outdated philosophic model of science. Supporters of scientific historiography that upheld this nineteenth-century model of science, attempted to create scientific historiography modeled after Newtonian physics, mechanistic, deterministic, prognostic, and deduced from laws of human nature. Scientistic strands of Marxism shared this nineteenth-century model of science, claiming that Marx was the Newton of historiography, who founded a deterministic prognostic science of historiography deducible from the economic laws of dialectical materialism. These intellectual debacles generated a bad reputation for scientific historiography and led historians to object to behavioristic and quantitative historiography (Lloyd, 1993, p. 21). The foes of scientific historiography directed much of their wrath against the nineteenth-century ideology of science, not against the possibility of scientific historiography in the modern sense of science, as stochastic, probabilistic, with limited powers of prediction, and irreducible to another science.

The most stubborn positivist characterization of scientific historiography is its deducibility from other sciences such as psychology, economics, or sociology. Rickert (1962) claimed that historiography and geology are sciences of concrete events that must borrow their general statements from other nomothetic sciences. Rickert was clearly wrong about geology (Laudan, 1992, pp. 63–4). But his analysis of historiography proved more tenacious. Berlin argued the case for the deducibility of scientific historiography:

If only we could find a series of natural laws connecting at one end, the biological and physiological states and processes of human beings, with, at the other, the equally observable patterns of their conduct – their social activities in the wider sense – and so establish a coherent system of regularities, deducible from a comparatively small number of general laws (as Newton had so triumphantly done in physics), we should have in our hand a science of human behavior. (Berlin, 1960, p. 2)

The attempts to deduce scientific historiography produced boring and shallow historiographic ad hoc interpretations of theories that could be relevant only for one facet of history, such as universal human nature in enlightenment historiography, or economic factors in doctrinaire Marxist historiography. On the contrary, as demonstrated in chapters two and three, historiography and other historical sciences have their own theories, about the transmission of information in time, which infer new interesting knowledge of the past.

The opposite inference from this deductive fallacy is that if historiography cannot be deduced from or reduced to another established science, scientific historiography is impossible. Fales attempted to disprove the possibility of historiographic covering laws by arguing that historical events are emergent:

> Like works of art, historical events are culturally emergent. The criteria for identifying and relevantly characterizing them depend upon the cultural milieu in which they occur; and the traditions, social institutions, and legal systems which provide the context required to make sense of history are the variable products, intended and unintended, of human cultural activity, not reducible to some uniform set of causal or even non-causal psychological laws. (Fales 1980, p. 275).

Emergence does not preclude the possibility of laws describing the regularities of emergent events and even their reduction. There are many known *sui generis* laws of a higher system that are not reduced to those of a lower level. Descriptions of biological events do not have to be explained by physical theories to be scientific. Social explanations need not be reducible to psychology (Dupré, 1995; Jackson & Pettit, 1992). If historiography is irreducible to psychology or another science because its concepts are supervening on an infinite number of concepts from a lower level, it does not disprove the actual or potential existence of historiographic theories that are *sui generis*, irreducible to psychology or economics. Such supervenience is just as characteristic of chemistry (Kincaid, 1996, pp. 59–60).

The deduction of scientific historiography from laws of human nature is consistent, and often associated with arguments for *methodological individualism*. From the mid-forties to the mid-sixties, philosophers argued about the kind of reduction that is appropriate for historiography and the social sciences: Should description of historical events be reduced to descriptions of the individuals who composed them, as in *methodological individualism* or to *social individuals*. The argument within philosophy of historiography, unlike in philosophy of the social sciences where the debate still rages on, was settled in an apparent agreement: Ontologically, all historical events are reducible to the individuals who participated in them. But for the purposes of hypothesis formation and explanation, descriptions of social individuals are more useful (Boudin, 1988; Brodbeck, 1966; Danto, 1985, pp. 257–84). Philip Pettit (1993) put it better when he interpreted holistic analysis of social units as ontologically supervenient on an individual level, much like mind is supervenient on body. The epistemic question whether or not scientific historiography is possible is independent of the ontology of history. Explaining and understanding social phenomena in holistic terms, *methodological* or *epistemic holism*, does not imply that social agents have no personal moral responsibility for their acts, *ontological holism*, so that each criminal could say that history/ his race/ class/etc. "made him do it" (Berlin, 1969; Danto, 1985, pp. 257–84). Politically, a scientific knowledge of history or society does not give states perfect techniques for changing history any more than scientific cosmology gives its practitioners the power to create universes. Holism was called in the fifties and sixties *methodological collectivism* or *methodological socialism* and was associated with giving states legitimization for totalitarian control of the lives of their citizens in the name of a visionary scientific social engineering plan. This association followed the Soviet ideological coupling of Marxist dogma with totalitarian control. But, the social sciences often generate knowledge that some social problems cannot be solved or that their solution would generate worse problems in other spheres (Jervis, 1997).

Conversely, the positivist metaphysical deductive argument for the possibility of scientific historiography assumed that since supra-atomic physics draws a deterministic picture of the universe, there are deterministic laws of historiography that, at least in principle, can be deduced from physics and are shorthand for complex interactions of physical laws (Oppenheim & Putnam, 1958). Yet, this repeats the same fallacy, confusion of the metaphysics of history with historiographic epistemology and methodology. If we live in a deterministic universe, this metaphysical tenet does not warrant the epistemic conclusion that this universe is decipherable by displaying observable regularities. If deterministic laws govern history, it does not imply that humans can discover them. Arguably, the picture of the universe that contemporary science draws is inconsistent with the unity of science (Dupré, 1995).

Some arguments against the possibility of scientific historiography confuse a description of some of the aspects of traditionalist historiography with its epistemic limitations. Many of Berlin's (1960) arguments against scientific historiography are based on this confusion. Berlin was right to argue that some historiographic generalizations are tautologies, or vague, or inaccurate. It is impossible to deduce from these generalizations mechanically, they require empirical intuitive judgment, ad hoc interpretations in the terminology of chapter four. But this does not imply that historiography is doomed to be so. Berlin cited only August Comte's early nineteenth-century model of science in support of his argument: Science stretches from mathematics to sociology, in descending order of comprehensiveness and precision, and ascending order of concreteness and detail. But this model is clearly false (Dupré, 1995). Chemistry is more precise than quantum physics, and economics is more precise than psychology. It is an utter fatuity even to attempt "to demarcate, at any given time, the ultimate cincture of any branch of field of any variety of research" (Tennessen, 1969, p. 129). Berlin ignored the larger part of historiography that has been scientific for two hundred years, the part that has been providing highly reliable and accurate knowledge of history. Conversely, Popper (1964) and Berlin (1960) confused philosophy of history with scientific historiography, probably under the influence of scientistic Marxism. They criticized philosophies of history that had scientific pretensions. But though some of their arguments are valid, they are irrelevant for evaluating the limits of scientific historiography.

Dilthey, Weber, Collingwood, and others claimed that historiography is not a science because it is based on nonscientific empathy or *verstehen*. Even had historiography relied on empathy as a basic method, which I doubted in the previous chapter, it would not have excluded the possibility of scientific historiography:

That normal humans with no special expertise have a special means of identifying motives is no more surprising than that they have special means of identifying shapes. Of course, emphatic imaginings are not infallible, and, if further experience sometimes extends the scope of the technique, it sometimes reveals limits of culture and temperament beyond which emphatic inferences are foolish. But the same kinds of warnings are appropriate when people discern shapes by looking and touching. . . . Fundamental reliance on *specific* means of detection is *common* to all fields. (Miller, 1987, pp. 129–30)

It has been claimed at least since Dilthey (1988) that historiography and the human sciences use unobservable theoretical terms such as intentions, reasons, and agents to describe and understand human action. But except for vulgar empiricists all philosophers of science accept that each science uses different unobservable theoretical entities. Physics uses *black holes*, historiography can talk of motives and reasons.

It was argued that history, like other human phenomena appears in consciousness imbued with meaning that reflects internationality. But the interpretation of the meanings of historical events in historiography belongs to historiographic interpretation, rather than to historiographic knowledge (cf., the introduction for an explanation of this distinction). It is certainly possible to develop Husserl's phenomenology to encompass consciousness of history, but such a project does not exclude the possibility of scientific knowledge of the past anymore than the discovery of Husserl's life-world through epoché excludes the possibility of abstracted science in general.

COMPLEXITY

The alleged complexity of history was proposed as a reason for its essentially nonscientific status, or as an explanation for a delay in its transition to science. John Stuart Mill's theory of the history of science correlates the emergence and development of the distinct sciences with the degree of complexity of their subject matters, measured by the number of types of causes that affect, and laws that govern, a realm of nature, which today we may call a *system*. Mill held that the progress of science, measured by accuracy in description and prediction depends on the complexity of its subject matter and time. Human intellect is applied at a constant rate, equally to all the sciences. The complexity of the subject matters of the sciences determines which sciences develop first and at what pace. If Mill is right, the progress of science measures the complexity of its subject matters. The sciences with simpler subject matters describe fewer types of causes and laws and hence develop first and faster, for example astronomy. The sciences with more complex subject matters develop later and slower, like the social sciences. The complexity of society, the number of types of causes and laws, accounts for the relative backwardness of the social sciences (Mill, 1976, VI: I).

John Stuart Mill assumed an evolutionary model of the history of science. Each science goes through three stages of development. At the first prescientific stage, fields of knowledge are cultivated only for particular practical purposes, for example, medicine before the study of physiology and Mill's contemporary social and political sciences. At this stage, inquiry attempts to solve particular questions about the cause or effect of a certain phenomenon that has practical

consequences, without systematic research and subjection of the phenomena to general laws, as in the next two stages (VI: VI: p. 1). The
second stage is already scientific because general laws describe the
principal parts of the phenomena in a part of nature. Yet, the interactions between the phenomena in the given field are still too complex
for the science to be exact. Known scientific laws account only for
the greater causes. Science at this stage is not yet able to explain and
predict, precisely because many minor causes affect the effects of the
greater causes and make it difficult to predict them. Explanations and
predictions are imprecise, subject to modifications and variations, due
to the effects of intervening variables. For example, astronomy passed
through the second stage of its development when it was able to explain
"the general course of the planetary motion" though its "calculations
had only mastered the main phenomena, but not the perturbations."
Mill considered his contemporary "tidology," and "meteorology" to
pass through their second evolutionary stage (VI: III: pp. 1–2). The
sciences of human nature are still far from this stage, though for all
practical purposes, when they reach this stage, they will be almost
as good as complete exact sciences, since in Mill's opinion statistical
generalizations about masses of people are almost as good as full generalizations that account for individual variations and perturbations.
At the third and final stage in the evolution of each science it becomes
exact and predictive. All the phenomena in its realm of nature are subjected to deterministic laws. Mill thought that mid-nineteenth-century
astronomy reached that final stage because it "enables us to predict
the places and the occulations of the heavenly bodies." When the human sciences reach this stage they will "enable us to foretell how an
individual would think, feel, or act throughout life" (VI: III: p. 1). The
human sciences are far from such a stage in their evolution because
the data necessary for making such predictions is far greater and more
complex than that of astronomy. Still, Mill predicted that, following
his evolutionary scheme, one day the sciences of man would achieve
this stage in their evolution (VI: X: p. 8).[1]

    Mill's assumption that human intellect has been applied in con-
stant measures to all branches of knowledge at all times and places is
probably wrong. The development of the sciences in concentric circles
around the human subject, from the outside inward, may be ascribed
to the difficulty in challenging old religious and other traditional

notions that are closer to the subject. Mill's theory of the history of science was ad hoc, modeled after a single case, the history of physics and astronomy from Newton to Mill's era. Since then, it had been falsified, since contemporary physics draws a far more complex picture of reality than, say, contemporary chemistry.

Hayek agreed with Mill that social phenomena are more complex than natural phenomena but reached the opposite conclusion: History is quite likely too complex for scientific analysis. Hayek claimed that an inductive science of society and history is unrealistic because it is impossible to isolate the various processes in a complex society (Hayek, 1973, Vol. I, pp. 63–5).[2] Yet, it is impossible to determine a priori whether society is indeed as complex as Mill and Hayek asserted. Hayek's protégé, Popper, rejected altogether Mill and Hayek's opinion. Popper thought that society is not likely to be more complicated than nature because social situations involve rationality. Popper ascribed the belief in the complexity of social systems to inappropriate comparison of the complexity of concrete social situations with the complexity of artificially isolated experimental physical situations, and to Mill's belief in the deduction of social situations from the laws of human nature (Popper, 1964, pp. 139–40).

There are no independent grounds for deciding among the conflicting metaphysical intuitions of Mill and Hayek versus Popper, or between their conflicting opinions regarding the prospects of scientific historiography. "It is not evident that natural events and processes are any less complex than social ones, and it is not clear how one could even begin to evaluate this claim" (Rouse, 1987, pp. 198–9). "There is no reason to suppose that the Book of Nature is simpler for us to read than the Book of Human Life or Society" (Miller, 1987, pp. 132–3). Whatever can be known about the subject matters of the sciences and their degrees of complexity is known through the sciences themselves. It is possible to compare the complexity of the sciences, the complexity of what they tell us about the systems they describe. For example, Lewontin argued that biology is more complex than physics because its "list of conditions is extraordinarily large, the action of each causal pathway is extremely weak, and nonadditive interactions among pathways are extremely important" (Lewontin, 1994b, pp. 508–9). But comparing the ultimate complexity of natural systems, like achieving ultimate knowledge of them, is pure metaphysical speculation.

Without an established scientific theory of a system, its complexity can only be assessed through trial and error. For example, when Gregor Mendel was conducting experiments in the garden of his Brno monastery about the heredity of observable features of peas, he had no idea how lucky he had been to pick such a simple genetic system. Later, Mendel followed the advice of a famous botanist, Karl von Nageli to work with hawkweed, which has a much more complex genetic system. Mendel never grew out of hawkweed, eventually quitting research and moving to the administration of his monastery. Genetics was established a generation after Mendel, with work on the relatively simple genetic system of fruit flies, with the introduction of an appropriate research program in genetics (Shapiro, 1992, pp. 13–45). The degree of complexity of history, or of relatively isolated historical systems, can only be assessed through historiographic trial and error. Jervis (1997) argued that the international system is complex. He supported his argument by explicating many examples from the historiography of international relations. Yet, the fact that Jervis was able to make his case, to prove that complex processes in international relations led to unforeseen results, implies that these complex system effects are not beyond the purview of political science. If a system is complex it does not imply that we cannot understand it, at least after the fact, as is the case in historiography. Much of the recent progress of science has been in developing methods for the analysis and modeling of complex systems (Coveney & Highfield, 1996). So, even if we found a system that is currently too complex for our contemporary scientific tools, it does not imply that it must be so for all eternity.

COINCIDENCE

Philosophers and historians have been arguing that historical coincidences such as the weather or the traits of particular leaders exclude the possibility of scientific historiography. For example, the storm that destroyed the Spanish armada in the sixteenth century and the consequent ascendancy of England were arguably coincidental. Tolstoy proposed Napoleon's cold on the eve of battle and Pascal explored Cleopatra's nose as chance happenstances that influenced the course of history. It is necessary first to clarify the meaning of historical coincidence or accident. Nagel (1961, pp. 372 ff) and Mandelbaum (1977, pp. 105–108 ff) explicated historical accidents as the intersection of two or more independent causal chains. For example, if "coincidentally," I meet an acquaintance in the street on my way to a concert, it means that two independent causal chains, one causing me to go to the concert, and another causing my acquaintance to go to, say, a bookstore, intersected. This explication of coincidence is objective, since the intersection of two independent causal chains is a fact in the world. A fully determined scientific modeling of a system is possible only in relatively closed systems that are not subjected to frequent effects of intervening variables external to it. Unlike the solar system, for example, historical processes are insufficiently isolated for noncoincidental description. Factors external to processes studied by historians may intervene and affect the outcome. Thus, historical accidents are relative to a system; they do not imply metaphysical indeterminism (Mandelbaum, 1977, pp. 105–108ff).

But consider the case of meeting a friend in a concert hall. The causal chains that led us to be at the same place at the same time are independent of each other. Still, if I have background information about my friend's musical taste and the concert performance reflects that taste, I sense no coincidence. Coincidence seems then to be relative to background information, factual and theoretical, rather than to an objective system. When I meet an acquaintance who shares my musical tastes at a concert, my reaction would be: "Of course, I expected to meet you here." Whereas, if I am not familiar with my acquaintance's musical taste or other reasons for him to be at the concert, I say: "What a coincidence! Fancy meeting you here!" Dray (1993, p. 131) suggested that "to call a historical event a matter of chance implies not an absence of causes, but an absence of specifically historical causes." This covers nonhuman intervening variables such as the climate. If a meteor hits earth at a historical period, it is considered coincidental from a historiographic perspective but may be determined from an astronomical perspective. J. B. Bury, the historian of Rome, described the invasion of the Huns as coincidental. A historian of the Huns or of world history would not consider this invasion coincidental. Dray concluded that chance in history is standpoint-relative. But in Dray's opinion judgment of chance is relative to the chosen subject of inquiry, "a point of reference for judging what is intrusive and what is internally explicative" (Dray, 1993, p. 132) Dray did not consider how historians choose their topics of research. This choice is often guided by theoretical background. Historians tend to choose problems that their theoretical background leads them to expect they could solve. What appears like historical coincidence relative to a subject, is often relative to the historiographic theory or theories that influenced the choice of subject in the first place. What historians consider coincidental therefore, reflects their theoretical baggage.

The more limited is the knowledge that historiographic theories offer, the more coincidental history will appear. Coincidence then is not a metaphysical property of history, but an epistemic category, relative to background theory and knowledge. Coincidence is no hindrance for scientific historiography, because it is a corollary of the theoretical limitations of historiography. Accordingly, historiographic grand scope theories refer to coincidence whenever they cannot account for some evidence. Occasionally, history fails to proceed the way historiographic and social theories, such as Marxism or Braudelian theory of historiography, would lead us to expect. Instead of ditching the theory, it is useful to claim a coincidental development, which changed the course of history and intervened to prevent the expected outcome. Add an auxiliary ad hoc hypothesis to account for the "coincidental" occurrence and save the theory. Consequently, historical coincidence does not raise new issues, beyond those of traditionalist historiography. Describing an event as coincidental is equivalent to saying that our background theories and knowledge are incomplete in that respect. If our knowledge of historiography expands, events that appear coincidental will cease being so. From the perspective of world historiography, unlike from the viewpoint of Roman history specialists, the invasion of the Huns is not coincidental. There are theories that explain such migrations, for example, by demographic pressure on natural resources. Once my acquaintance tells me that he is also a Mahler fan, I do not consider our meeting at a performance of his Eighth Symphony coincidental, I expect to meet him next week when Masur conducts *Das Lied von der Erde.*

HISTORICAL CONTINGENCY AND NECESSITY

It has been argued that history is too contingent for scientific analysis. Some of these arguments demonstrate the extent to which such issues require philosophic analysis and articulation. For example, it was argued that historical contingency proves that history is indeterminate

(Ferguson, 1997, p. 53; Jervis, 1997, pp. 156–7; Telock & Belkin, 1996, p. 8). The metaphysical doctrine of determinism, which holds that all events have causes without which they would not have come about, has nothing to do with historical contingency. For historical events to be indeterminate they would have to come into existence without a cause as some quantum particles pop in and out of our universe according to the quantum indeterminacy principle. Clearly, this is not the case. Another misinterpretation of historical contingency identifies it with unintended or unexpected events from the subjective perspectives of historical actors who participated in bringing them about. For example, Clark (2000) argued that democracy in England was an unintended consequence of religious strife between High Church Anglicans and Protestant dissenters and Catholics. Elster (1989, pp. 42–51) described much of social life as unintended consequences and Jervis (1997) brought many examples from the historiography of international relations for unintended consequences. Unintended consequences are subjective, relative to the amount of knowledge an agent possesses. Other contemporaries and historians or social scientists, in hindsight and with the benefit of evidence that was unavailable to historical agents, can confirm hypotheses that explain why the unintended consequences came about. An unintended outcome is no challenge for scientific knowledge of the past.

Yemima Ben-Menahem (1997) following David Lewis, went a long way toward analyzing and clarifying these issues. She explicated historical contingency in terms of degrees of sensitivity to initial conditions. The more sensitive is a type of result to particular initial conditions, the more contingent it is. The less sensitive it is, the more necessary. Ben-Menahem observes a case of historical necessity when several independent causal chains lead to an identical type of result, the result is then over-determined, it occurs whether or not specific initial conditions are present. For example, death is necessary within certain time limits because some chain of events will bring it about irrespective of any particular initial conditions. In mathematical terms, in systems theory, the most necessary, overdetermined system is hyperpredictable. In a hyperpredictable system, irrespective of initial conditions, the end-state of the system is identical. Other systems, such as demographic systems, may be hyperpredictable not in their end state, but in a cycle of end states, such as the one determined by rates of procreation in relation to natural resources (Maudlin, 2000).

Other events or processes are very sensitive to initial conditions: If they change minutely, their outcomes would change radically. For example, Asimov (1994) construed a contingent narrative in which the replacement of a single letter in the forename of a scientist prevents a nuclear war. Mathematically, events most sensitive to initial conditions, most contingent, are chaotic. Chaos theory describes stochastic behavior in deterministic systems that are sensitive to minor changes in initial conditions. Deterministic laws may govern chaotic events, but their complexity usually prohibits prediction (Ben-Menahem, 1997).

A linear, nonchaotic, system may include a critical point when one and only parameter in that system is very sensitive to initial conditions and is governed by nonlinear algorithms. Hypercriticality takes place in a system when there are many such parameters. When most states of a system are hypercritical, it is chaotic (Maudlin, 2000). "Chaos theory is the qualitative study of unstable aperiodic behavior in deterministic nonlinear systems" (Kellert, 1993, p. 2). Chaotic systems display unstable behavior and are aperiodic, no variable has repeating values. Typically chaotic systems are deterministic, governed by no more than five simple algorithms. Extreme sensitivity to initial conditions prevents the prediction of states of chaotic systems because it is difficult or even impossible to achieve sufficiently detailed and accurate descriptions of the initial conditions of such systems. Scientific measurements usually specify their margins of error. The accuracy that is required for prediction of chaotic systems is beyond the margins of error. The further into the future is the prediction, the more accurate must be the measurement of the initial conditions. Kellert (1993, pp. 33–42) called this "predictive hopelessness," because the required extreme accuracy in measurement in such cases is hopeless, as distinct from impossible as some measurements are in quantum mechanics.

If "'Chaos' . . . is essentially a mathematical concept, and 'chaos theory' is a mathematical theory" (Smith, 1998, p. vii), then it makes little sense to discuss "chaos," "criticality," or "linearity" in history. Smith did not consider the assassination of a political leader that has wide-ranging historical effects to be a chaotic event: "It is no news that minuscule changes can have huge effects" (Smith, 1998, p. 1). Chaos theory goes beyond the old observation that microchanges can produce unpredictable macroeffects to define such causes and effects mathematically. If we accept Smith's position that chaos is an exclusively mathematical concept, it is impossible to find out if history is chaotic or not until historiography builds quantitative models of history. In historiography, such analysis is possible only in well-defined systems that can be quantified and generate a time series of values for variables, for example in demographic historiography or in parts of economic historiography. Demographic history is not chaotic though the history of stock markets does display some critical episodes.[3] Models of chaos are rarely confirmed empirically. Often they are tested by computer simulation that reiterates a small group of algorithms, given initial conditions. At present, computers can simulate simple systems in international relations (Cederman, 1996), economics, and demography. The history of stock markets and other price movements has received special attention because of its potential for generating profits. Such computerized mathematical models have not predicted critical points in the financial system. For example, the collapse of the real estate market in Thailand and the Russian government's default on its external debts had critical effects on the world financial system, far beyond their relatively small value in that system. Even the most sophisticated computerized models used by Long Term Capital investment fund did not measure such marginal variables and so did not predict their effects. Consequently, the investment fund that was led by Nobel laureates had to be saved by the U.S. Federal Government. Models of demographic changes have proved critical or even chaotic with bacteria and animals, but I have never encountered such a model for human populations. Cederman (1996) presented a rudimentary simplified model of stability and change in international relations, but that model is linear. All such models, as Cederman conceded, are oversimplified, cannot predict, and are mutually inconsistent because they are based on inconsistent theories. Though it seems reasonable to avoid attributing chaos or linearity to historical systems unless they are clearly quantifiable, chaotic or critical attributions have often been attached to historical processes. Kellert's example for a chaotic, unstable, and aperiodic system is human history:

Although broad patterns in the rise and fall of civilization may be sketched, events never repeat exactly – history is aperiodic. And history books teem with examples of small events that led to momentous and long-lasting changes in the course of human affairs. The standard examples of unstable aperiodic behavior have always involved huge conglomerations of interacting units. The systems may be composed of competing human agents or colliding gas molecules, but until recently our primary image of behavior so complex as to be unstable and aperiodic was the image of a crowd. (Kellert, 1993, pp. 4–5)

Yet, Ben-Menahem reached the opposite conclusion for similar reasons:

Where large ensembles of systems are concerned, we might find a large degree of overall necessity due to the law of large numbers, but low degree of necessity at the level of individual events. (Ben-Menahem 1997, p. 102)

Specifically, regarding historical events, she did not commit herself: "The sensitivity of historical events to initial conditions may or may not be as radical as that of chaotic phenomena, but it can certainly be very significant" (p. 102).

Reisch wrote:

Of course I cannot demonstrate that history is chaotic. . . . The subject of histories do not constitute isolated systems, and even if they did their histories are not repeatable. But I will stand by the claim [that history is chaotic] nonetheless, for I am only applying a technical term to highlight what is an obvious feature of history. (1991, p. 9)

Reisch provided no empirical evidence for which historical processes are obviously chaotic. McCloskey (1991) acknowledged as well that it is impossible to know whether many systems are linear or not. Still, McCloskey opined that history may well be chaotic and suggested a few anecdotal qualitative examples from the historiography of the Civil War in the United States. But though it seems likely that the exact course of some of the events of the U.S. Civil War may have been sensitive to initial conditions, McCloskey did not prove that something similar would not have been brought about by different initial conditions and certainly neither McCloskey nor Reisch introduced the kind of mathematical modeling that scientists associate with chaos.

Roth and Ryckman (1995) questioned the plausibility of Reisch and McCloskey's intuition that history is chaotic. A proof for chaotic history necessitates the confirmation of counterfactuals in which the initial conditions are slightly different but the outcome radically different. In Roth and Ryckman's opinion, since it is impossible to know which causes were necessary for particular historical events such as the Great Depression or the Civil War in the United States, it is impossible to confirm counterfactuals about them. They argue that since there is no concrete proof that history is chaotic, and since there are no quantifiable models of history that use chaotic mathematical models, chaos is just a scientistic analogy or metaphor of limited value for historiography.

Reisch (1995) conceded that it is impossible to rerun history to examine empirically how sensitive it is to initial conditions. Though there are no precise quantifiable nonlinear historiographic models in the natural sciences, Reisch suggested a counterfactual: If such models had been knowable, they would have been chaotic. A completely linear history would be inconsistent with too many historiographic anecdotes. The open question is how much of history is nonlinear, where and when? Shermer (1995) attempted to satisfy the requirement for concrete examples of chaos in history, claiming that historians have been discussing contingency and necessity for centuries, though their use of these terms was ambiguous (as is Shermer's who confuses it at times with unforeseen consequences). Shermer's examples for chaotic elements in history include inventions, discoveries, ideas, paradigm shifts, earthquakes, avalanches, economic depressions, ecological disasters, and possibly wars and revolutions. The sensitivity of historical sequences to leaders and exceptional men are dependent on the stability of social circumstances. Shermer analyzed cases of mass hysteria such as witch hunting, repressed memory syndrome, and alien abduction as chaotic.

Intuitive assessments of the degree of contingency of a system may lead easily to mistakes. For example, the weather system and the system of tides appeared to Mill less complex and contingent than social systems but more complex than physical ones. Though Mill spent most of his life in the British Isles, he grossly underestimated the contingency of the weather. Edward Lorenz developed chaos theory in the early sixties as an attempt to model the weather. To avoid insubstantial quibbling over terminology, I avoid using "chaos," "criticality," and "linearity" except when applied to mathematically modeled systems. Instead, I refer to *contingency* and *necessity*, bearing in mind that if it becomes possible to quantify those parts of historiography that indicate today contingency or necessity, they may be expressed by chaotic, or more probably by critical or linear models. The extent and location of contingency in history are theoretically contested. The Marxist and Annales schools are generally hostile to historical contingency, upholding that individuals cannot exert significant influence on the course of history. British revisionist historians like Jonathan Clark (2000) think that much of history is contingent. In my opinion, evaluating how contingent history is can only be done empirically. There is no philosophic superhighway to bypass the careful historiographic study of concrete historical processes through the evidence. Sound counterfactuals should discover how sensitive were particular historical outcomes to initial conditions.

Historians and social scientists use counterfactuals regularly though implicitly when they assign necessary causes or justify the assignments of degrees of importance to causes. For example, when Ranke wished to support his claim that the Aragon dynasty and the house of Sforza achieved for the Italians a degree of freedom from the influence of foreign nations that allowed them to develop culturally, he wrote:

If Francesco Sforza had not become Lord of Lombardy, the French would have been; had Alfonso not given Naples to a spurious son, a Spanish viceroy would have been even at that time established there. It was due to this assertion of their independence, that the Italians, untrammeled by foreign influence, and in progressive movement and rivalry within, were enabled within a somewhat limited sphere to develop their intellectual energies to a degree that the Germanic-Latin nations have always regarded as the highest perfection of culture to which they ever attained. (Ranke, 1909, p. 180)

The assignment of necessary causes assumes that had the causes not occurred, nor would have the effects. More ambitious attempts to explicate causation and natural laws by using counterfactuals have failed (Dray, 1980, chap. 4; White, 1965, chaps. 4–5). Counterfactuals that isolate the effects of individual causes may support the assignment of degrees of importance to causes by comparing the effects of a counterfactual antecedent with history. The greater the difference, the more important is the cause. Though historians use counterfactuals to support the assignment of degrees of significance to causes, the use of contrast classes and criteria of relevance are more common (Hammond,

1977). It is necessary then to analyze historiographic counterfactuals and how they can be evaluated, in view of using them to assess how contingent or necessary is history.

COUNTERFACTUALS AND THE EVALUATION OF HISTORICAL NECESSITY AND CONTINGENCY

Elster (1978) suggested that theoretical background participates in two aspects of the construction of historiographic counterfactuals: It infers the consequent from the hypothetical antecedent and it decides on the plausibility of the counterfactual antecedent in the given historical context in the first place. Every counterfactual has a *ceteris paribus* clause, the historian assumes that historical reality remained constant, except for the examined factor. For example, we may ask what would have been the effect of the death of Hitler in the First World War, assuming that otherwise the historical context of the First World War remains constant. Elster argued that some counterfactual antecedents are inconsistent with their *ceteris paribus* historical context and therefore are filtered out by a theory. For example, if a historian asks what would have been the effects of a Nazi racial ideology that assumed that the Jews are the master race, background theories and information imply that a history where the Nazis adore Jews is inconsistent with the context of Germany in the relevant period. Such a counterfactual is internally inconsistent. Elster argued that the dual role of theoretical background in constructing counterfactuals constitutes an epistemic zero sum game: The better is our theoretical background, the greater support we have for connecting counterfactual antecedent with consequent, but the fewer counterfactuals will be consistent with their *ceteris paribus* conditions (Elster, 1978, pp. 175–221). Elster's considerations exclude some of the historiographic counterfactuals that the cliometric school presented, for example, R. W. Fogel's attempt to quantify the effects of railroads on the U.S. economy by a counterfactual in which the nineteenth-century United States had no railroads. Economic theory that should assist in deriving the counterfactual also explains why railroads were adopted in United States in the first place, so the counterfactual is internally inconsistent.

However, the theoretical backgrounds that determine the consistency and justify counterfactuals are not necessarily identical. For example, the evaluation of the consistency of Hitler's death in the First World War with all else that is known of that war, what could and could not have happened to soldiers during the war, has little to do with considering the effects of that death on European history. The latter requires the examination of the evidence for the early stages of the formation of the Nazi party and later German history to infer who would have been likely to lead the party in Hitler's absence, and how different would have been its electoral appeal, policies, and so on. For example, Ian Kershaw (1998), Hitler's biographer, thinks that without Hitler, a similar regime to the Nazi regime would have emerged in the thirties out of the German crisis, but without Hitler such a regime would not have been so virulently anti-Semitic. I suspect that Elster's example from cliometrics, where the same economic theory is used both to infer the consequent of a counterfactual antecedent and to prove that the antecedent is inconsistent with its historical context, is the exception rather than the rule in historiography. As I argued especially in chapters three and five, causal or explanatory propositions in historiography are typically confirmed by the evidence and theoretical background that connects hypotheses with the evidence, not cause with effect or explanans with explanandum. Counterfactual hypotheses may be just as atomic, and the relevant theoretical background for evaluating them may connect them with the evidence.

A broader reformulation of Elster's position that would replace theory with information would be consistent with the epistemology of historiography that I expounded in this book. The more information, including theoretical information, we have about the past, the fewer possible alternative pasts there are. This follows the meaning of "information" in information theory (see the introduction and chapter three of this book and Dretske, 1981, pp. 1–12). Conversely, the more evidence there is about the past, the more information about historical agents and situations there is, the more accurate can be the evaluation of proposed counterfactual hypotheses. The historical consistency clause can certainly dispose of counterfactuals whose antecedents are inconsistent with information we have about their *ceteris paribus* conditions. For example, Clark (1997, pp. 125–74) asserted that had there been no Glorious Revolution, the American colonies would have remained in the British Empire. Mark Almond (1997, pp. 392–415) held that had the Russian *nomenklatura* elite headed by Gorbachev not conceptualized the crisis of Communism as it did, their empire would not have collapsed. Here changes in the initial conditions, the Glorious Revolution and the world view of the Russian Communist elite, are inconsistent with their *ceteris paribus* conditions: For England to have no kind of Glorious Revolution, for English society to accept absolute monarchy and Papism or something similar, it would have had to be a different country with a different history. Almond's claim that had the *nomenklatura* had different beliefs, it would have acted differently and Communism would have survived is logically equivalent to noting that the Communist system collapsed rather than was destroyed by external forces. Almond's counterfactual is inconsistent with what we know of late Communism.

Tiny counterfactual variations on actual history, such as Hitler's death in World War I, are too small to be inconsistent with our information about their contemporary historical context, but still could have had enormous effects on history. Since we understand history backward, it is possible to assess the effects of contingent minute causes, though it is impossible to predict such effects from examining minute causes in the present. For example, it is always possible to pose a counterfactual to examine the effects of individuals in history, by asking what would have happened had they died in the crib. Still, information about minute events that may have generated contingent processes may not have been recorded. For example, any information about a painful encounter that Hitler may have had with a Jew would be extremely important for historians, given Kershaw's hypothesis about the crucial effect Hitler had on Nazi anti-Semitism. Yet, no information that could confirm or deny such an encounter reached the present. The minutiae of Hitler's life prior to the 1920s were not recorded; much like a butterfly in China whose fluttering wings cause a hurricane in Texas is beyond the most sensitive scientific measuring devices. Indeed, scientific historiography may be unable to discover the very origins of contingent processes.

The degrees of beliefs we have in historiographic counterfactuals depend on the available evidence. I argue that counterfactual historiographic hypotheses are tested just like factual historiographic hypotheses. The difference between factual and counterfactual hypotheses is ontological, not epistemic. Counterfactual hypotheses only require a *ceteris paribus* clause applied to the evidence: We suspend belief in a body of evidence that proves that the counterfactual never happened while maintaining all the rest of the evidence. The probability of the counterfactual depends then on the likelihood of the rest of the evidence given a counterfactual hypothesis. That probability can be high or low. For example, consider the counterfactual: Had George Bush Sr. died in 1990, Vice-President Dan Quayle would have become the 42nd President of the United States. Of course, there is plenty of evidence that George Bush did not die in 1990 but continued to serve as president through 1992. But we suspend our belief in that evidence, while maintaining our beliefs in the rest of the evidence. The Constitution of the United States stipulates that the vice-president becomes the president in the event of the death of the president, and plenty of evidence for the behavior of American political elites during and before 1990 confirms that they followed the Constitution. Accordingly, the degree of belief we have in this counterfactual hypothesis is comparable to that in the factual hypothesis that George Bush was the 41st President of the United States. However, the degree of belief we have in the counterfactual hypothesis, *Had George Bush senior died in 1990, Governor Mario Cuomo would have been the 43rd President of the United States,* is lower. The relevant evidence is:

1. The economic recession of 1991 was a major reason for the Republican defeat in the 1992 U.S. presidential elections according to contemporary opinion polls.
2. The reasons for the recession, such as overinvestment in construction, were independent of the policy of the administration or the identity of the president.
3. All opinion polls during Bush's presidency reported that Vice-President Quayle was less popular than President Bush.
4. The most popular Democratic party leaders did not present their candidacy for the Democratic primaries because, following the victory in the first Gulf War, President Bush's popularity sky-rocketed, and they assumed the counterfactual, that if they ran, they would be defeated by Bush and destroy their chances to run in 1996.

Still, there is insufficient evidence for evaluating how a Quayle administration would have fared on the main challenges of those years such as the collapse of Communism and the Iraqi occupation of

Kuwait. Nor is there evidence for the relative popularity of competing Democratic leaders in the event they became presidential candidates. All in all, this counterfactual hypothesis has a certain plausibility, but it is far from being as high as the previous one. When historiographic counterfactual hypotheses are overstretched across many causal links, evidence is missing for determining them. It is one thing to examine whether the fall of the Stuarts was contingent. It is quite another, to hopelessly attempt to outline the next 300 years of Stuart rule in 25 pages or less (Ferguson, 1997, pp. 416–40).

In sum, the evaluation of our degrees of beliefs in counterfactuals, is similar to the normal Bayesian likelihood of the evidence given the hypothesis multiplied by the prior probability of the hypothesis:

$$\Pr(H_{cf}|E') = \Pr(E'|H_{cf} \times \Pr(H_{cf}|B_t)$$

The hypothesis H_{cf} is an atomic counterfactual. The evidence E' for H_{cf} is a subset of the evidence that does not contradict the antecedent in the counterfactual hypothesis. Background information B_t is the one we have prior to the time t of the counterfactual antecedent. This analysis explains both Elster's conditions and the actual degrees of belief we have in counterfactuals. Another way of putting Elster's consistency clause is by assessing the prior probabilities of the counterfactual hypothesis, given background information about history prior to the time t when the counterfactual antecedent would have taken place. For example, given everything we know about Nazism, the prior probability of them believing since 1924 that the Jews are the master race is nil. By contrast, given everything we know about the First World War, it is possible that Hitler would have died by 1918. The precariousness of human life throughout history implies that any counterfactual hypothesis whose antecedent is the death of an individual is sufficiently probable given background information. Competing counterfactuals typically compete over the explanations of a similar body of evidence E'. Often, they also have a similar antecedent.

In cases when evidence is insufficient, counterfactuals are underdetermined. Tetlock and Belkin (1996, p. 9) noted the general scarcity of evidence relevant for confirming counterfactual statements in the social sciences. Lebow and Stein (1996) argued that paucity of evidence about Khrushchev's policies, beliefs, and purposes prevents us from evaluating conflicting counterfactuals about alternative U.S. reactions to the Cuban missile crisis, though the prior improbability of some counterfactual hypotheses is sufficiently low to consider them invalid. "The greater the paucity of reliable data, the greater the dependence of counterfactual claims on the analyst's theoretical apparatus, cognitive imagery, or philosophy of history" (Breslauer, 1996, p. 83). Breslauer documented the normal multiplication of schools as a reaction to insufficient evidence, as discussed in chapter four. Competing schools, founded on conflicting theories in international relations, different theories of the Soviet Union, and conflicting political opinions generated inconsistent counterfactual hypotheses about Soviet foreign policy. As with traditionalist historiography in general, underdetermined counterfactual hypotheses are chosen on the basis of vague or inconsistent theories, associated with schools. "Each school ... can foster its own favorite set of supporting counterfactuals.... These schools sometimes prescribe contradictory rules for assessing counterfactuals" (Tetlock & Belkin, 1996, p. 27). For example, historians have been revising their opinion of the effect of Neville Chamberlain's premiership on the outbreak and course of the Second World War. Khong (1996) divided the debate into three stages, after the war, following the discovery of Chamberlain's private correspondence, and following the publication of contemporary government papers.

The evaluation of any historical event or process as contingent or necessary requires much more than the examination of a single counterfactual causal chain. Historians must conduct a thorough examination of the historical context of the counterfactual causal chain to discover whether alternative causal chains would not have led to a similar effect, in which case the process is necessary. For example, if I excuse my absence from work yesterday by claiming that my regular train was early so it missed me, my employer may rightly inquire why did I not take the next one; in a big city with an advanced public transportation system, there are many alternative causal chains that get people from home to work; if one fails, any other should generate a similar result. The process of commuting to work is then necessary. Arguably, events such as the First World War, the Holocaust according to Goldhagen (1997), or the development of calculus were necessary in the sense that had not one chain of events led to them, others would have. This requires historians to work harder to be attentive to the evidence for historical contexts of processes in which they are interested. But these are local practical difficulties, not global reasons to reject in principle the possibility of scientific counterfactual analysis in historiography.

Jervis (1997) argued that parts of history are contingent, while other parts are necessary. "Small and often accidental differences between two actors at an early stage can lead to enormous divergences later on; many aspects of politics and society are to be explained . . . by quirks and small perturbations that occurred earlier" (p. 155). *Path dependence* in the social sciences reflects the contingency of processes where a detailed description in minute details of the initial conditions explains the major differences between parallel processes with similar initial conditions and influences. Yet, on the other hand, "Intuitive analysis of changes in outcomes . . . is often flawed by a focus on a single factor on the assumption that others are constant" (p. 43). Jervis (pp. 61–72) demonstrated necessity by showing that some political systems tend to remain stable irrespective of the introduction of policies designed to change them. Most notably, regulation in one part of the system tends to cause changes in other parts of the system that result in a stable equilibrium. The extent of necessity and contingency in society is debated in various parts of the social sciences. For example, it is debatable whether the economic results of the transition from Communism in East Central European countries were contingent, or depended on minor differences in 1989. Some argue for path dependence, others claim that the stages in transition were forced on all post-Communist governments by common economic constraints, global conditions, and social structures irrespective of the precise initial conditions, the political party in power and its ideology (Tucker, 2000).

The most interesting counterfactual studies demonstrate where, when, and how history was necessary or contingent. Alvin Jackson (1997, pp. 175–227) argued convincingly for a contingent turn in British and Irish history in 1912. Had the political constellation been slightly different in Westminster in 1912, had a handful of MPs voted differently, the Irish Home Rule Bill would have passed and the subsequent history of Ireland would have been different, most notably the Northern Ireland conflict in its current form would have been averted. Diane Kunz (Ferguson, 1997, pp. 368–91) made a strong argument for necessity by examining how different U.S. history would have been had Oswald missed and President Kennedy survived. An examination of U.S. politics in the sixties demonstrates that the constraints that forced President Lyndon Johnson to maintain and escalate the war in Vietnam would have forced Kennedy to do the same. Nor would Kennedy have pushed the liberal policies of civic rights and welfare beyond what L.B.J.'s agenda. Jonathan Haslam (1997, pp. 348–67) examined several possible causal chains that led to the outbreak of the Cold War, and proved, using counterfactuals, that none of them was necessary because alternative causal chains were sufficient to bring about the Cold War. Lebow and Stein (1996) proved that irrespective of various U.S. counterfactuals, the Soviet missile deployment in Cuba was necessary. Andrew Roberts (1997, pp. 281–320) denied any contingency in the process that led to the outbreak of World War II. Though it is easy to analyze in hindsight what democratic countries could have done better to curb Nazi expansionism, at the time these reasons were unknown and there is no nonlinear gap in the causal chains that led to appeasement. Roberts noted, as many historians had before, that had Hitler not decided to avoid obliterating the British expedition force in France before it was evacuated from Dunkirk, the British Isles would have been left with little ground defense and the Germans could have attempted to launch an invasion of England in 1940. Still, Roberts claimed that irrespective of Hitler's decision, the outcome of the war would have been the same. For the Germans to launch a successful invasion of the British Isles, the German fleet would have had to control the English Channel for about 12 hours facing the Royal Navy and the possible use of huge amounts of mustard gas by the RAF against the invading force.

Some judgments of historical contingency result from historiographic sloppiness, they consider only a single chain of events that led to a particular result, ignoring the possibility that other chains of events could have resulted in the same necessary outcome. This kind of counterfactual exemplifies the logical fallacy of denying the antecedent:

> If p then q.
> Not p.
> Therefore not q.

This is a fallacy because q may be conditioned or caused by other factors than p. If historians establish a causal relationship between two descriptions of events, it does not imply that the cause was necessary for the effect. Some revisionist anti-Whig historians who argue for historical contingency fell for this fallacy. They examined single causal chains and ignored their historical contexts: John Adamson (1997, pp. 91–124) demonstrated that had Charles I had better intelligence about the weakness of the Scottish Covenanter army, he would have decided to fight and would have defeated it. Adamson further speculated that a Scottish defeat would have prevented the Puritan Revolution. The first conclusion appears more convincing than the second. The deep rifts within English society would have probably caused something similar to the Puritan Revolution even had the Scots been defeated. Adamson does not consider the possibility that the English civil war was necessary because several independent causal chains led to it. Ferguson (1997, pp. 228–80) analyzed the causes for the British participation in the First World War and concluded that it was contingent. He analyzed the day-to-day decision-making processes of European political elites. But he ignored the social, ideological, and economic contexts in which these elites operated. Ferguson suggested that Asquith's government decision to send the British expeditionary force to France was a contingent causal factor. Had the government delayed its decision, France would have fallen to the Germans and Britain would have never joined the war. But as Ferguson mentioned, most members of the Liberal government and all the Conservatives sensed compelling reasons to go to war over Belgium and France. Ferguson suggested that had the dissenting ministers in Asquith's government brought down his government, by the time a new government would have been established the defeat of France would have been a *fait accompli* and there would have been no reason for Britain to continue fighting alone. Yet, as he himself noted, the dissenting ministers consented to postpone their public resignation to prevent sending a message of disunity to Germany that could have facilitated the occupation of Belgium. Winston Churchill, then a liberal, communicated with the opposition conservatives precisely to prevent the possibility that the dissenting ministers would bring down the government and prevent the British involvement in the war. Further, twenty-five years later, the British government did decide to stay the course of war after the fall of France and Belgium. It is far from clear that similar geo-political reasons would not have prevailed in 1914, even had France fallen before the British military intervened. In the name of anti-presentism, Ferguson constructed decontextualized historical agents, isolated from the forces and constraints under which they had to act. Clark (2000) seems to argue that democracy in England was contingent rather than necessary. But his terminology is confused. On the one hand, he seems to interpret contingent as unintended. On the other hand he wrote: "The 1832 [reform] Act seems to be under-determined, to be the result of contingency, only if it is isolated from the themes of Repeal and Emancipation" (p. 548). This seems to imply that the development of democracy in England was necessary, given the religious struggles of the first third of the nineteenth century. Elsewhere, Clark seems to claim that had the exact political constellation in the upper and lower houses of parliament been a little different, reform would have been resisted, as it had for a century and a half, though he did mention that when reform was blocked, it resulted in popular protest and fears of a civil war among the aristocracy. Clark's book is too confused on the topic of the contingency or necessity of English democracy to determine his position on this topic, let alone to judge it.

When historians talk of "deep" factors, they often mean that alternative causal chains emanated from the same "deep" factors and overdetermined the kind of outcomes. Social or economic rifts in society would result in social conflict irrespective of particular trigger events. For example, the conditions in the South in the United States would have resulted in the civil rights movement after the Second World War whether or not Mrs. Rosa Parks decided to insist on sitting in the front of the bus or a group of Arkansas students insisted on going to the state university in Little Rock despite the rules of racial segregation. The revisionists are right to reject teleologic considerations in historiography, such as the Whig interpretation of English history that considered constitutional democracy to be its manifest destiny. Yet, rejection of destiny does not imply the endorsement of contingency. The democratization of England may have been necessary because several alternative processes were leading to it.

Consideration of contingency and necessity are just as relevant for the historiography of nature. Stephen Jay Gould (1989) claimed that life as we know it is contingent. "Alter any early event, ever so slightly and without apparent importance at the time, and evolution cascades into a radically different channel" (1989, p. 51); Gould argued correctly that such issues should not be discussed in the abstract, but concretely, in his case he analyzed Cambrian fossils found in the Burgess Shale. Gould argued convincingly that a slightly different pattern of extinction during the Cambrian would have changed completely the subsequent history of life. There were apparently several such episodes of mass extinction in the history of life. The results of these mass extinctions were contingent because almost all life forms became extinct in a relatively short period of time, quite possibly as a result of some catastrophic cataclysm such as the impact of a large meteor. The forms of life that survived and form the basis for all subsequent life were not more fit than many of the forms of life that became extinct. The theory of evolution cannot explain their survival by their relative fitness; they just got lucky because of minute differences in the circumstances of extinction.

Yet, Gould (1989, p. 283) made the much grander claim that history, natural and human, is contingent, that contingency is its central principle. Gould's examples are not just from natural history, but also from human history, the Civil War in the United States (pp. 283–4). In one sense of "contingent," if history includes a single contingent episode such as mass extinction, then the rest of it is contingent in the sense of being the effect of this contingent episode. But before and after contingent episodes there can be historical periods that are not contingent, given the results of previous contingent processes. This second sense of "contingent" does not apply to the whole of natural or human history, only to a period, a process, or an event. In the first sense, natural history and probably human history are contingent. But in the second sense, natural and human histories are divided into many processes that may be contingent or necessary.

Gould (1989, pp. 277–91) found the plot of Frank Capra's American film classic *It's a Wonderful Life* sufficiently contingent to name his book after it. In that movie, George Bailey, the owner of a Savings and Loan bank, like Job wishes he was never born. An angel named Clarence shows Bailey how different the world would have been had he never been born. After witnessing this dismal counterfactual, George Bailey realizes that his life has been valuable for his fellow denizens of Bedford Falls. He chooses to live and returns to his previous life and family to a happy movie ending. But how plausible is the film's counterfactual? Capra's movie suggests that had Bailey never been born, his wife would have become a stereotypical old spinster. But the film also presented Mrs. Bailey as an attractive young woman who had many suitors. Given the plot of the movie, had George Bailey never existed, Mrs. Bailey probably would have married somebody very much like Mr. Bailey and would have had the same kind of family and middle-class life style she had with him. The counterfactual suggests that had Bailey never existed, the Savings and Loan bank he inherited from his parents would have collapsed, and a middle-class suburban neighborhood it financed through affordable mortgages would have never been constructed, with dire repercussions for the social structure of the town of Bedford Falls. Still, Bailey's business existed because he was able to provide low interest mortgages to middle-class homeowners. Had Bailey's S&L not existed, it is likely that some other firm would have filled that market niche. Bedford Falls would have looked pretty much the same. In the movie, George Bailey saves the life of his little brother after an accident. In the counterfactual universe, the brother dies, and consequently their mother ends her life among the working poor. Yet, the Bailey parents followed the norm of their social class in having two children, "an heir and a spare." Had George not been born, there most likely would have been another child. Even had the brother died, the other child, would have functioned as "the spare" and would have cared for his or her aging parents.

Frank Capra presented in counterfactual narrative form the values of American individualist culture, one of which is that each individual matters. Much though I would like to believe it, social effects are not so clearly contingent on individual action. The price mechanism of the market, the other aspect of American individualism, provides incentives to supply substitutes to lost resources, including human resources. If a firm goes out of business, the product it provided will become more expensive and another firm will step in to provide the same or similar product, given sufficient demand. If a worker is lost, the market will mediate the hiring of a substitute. Even technological innovations are probably necessary over a period of time. "Nozick (1974) explained the limited period of time granted for patents, by suggesting that beyond the period of patent rights, patented inventions would have been necessary, independently of the patent holders." Usually patent holders are the first to come with an invention. Accordingly, they are entitled to its rewards because had they not introduced the invention at the time they did, it is unlikely that anybody else would have. As time passes the probability that the invention would have been introduced by somebody else increases gradually. Patents expire at the point of necessity, when it is more probable that the invention would have been introduced anyway. At that point the patent holder loses the right to a monopoly over the invention. Current proposals to shorten the period of patent rights may be explained by the accelerating rate of innovation. Since more people work to innovate, it is increasingly probable that had an invention not been introduced when it was, somebody else would have invented the same thing shortly thereafter.

Gould claimed that the contingent nature of history corresponds with a narrative form of historiographic presentation and explanation. Gould held a romantic view of life that blurs the distinction between fact and fiction. People read popular fiction because it is more interesting and more surprising, than life. If we consider romantic love, for example, we will find in literature many cases of what would appear from the perspective of the protagonists contingent, boy meets girl sort of chance encounters. Yet, from the perspective of the historiography of the family, there is little contingency and much necessity. The kind of generalizations that historians and social scientists make imply that had Jack not met Jill, he would have encountered Jane who would have had similar socioeconomic and other properties. The lives of most people, certainly in eras with less mobility than our own, were quite necessary. We may be actors in a historical script we did not author, and if we call in sick, there is always an understudy to take our place.

Particular studies of concrete historical events and processes can assess degrees of contingency or necessity. Determined counterfactuals can distinguish historical necessity from contingency, within the constraints of evidence. But then historical contingency is not a special problem for scientific historiography, because counterfactual hypotheses are determined or underdetermined by the evidence just like any other historiographic proposition.

REFORMULATING THE QUESTION

I divided historiography into evidence, hypotheses, and theories about the transmission of information from events to evidence. Accordingly, the scientific prospects of areas of historiography that are currently underdetermined depend on the prospects for progress in these three parts, expansion in the evidential base, better hypotheses, and theoretical innovation that discovers nested information.

The chief reason for underdetermination in historiography is the paucity of evidence. Each historical event generated a burst of information. However, most of it deteriorates rapidly and vanishes. We will probably never obtain knowledge of most historical events and never be able to determine answers to extremely interesting questions such as: What was the nature of the first human language? Why did Hitler hate Jews so much?, How did Beethoven intend his Ninth Symphony to sound exactly? How did Mahler intend to finish his Tenth? New historiographic evidence has been discovered. But it is impossible to predict such discoveries except when known evidence is temporarily unavailable, for example secret government documents in state archives. Nor is it possible to predict theoretical innovations that infer new knowledge of history from old evidence, such as Bloch's work on field patterns or Burckhardt on fourteenth-century art.

The assessment of possible improvements in the forms of historiographic hypotheses is more complicated and deserves an extended discussion. It has been argued that descriptions of historical events, which I consider a kind of historiographic hypothesis, are unique. This alleged uniqueness arguably excludes a scientific account of history. I think there is something to this claim, but many confusions need to be cleared first.

UNIQUENESS

Unique events entered philosophic discourse during the nineteenth century following the establishment of psychology as a science with a human subject matter. Psychology collapsed the traditional differentiating correspondence between scientific methods and nature on the one hand, and nonscientific methods and human subject matters on the other. Psychology seemed to share the methods of the natural

sciences and yet have a human subject matter (Köhnke, 1991). Consequently, Neo-Kantians like Windelband (1980) and Rickert (1962) proposed to redraw distinctions among the sciences on the basis of their
value-laden methodologies, on whether they aim to describe events as
unique or as instances of universal laws. Instead of the older ontological
distinction founded on domains of nature, Windelband and Rickert
introduced a methodological and conceptual distinction, founded on
how the sciences conceptualize events they study. Windelband held
that *nomothetic* science is interested in eternal and unchanging laws
of nature that have many instances. The *ideographic* sciences are interested in: "(1) Complete and exhaustive description (2) of a single,
more or less extensive process (3) which is located within a *unique*,
temporally defined domain of reality" (Windelband, 1980, p. 174
[italics added]). These criteria are not very useful. There is no exhaustive description of anything. Science describes and explains short and
long events and processes. The description of events as taking place
in a unique space and time, individuation, does not preclude scientific explanation of such descriptions as tokens of theoretical types.
Windelband thought that a phenomenon may be described from one
perspective as unchanging and subject to nomological explanation,
and from another perspective as transitory and subject to ideographic
description. Windelband's examples are not helpful: Language obeys
unchanging formal laws, but is also a transitory process in history.
Windelband did not consider that as a transitory process in history
language is subject to the scientific laws of diachronic linguistics. He
considered systematic organic biology nomothetic and evolutionary
biology ideographic. But individual cases of evolutionary change are
explained by evolutionary theory as adaptations to an environment
that best explain fossil and geologic evidence.

    Rickert (1962, pp. 14–15) tread in the footsteps of his mentor,
Windelband. Rickert suggested that historiography aims to study unrepeatable events in their significant particularity and individuality,
in contrast to understanding them by subsuming them under universal scientific laws or general concepts. For example, the scientific
description of the development of the chicken inside the egg is what
is common to many such processes (Rickert, 1962, p. 58). By contrast, Ranke's (1881) descriptions of the popes brought them under
particular and individual concepts. Phylogenetic biology did not quite

fit either of Rickert's classificatory terms, so, writing at the beginning of the twentieth century, he dismissed it as a fashion for drawing genealogic trees whose time may have passed (Rickert, 1962, pp. 104–8). But he stressed that to the extent that phylogenetic biology uses general laws, it is not historical. Historicists like Friedrich Meinecke (1972; Iggers, 1995) and Oakeshott (1985) accepted from the Neo-Kantians that universal or general statements are inapplicable to historiography because historical events are unique. The purpose of historiography is then to describe unique and unrepeatable events, the necessary preconditions for a significant past. Rickert's characterization of historiography is clearly mistaken. Ranke used quite a lot of theories to infer *The History of the Popes*, the third volume of which is devoted to reproduction and analysis of the documentary evidence, using general principles to assess its reliability along the lines discussed in chapter three. In his introduction to the English translation of Rickert's book (1962, p. vi), Hayek also noted that both theory and history are significant in all the branches of knowledge without distinction. Yet, though Rickert clearly did not understand scientific historiography, his suggestion that uniqueness is conceptual and connected to descriptions of events that are not repeated and therefore not subjected to general laws is valuable.

Critics of Hempel's (1965) covering law model of historiographic explanation claimed vaguely that if historical events are unique, they cannot be subjected to generalizing laws. This attempt may have been inspired by Windelband.[4] This is not an effective criticism of Hempel. Hempel presented a formal model of explanation; he said nothing of events and their relation with the alleged covering laws. The formal structure of explanation could be as Hempel put it, and the alleged covering laws could be false (Davidson, 1980, pp. 261–76). Philosophers who defended the covering law interpretation of historiographic explanation retorted that historiography uses concepts (states, revolution, wars, etc.) that are concrete particulars only in the sense of taking place in a definite time and space to describe historical events. Otherwise, historiographic concepts refer to several historical events (Joynt & Rescher, 1961). Fetzer argued that since it is impossible to describe, let alone explain, the myriad aspects of any event, scientists describe and explain only aspects of events that fit their theories. Thus, scientists can offer a partial explanation of any event by concentrating on descriptions of those of its aspects that can be explained by an acceptable theory (Fetzer, 1975). Fetzer acknowledged only a single context of scientific explanations, the context of an established scientific theory that connects explanans with explanandum. But there are other contexts of explanation in science. Atomic explanations are supported by the evidence (see chapter five). The evidence underdetermines some atomic explanations. Such explanations are either not connected with a general theory or are ad hoc interpretations of vague grand scope theories. They are advocated despite being underdetermined for a host of pragmatic reasons, like underdetermined historiography in general (see chapter four). For example, historians feel they must try to explain Hitler's pathologies, though they probably have much more relevant evidence to determine an explanation on why he sported a funny little mustache, given contemporary male facial hair fashions in Europe.

Hull argued like Joynt and Rescher and Fetzer that unique historical events can receive scientific explanations.

Caesar's crossing the Rubicon . . . was a unique event. . . . But this event, unique though it may be, can be assimilated to a variety of reference classes; e.g., people crossing rivers, generals disobeying orders, ambitious men making their big moves. Certainly under some of these descriptions the event is an instance of a significant generalization, though perhaps not a law of nature. (Hull, 1975, p. 268)

Historians do not usually care if Caesar crossed an existing bridge, constructed a new one, crossed the river with ferry boats or at a shallow point. In ordinary historiographic contexts, Caesar's crossing of the Rubicon was a historical-political event. The historian is interested "in the crossing of the Rubicon only in its relation to Republican law, and in the spilling of Caesar's blood only in its relation to a constitutional conflict" (Collingwood, 1956, p. 213). Joynt and Rescher, Fetzer and Hull repeated the mistakes of Hempel, in attempting to deduce a historiography a priori. Their model is irrelevant for the concerns of historians who do not and need not limit their explanations to descriptions of events that can be covered by scientific laws (see chapter five). If uniqueness should prove a challenge to scientific historiography it must mean more than individuation of concrete particulars (Murphey, 1994, p. 106) since there is nothing to prevent the scientific explanation of individuated events under one description or another (Dray, 1957; Hempel, 1965; Fetzer, 1975). Murphey suggested that scientific knowledge of unique events is impossible or at least problematic.

> There are events that do appear to be unique in the sense that no presently imaginable classification could bring them under a law-like generalization. The Big Bang in which our universe began is a unique event, and certainly it is obvious that none of the Humean criteria [of causation] can be applied to the Big Bang, at least as it is currently understood. Whether there are other such events is not clear. (Murphey, 1994, p. 106)

The problem with this characterization of "unique" is that it applies to events rather than to their descriptions. Joynt and Rescher (1961), Fetzer (1975), and Hull (1975) noted correctly that aspects of practically any event can receive scientific explanation, however irrelevant. We do know certain things about the Big Bang because they can be inferred from scientific theories and the evidence. As a singularity, the Big Bang is defined theoretically in Einsteinian physics. The problem scientists have with the Big Bang is that they cannot have a scientific explanation of why it occurred when it did, why is there something rather than nothing, as Leibniz put it. This has to do both with the fact that there is no evidence for other Big Bangs that could determine theories about them and the physical limits on gaining information about anything below an event horizon.

I consider "unique" a predicate of historiographic hypotheses. I suggest that unique historiographic hypotheses describe events, processes, explanations and so on, as occurring once and only once. Their significant properties or parameters, specified in the description are either:

A. Not shared by anything else, apart of spatiotemporal location and self-identity, or it is unknowable whether they are shared by anything else.

Or

B. Too complex for effective comparison with other hypotheses.

Unique hypotheses can be confirmed scientifically and offer knowledge of the past. Historiographic evidence with the usual information theories that historians use habitually can confirm hypotheses that describe all kinds of events in terms that cannot be compared with other historiographic hypotheses. But if historiography, or for that matter any other field of knowledge, is composed of unique hypotheses, it cannot offer a unified theory or group of theories of that domain of nature. Scientific historiography composed of unique hypotheses would be a complex amalgamation of little hypotheses that can never amount to a larger simple theory of wide scope of social change in time. Such unique historiographic hypotheses can form some kind of simple unity only through interpretative relations with a grand scope vague theory. But as noted in chapter four, such vague theories are insufficiently accurate to be considered scientific.

Unique hypotheses cannot be inferred from larger theories and therefore are more difficult to confirm. For example, if we describe the French Revolution as unique, evidence generated by other revolutions is irrelevant for determining hypotheses that explain its outbreak because no scientific theory can mediate between evidence for other revolutions and hypotheses about the French Revolution. By contrast, Wolf's hypotheses about the origins of the Homeric poems as orally transmitted distinct poems was not phrased in unique terms and thus could be confirmed by anthropological evidence from Finland and Yugoslavia about oral sagas in illiterate societies.

If an atomic explanatory hypothesis is unique, it depends exclusively on the limited evidence generated by the event to which the hypothesis refers. If this evidence is insufficient for determining one of several competing hypotheses, it is impossible to expand the scope of the evidence by using evidence for other comparable events. Trifold, non-atomic explanations of unique events are always underdetermined because any theoretical background that is relevant for their explanation is underdetermined (Tucker, 1998).

Historically, many hypotheses that had been considered unique have been superseded by discovering evidence that the events that appeared so were not unique after all. For example, the appearance of individual comets appeared a unique event for most of history. Knowledge of what came to be known as Halley's comet preceded Halley's discovery: Comets appeared in the sky and people recorded these appearances. However, each of the hypotheses about these appearances was unique. Explanatory hypotheses were underdetermined because each appearance of the comet was explained as a different omen. Halley discovered that all the unique appearances were actually cases of the same comet that followed the same trajectory. Scientists often discover that events and process that were described as unique are not unique by discovering the properties that were considered unique elsewhere and by inventing techniques for managing the complexity of unique hypotheses.

Hypothetical descriptions of events may appear unique relative to a scientific context, but may be discovered as nonunique in a different scientific context that may include the discovery of new relevant evidence and new and better theories with broader scope. If a unique hypothesis had been determined prior to the discovery, a new hypothesis that explains the old and new evidence will be better in having a wider scope, it will explain the evidence generated by more than a single event, for example, the discovery of the recurrent appearances of Halley's comet led to their elegant explanation by Newtonian physics. Similarly, scientific medicine discovered that many groups of clinical symptoms that were considered unique by traditional medicine were actually tokens of disease types, and consequently could be subsumed under scientific generalizations with obvious practical advantages. The discovery of further occurrences of events that were previously described as unique may be guided by a scientific theory, as in the case of Halley's comet and Newtonian physics. Some classification efforts in sciences as diverse as botany, biology, astronomy, medicine, historical linguistics, and the social sciences may be interpreted in such terms. Classifications may change with scientific theories; for example, cladistics has been replacing morphology as the main system of classification in biology on the basis of evolutionary theory.

Some unique hypotheses describe events or processes as complex beyond comparison. For example, a historian may describe the French Revolution as a complex interaction between myriad factors. Though each of the factors, class structure, state type, leadership kind, economic background, French national character, and so forth, can be linked to a wide scope of evidence generated by many different historical events, the complexity of their interaction in the particular context of the French Revolution makes such comparisons useless for determining hypotheses about it. Scientists attempt to simplify unique descriptions of events that are too complex for comparison with other descriptions of events that may share some of their predicates by using statistical methods, system theory, and computers to compute recurring algorithms. One scientific method that is mentioned often in connection with attempts to replace unique descriptions of events is *reduction*. Wimsatt suggested that the kind of reduction scientists use and discuss most is *explanatory methodological reduction* in which the familiar properties of higher level entities are explained in terms of unfamiliar properties and interrelations of lower level entities. Wimsatt characterizes "level" as "local maxima of regularity and predictability in the phase space of different modes of organization of matter.... The simplest and most powerful theories will be about entities at these levels" (1984, p. 484). Explanatory reduction is valuable for:

> cases that are anomalies for or exceptions to the upper-level regularities. Since an anomaly does not meet the macro-regularity, the macro-regularity *cannot* "screen-off" the micro-level variables. If the class of macro-level cases within which exceptions occur is significantly non-homogeneous when described in micro-level terms, *then* going to a lower-level description can be significantly explanatory, in that it may be possible to find a micro-level description partitioning the cases into exceptional and nonexceptional ones at the macro-level. We would then have a micro-explanation for the deviant phenomenon. (Wimsatt, 1984, p. 492)

The anomalies that explanatory reduction should explain may well be described by unique hypotheses. Explanatory reduction is a common method by which scientists expand science when encountering unique descriptions of events. When scientists face complex properties of an event that occurs only once, they attempt to explain them by other properties of a more manageable number and complexity from a lower level (Ruse, 1989). The depth of the reduction depends on the complexity of lower levels. Beyond a certain level, the relations among the reducing properties may be more complex than those they are supposed to reduce, and the reason for *methodological*, as distinct from *ontological*, reduction disappears. For example, Dalton's atomic theory explained unique descriptions of events in terms of smaller and more manageable number of recurring properties of atoms and their less complex interactions. The reductions of descriptions of social events to descriptions of the individuals that compose them and the psychological laws that govern them will in most cases create greater methodological difficulties because complexity would likely increase.

Nagel's (1961) classical formulation of intertheoretic reduction is of the deduction of reduced theory or hypothesis from reducing theory with the help of bridge laws. The bridge laws that should connect reducing theory and reduced hypotheses may be confirmed only in the case of properties/parameters of unique descriptions of events that are recurrent though complex (Tucker, 1998). But as critics of Nagel's model of reduction (Churchland, 1985; Feyerabend, 1962; Ruse, 1984; Schaffner, 1984) argued, Nagel-like derivation reduction is rare in the history of science. Schaffner (1984), Ruse (1984), Churchland (1985), and Churchland and Churchland (1995) suggested weaker models of epistemic intertheoretic reduction in which reducing theories entail only a strong analogy or isomorphic approximation of reduced theories that account for the extensions, evidence, explanatory and predictive powers of the reduced theory. Feyerabend (1962) and Hull (1984) claimed that the derivation of analogies or approximations of theory/concepts is actually theory/concept replacement. Replacing theories share the extensionality and exceed the predictive powers of the preceding theories.

Wimsatt (1984, p. 482) listed three reasons for establishing weak reductive relations between succeeding scientific theories: First, following Nickels (1973), weak reduction gives prepackaged confirmation of the reducing theory by showing that it generates the reduced theory as a special case. Second, following Sklar (1967), weak reduction "explains away" the old theory, or explains why we were tempted to believe in it. Third, following Nickles (1973), a weak reduction delimits acceptable conditions for use of a reduced theory as heuristic device, by determining conditions of approximation. Further, weak reduction "provides us with a much deeper insight into, and thus a more effective control over, the phenomena within the old theory's domain" (Churchland & Churchland, 1995, p. 71) since the reducing theory provides us with a simpler account of its domain and explains more phenomena than the reduced phenomena.

The possibility of reductions of descriptions of properties is debated in the philosophies of biology, mind, history, psychology, and the social sciences. For example, Campbell (1997, pp. 128–9) expressed optimism that all the events in nature (including black holes) may be methodologically reduced to a set of basic recurring tropes. Churchland (1985) proposed that folk psychology might be reduced to a neurological science that would preserve the ontology of folk psychology, the things and properties it postulates. Ten years later, while considering the methodological reducibility of individual mental events Churchland concluded that "It may indeed be unrealistic to expect an exhaustive global account of the neural and behavioral trajectory of a specific person over any period of time. The complexity of the neural systems we are dealing with may forever preclude anything more than useful approximations to the desired ideal account" (Churchland & Churchland, 1995, p. 74). Opponents of reduction in these fields claim that certain types of descriptions of properties are irreducible; or holistic, dependent on other properties of the higher level; or are complex beyond human and machine computational capacities. There are generic counterarguments for some of these arguments (Hoyningen-Huene, 1989). The resolutions of these debates are likely to come from scientific research, trial, and error, rather than from philosophic speculation. Historically, explanatory reduction of unique hypotheses seems the normal method by which science expands into new realms. When biologists, geologists, and chemists encountered *prima facie* unique hereditary sequences or chemical reactions, they invented successful reductive theories, genetics, and atomic theory.

What could a historiographic reducing theory be like? It is impossible to know. One can only speculate that it may govern the kind of entities and properties that are repeated in history: States, social institutions, economic organizations and forces, demographic forces, and and so forth. There hardly has been a serious attempt at a reduction of unique historiographic hypotheses. Grand historiographic theories are too vague to reduce anything. Social science theories abstracted general features that several or even many unique and nonunique historiographic hypotheses share. But abstraction does not amount to a reduction. Abstractions cannot explain or replace unique historiographic hypotheses, only aspects of them. The combination of several social science theories does not amount to a unified theory that can explain historiographic hypotheses because the theories are incomplete and sometimes mutually inconsistent.

A search for uniformities that can be described only on a very abstract plane clearly inhibits a detailed comparison involving the kind of variables that historians usually stress. (Fredrickson, 1980, p. 458; see also, Carr, 1987, p. 65)

Overcoming the uniqueness of historiographic hypotheses would require expanding the evidence base to discover recurrences and to determine reductive theories. Murphey believed that comparative historiography would generate scientific historiography by discovering a variety of evidence to confirm or falsify historiographic theories and hypotheses that are currently underdetermined:

Before the process of [historical] change can be conceptualized and its determinants defined, it is usually necessary to examine a number of instances of the process, and this requires the comparative study of many societies. History as a discipline is not well organized for this undertaking, and as a result few such comparative studies have been done. (Murphey, 1973, p. 123)

The absence of good comparative historiography reflects

the tradition of humane scholarship which has dominated the profession and which has defined the appropriate working unit as the single scholar rather than a team of scholars. But it also reflects the hard economic fact that funding for large-scale multi-person projects has been, and is now, largely non-existent. (Murphey, 1973, p. 156)

Murphey perceived in 1973 two developments that might have enabled historians to develop scientific comparative historiography: The use of computers in historiographic research and new institutional arrangements based on teams of historians and social scientists working together on a problem. But computers cannot generate theories and new institutional structures in academic historiography did not expand beyond the experimental.

Ingenious historiographic theoreticians, if such a breed of scholars is possible, are unlikely to emerge under current academic conditions requiring academic historians to specialize in a period and geographic area, thus inhibiting the development of extensive rather than intensive knowledge of evidence, necessary for the development of creative and imaginative historiographic theories:

Historians become experts on delimited times and places, often specializing in particular kinds of subject matters within those limits: for example, early modern French political history; twentieth-century U.S. economic history; or

Ming-Ch'ing Chinese intellectual history. For the most part, historians address established problems, bringing to bear new sources of evidence, new arguments, or perhaps new methods of analysis; occasionally a professional historian may also redefine the key problems to be addressed in his or her specialty. As research proceeds, most professional historians must also teach established university courses and train graduate students within their specialties. At the peak of their careers, premier historians may write syntheses of existing scholarship, covering several countries and subject matters for a major epoch, or covering many centuries of one country's past. A project on the scale of [Perry Anderson's] *Passages-Lineages*, surveying over two millennia for all of Europe, with discussions of major non-European civilizations as well, would rarely make sense within the operating frame of reference and even of a premier professional historian. (Fulbrook & Skocpol, 1984, p. 172)

The academic division between history departments and social sciences departments precludes extensive interaction that may have led to simpler and more accurate theories of wider scopes.

Projects involving teams of historians should have been able to test reductive historiographic theories. Already in 1900, Henri Berr asserted that teams of historians are necessary for scientific historiography (Iggers, 1985, p. 52). In the natural sciences, team projects are the norm. But even there institutional changes that increase the size of research units and decrease the importance and independence of individual researchers have been meeting resistance. For example, geneticists protested against the Human Genome Project because they wished to preserve the decentralized, small-group type of research in molecular biology. In historiography the tradition of humane scholarship dominates, excluding new, less individualistic, research methods. This reflects the position of most professional historians, who would find it difficult to participate in such a project, because of their training, temperament, and experience. When Charles Tilly initiated such large projects involving teams of historians that gather massive quantifiable evidence for historiographic hypotheses that are at once precise and of broader scope about topics like strikes in France and the character of the French working class in the nineteenth century, backward historians accused him of being an entrepreneur who mass produces studies of strikes, food riots, and tax rebellions (Hunt, 1984, pp. 254–5). This kind of academic resistance to innovation and change is hampering scientific progress, much like similar attitudes in what used to be the Soviet bloc blocked innovation and led to stagnation, decline, and fall.

Some social scientists failed to understand what would be involved in a reductive historiographic project: Ragin (1982) claimed that a rigorous comparative method is impossible in historiography because causal hypotheses in sociology or historiography are usually of a plurality, a configuration, of causes. It is impossible to examine rigorously hypotheses involving such configurations because there is no evidence for all possible configurations. Ragin proposed as an example, the hypothesis that explains educational attainment and occupational mobility by a configuration of three causes, modernity, capitalism, and industrialism. To substantiate such a hypothesis rigorously, claimed Ragin, it is necessary to study all eight possible configurations of these three causes and their negations. Ragin argued that since not all eight possible configurations occurred in history – there is no modern society that is neither capitalistic nor industrial – it is impossible to confirm comparatively configurational causal hypotheses. Ragin's argument can be properly assessed when applied to a scientific example: Scientists explain the explosion of an atomic bomb by the configuration of three necessary conditions:

1. A conventional explosion within the bomb.
2. The fission of two masses of plutonium.
3. The total mass of plutonium in the bomb is critical.

Since a conventional explosion causes the fission of plutonium in all atomic bombs, it is impossible to find a case where there is critical mass, a fission of plutonium inside an atomic bomb, but no conventional explosion. It is unnecessary to study all the logically possible configurations of causes to comparatively confirm theories about them. The absence of certain configurations of causes from history is evidence, not a problem. In Ragin's example, it is no accident that there has not been a society that was modern, but neither capitalistic nor industrial. A theory might explain this evidence either by modeling modernism, capitalism, and industrialism as affecting each other, or by discovering other hidden factor(s) that explain the correlation.

Though the question concerning scientific historiography, the limits of historiographic knowledge, is important, it is impossible to know whether the reduction of traditionalist ad hoc historiography, in whole or in part, to scientific historiography and the reduction of unique hypotheses that are already part of scientific historiography to more elegant and simple theories of wide scope/consilience is possible or even plausible. Further, under current social conditions it is unlikely that we will approach an answer in the foreseeable future. For now, fully scientific historiography is science fiction. Indeed, one of the greatest classics of science fiction, Isaac Asimov's *Foundation Trilogy*, tells of the discovery of quantitative scientific theory of historiography, "psychohistory" and its use by a group of social scientists in the context of a declining empire.

Psychohistory... that branch of mathematics which deals with the reactions of human conglomerates to fixed social and economic stimuli....

Implicit in all these definitions is the assumption that the human conglomerate being dealt with is sufficiently large for valid statistical treatment. The necessary size of such a conglomerate may be determined by Seldon's First Theorem. [Of] which... a further necessary assumption is that the human conglomerate be itself unaware of psychohistoric analysis in order that its reactions be truly random....

The basis of all valid psychohistory lies in the development of the Seldon Functions, which exhibit properties congruent to those of such social and economic forces as... [*Encyclopedia Galactica*] (Asimov, 1966, p. 17).[5]

7

Conclusion: Historiography and History

Historiography is the best explanation of historiographic evidence, it makes it most likely. The clear advantages of the common cause hypotheses over competing separate causes hypothesis in some cases, and of particular common cause hypotheses over their alternatives in some of these cases, allow historians of heterogeneous backgrounds to reach an uncoerced consensus on historiography. Other parts of historiography are underdetermined, too vague and imprecise or too ad hoc and of narrow evidential scope, too complex or too inconsistent. Schematically, we can model underdetermined, traditionalist historiography in a Cartesian space where the vertical parameters vary between complexity and inconsistency and the horizontal parameters are between wide scope and accuracy. Diagonal lines represent the possible positions of traditionalist historiography:

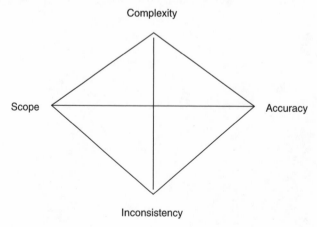

Fully scientific historiography is the introduction of social historiographic theories that are at once simple, accurate, consistent, and of wide scope.

The final question we should raise is about the relationship between historiography and history, the question of historiographic realism. Realists claim that historiography is a representation of history; historiography is largely a true account of the events of the past (Bunzl, 1997; Murphey, 1973, 1994). Constructionists claim that historiography is not a representation of the past, but a construction in the present (Goldstein, 1976, 1996). Realists think that historiography interprets or explains historical evidence to infer from descriptions of directly unobservable history, past events. The realist information causal chain leads from history to historiography through the evidence, the confirmation chain leads back from historiography to history through the evidence:

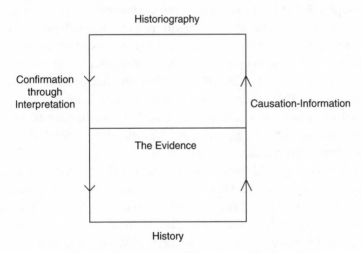

A 3-Tier Realist Scheme of Historiographic Knowledge

Constructionists deny the lowest tier of the realist three-tier scheme. Constructionism denies that historiography refers to history, to the past. Dummett (1978) argued that sentences about the past are not assertoric, they do not assert anything, they are neither true nor false, because there are no clear truth conditions that would allow or disallow us to assert them. Constructionists regard historiography merely as a construct, an interpretation of present evidence. Since the past is inaccessible or cannot be asserted, all we have is what historians tell us, further ontological assumptions about the past are to be taken at one's own risk.

There are three types of antirealist constructionism: First, *determined constructionism* regards historiography as having established a consistent family of theories and methods for the interpretation of evidence. Consistent application of these methods yields determined interpretation of evidence according to strict professional norms. Determined constructionism would balk at making any claims about the past. Determined constructionism denies that determined historiography is a true representation of the past or anything more than the most plausible interpretation of the evidence. Historiographic realism and determined constructionism agree on their epistemic descriptive analysis of historiography, on the determined relations between historiography and evidence; but disagree in their ontological interpretation of historiography. Second, *underdetermined constructionism* holds that there are several historiographic methods of interpretation of evidence. Though different interpretations lead to inconsistent results, there are no independent criteria to decide among them. Inconsistent historiography cannot be a representation of history because historical reality must be consistent. Third, *skeptical constructionism* holds that there is no privileged set of historiographic propositions because they are all equally indeterminate. Historiography is ontologically and epistemically indistinguishable from literary fiction.

The historiographic practices examined in this book do not neatly fit any of these positions. Historiographic textbooks clearly make realist assumptions. They claim to convey correct knowledge of the past, to tell us what history was really like. Many of the hypotheses that compose historiography, for example that Washington was the first President of the United States, are so entrenched, so well corroborated that many consider them facts. Some historiographic textbooks even attempt to create the impression among their readers that historians possess certain and extensive knowledge of the past by avoiding raising historiographic questions that have no determined answers; by ignoring what we do not know of the past but would like to. The worst textbooks present some underdetermined opinions as the truth about history. However, textbooks are hardly a guide to the practices of historians, to historiography.

If historiography is the best explanation of the historical evidence, it does not imply that it is a representation of the past, it could be wrong, it is fallible (Langlois & Seignobos, 1926, p. 195). Yet, the theories and methods of historiography are shared by a large heterogeneous and uncoerced community of historians, as well as by textual critics, philologists, detectives, and judges. I have argued since the first chapter that when historians reach an uncoerced, uniquely heterogeneous and large consensus on historiography, the best explanation is that they possess knowledge of the past. When one historiographic common cause hypothesis is clearly superior to all its alternatives, when it increases the likelihood of a broad scope of evidence, it generates a sufficient degree of belief in it, similar to that we have in everyday facts. We are as confident in our belief that George Washington was the first President of the United States as we are in the presence of an arch on Washington Square in New York. In that respect, historiography is as open to realist interpretation as any established science that posits unobservable entities such as atoms and genes. It is impossible to refute determined constructionism. It fits determined historiography as evidence just as well as a realist interpretation. Yet, though constructionism is simpler than realism, it makes fewer assumptions, realism is a better explanation of the historiographic Rankean paradigm, why a uniquely heterogeneous and uncoerced large group of historians has come to agree on the theories and methods that define the historiographic community? Constructionism fails to offer a convincing explanation of the historiographic consensus on theories and methods for interpreting the evidence that has determined historiographic consensuses on beliefs for two centuries. The textual critic Paul Maas went to the heart of the matter when he stated that:

The methods most closely related to the method of "stemmatics" [the science of inferring lost original texts from their later exemplars] are those of historical criticism of sources. But whereas a literary tradition goes back to an original similar in character to all the witnesses, in that it also is a manuscript, an historical tradition begins with an event, which by its very nature resists being set down in literary form, and is misrepresented or falsified, often even consciously, by the earliest witnesses. A work of literary art is an organic whole, and the reader is conscious of each element as standing in a necessary relation to every other element in it; it can survive over thousands of years without suffering serious damage, particularly in a civilization susceptible to its effect.

But of the historical event often only the roughest outlines, and sometimes not even these, are free from doubt. (Maas, 1958, p. 21)

Historiography does not reconstruct events; it cannot bring Caesar back to life or reenact the battle of Actium. Historiography does attempt to provide a hypothetical description and analysis of some past events as the best explanation of present evidence. This knowledge is probably true, but it is not true in an absolute sense. The most that historiography can aspire for is increasing plausibility, never absolute truth (Lloyd, 1993, p. 143). Most of history has left no lasting information-carrying effects after it. Therefore, most of history is and always will be unknown and unknowable.

Imagine an ideal book of history that describes and explains everything that has ever happened, events and processes. Suppose this ideal book of history is lost, and all we have are possible fragments of mutated copies. Historiography resembles an attempt to reconstruct this ideal book of history from the similarities between possible mutated fragments. Historians must first determine whether a fragment is connected with the ideal book of history and then attempt to use it in comparison with similar ones to deduce the authentic or near authentic form of a small section of the ideal book of history. Though historians are able to infer with high probability some small sections of the ideal book of history and know something of the content of others, most of this book is lost and can never be recovered.

Underdetermined constructionism is the best explanation of the traditionalist part of historiography. Underdetermined constructionism would lead us to expect to observe historiographic schools, as we do. Historiographic hypotheses that do not have a clear advantage over some of their alternatives and are not believed by a consensus of historians clearly fit underdetermined constructionist interpretations. Their mutual inconsistency excludes the possibility of a realist interpretation.

Skeptical constructionism cannot explain historiography. Had the skeptics been right, they should have been able to explain why historians agree on so much of historiography by external factors. Why do so many historians of heterogeneous backgrounds agree on theories, methods, and consequently hypotheses, if they do not share knowledge.

One of the main skeptical arguments relies on the hermeneutic cycle of interpretation, on the indeterminacy of interpretation, especially of texts from cultures separated from their readers by time, space, and culture (Quine, 1960). Skeptics concluded that since the interpretations historians give to documents can differ, they could never be final. Radical developments in this tradition even claim that texts have no fixed meanings, that their meanings are indeterminate. However, unlike some readers of literature, historians are not interested in confronting or understanding single texts without caring for the identity of their authors. Single uncorroborated documents indeed are open to conflicting interpretations. If they use them at all, historians only quote single sources while explicitly referring to their origins without being able to pronounce judgment on them (Langlois & Seignobos, 1926, p. 197).

Historians always seek groups of documents as evidence. A text that is not corroborated by comparison with other evidence is of little value or interest to historians. Historians go to extraordinary lengths to avoid confronting single documents or testimonies (Evans, 1999, pp. 69–75). Theories that interpret texts can be tested like any other theory, by comparing the likelihoods of the evidence, composed of similarities between texts, given competing theories. In cases when the evidence is limited, for example, when an unusual word occurs once in a linguistic context, it is indeed very difficult or even impossible to determine an interpretation. Debates within historiography about the interpretation of documents are relatively rare, and occur on the margins, where there is insufficient evidence to determine an interpretation. When historians face documents written in a different natural or conceptual language than their own, they study the linguistic and conceptual contexts through other documents, in order to corroborate a theory of interpretation. If a historian misses documents that are significant for a historiographic conclusion or draws conclusions that do not consider the reliability of the sources, other historians correct such oversights, as scientists correct each other by replicating experiments. Hermeneutics in historiography is not about a reader, a text, or the relationship between them, but about a community of interpreters, their theories, and sets of documents. The world is not a text, but it can be interpreted as texts.

When scientists realized that the comparison of similar texts, first biblical, then classical and historical, languages and finally species and material remains, could infer knowledge of their common causes, original texts, ur-languages, historical events, and extinct species, they generated a third scientific revolution that followed Galileo's and Newton's revolutions and partly overlapped with Darwin's revolution. The examination of the origins of biblical criticism, classical philology, comparative linguistics, and scientific historiography indicated that a single scientific community is responsible for their emergence and development by utilizing practically identical theories and methods to infer common causes from similar effects by tracing back the information signals that were sent by the common cause. Consequently, it is necessary not just to rewrite the historiography of science, but also to redraw the boundaries between the sciences. The sciences are divided neither into human sciences and natural sciences according to their subject matters, nor into ideographic and nomothetic sciences according to the purpose of their inquiries, but between sciences that examine the similar effects of common tokens of causes that preserve information about their common causes and sciences that examine the similar effects of shared types of causes. Sciences that examine common tokens of causes study the information preserving or destroying processes that could connect a common cause with its similar effects. Sciences that study types of causes examine correlations between types of causes and effects.

The common scientific theoretical background that allows historians to reach uncoerced consensus concerns the transmission of information in time, not the evolution of society. This point was confused often because in textual criticism, comparative linguistics, and evolutionary biology the *evolution* of the studied system, texts, languages, and species *is* the *transmission of information in time* and its selection, whereas in historiography and archeology the *evolution of society* and the *transmission of information* on past events are *independent of each other*. The theoretical background allows scientists who examine possible common causes to prove first that the similarity between effects is more likely given a common cause than given separate causes. Once the common cause hypothesis is proved better than separate cause hypotheses, historians use their theories to prove which common cause or common causes hypotheses increase the likelihood of the evidence more than others. These hypotheses put together compose our probable knowledge of the past, the conclusion of historiographic scientific research. Such hypotheses may have all levels of generality or concreteness; they may be descriptive or explanatory. Historiographic explanations are hypotheses that should prove to be the best explanation of the evidence. Further analysis of such atomic explanations is usually redundant.

Our knowledge of history is limited by the information-preserving evidence that survived the obliterating ravages of time in the historical process that connects history with the writing of historiography. Paucity of evidence engenders underdetermination of historiographic hypotheses. Historians tend to add underdetermined theoretical backgrounds to their shared theories and evidence to infer new hypotheses. Such theories increase their scope by decreasing their accuracy, creating vague large scope theories that form the intellectual basis for schools. Members of schools interpret ad hoc the vague theory they share to fit local narrow scopes of evidence. Such interpretations are mutually inconsistent and as ad hoc, underdetermined by the evidence. Problems in communication follow the use of identical words to convey different meanings by members of schools who interpret their vague theories differently.

Finally, an analysis of the chief philosophical arguments against the possibility of scientific historiography dismissed them as stemming from misunderstandings of science, historiography, or both. I suggested though that unique hypotheses limit the scope of scientific historiography because they cannot form together a theory of history that would connect disparate confirmed hypotheses of limited scope to form a large scope simple theory of social change.

At the foundation of all work in the philosophy of historiography lies wonder. Wonder with social change in time, wonder about the conditions of knowledge of the past that is significant for our understanding of our social environment and ourselves. Does the past really matter? I happened to be born into a culture where that was taken for granted, probably too much so for its own good. But I also think that this is so whether we are aware of it or not. What we know, do not know, can and cannot know, what we should and should not believe about the past matters for our temporal orientation, personal identity, and, consequently, conduct in the presence.

Cultures where the present is considered a continuation of the past by other means, where the place of a person in the universe depends on its location in a larger historical scheme, challenge their members to question the epistemic foundations of historiography. In that respect, the philosophy of historiography is a philosophy of liberation from the tyranny of the present by means of controlling and limiting knowledge of the past, not to say its outright fabrication. The old philosophies of history attempted to be philosophies of liberation as well, but they just replaced one apocalyptic vision with another. Liberation emerges out of being able to criticize the historiographic therapeutic myths of our forefathers that would lead us to self-destruction without either ignoring the past, losing cultural depth and historical perspective on our lives, or accepting all historiographies as equally right or wrong and therefore ultimately irrelevant.

Many of the founders of scientific philosophy escaped cultures where misrepresentation of the past, therapeutic nonscientific historiography, was used to lure the young into self-destruction. In the name of modernity, they ignored the past and paid little philosophic attention to historiography. I think it is increasingly obvious that this was a mistake. Under the guise of a priori analytical philosophy, shallow and dogmatic philosophies of historiography, ignorant of and indifferent to the practices of historians became dominant, and consequently made the whole subfield irrelevant and marginal. Yet, he who controls what we believe about the past, controls our futures. Liberation of the tyranny of premodernity through its control of the past requires knowing, not ignoring, it (Tucker, 2001). Political liberation will not result from our own therapeutic historiography that is just as good as its competitors. Only the probable truth, knowledge of the past founded on scientific historiography, and philosophic understanding of it can liberate us.

References

Achinstein, Peter (1983). *The nature of explanation.* New York: Oxford University Press.

Adamson, John (1997). England without Cromwell: What if Charles I had avoided the Civil War? In Niall Ferguson (Ed.), *Virtual history: Alternatives and counterfactuals* (pp. 91–124). London: Picador.

Almond, Mark (1997). 1989 without Gorbachev: What if Communism had not collapsed. In Niall Ferguson (Ed.), *Virtual history: Alternatives and counterfactuals* (pp. 392–415). London: Picador.

Alter, Stephen G. (1999). *Darwinism and the linguistic image: Language, race, and natural theology in the nineteenth century.* Baltimore: Johns Hopkins University Press.

Amariglio, Jack, & Norton, Bruce (1991). Marxist historians and the question of class in the French Revolution. *History and Theory, 30,* 37–55.

Ankersmit, Frank (1995). Statements, texts and pictures. In Frank Ankersmit & Hans Kellner (Eds.), *A New Philosophy of History* (pp. 212–240). London: Reaktion Books.

Apel, Karl-Otto (1984). *Understanding and explanation: A transcendental-pragmatic perspective* (Georgia Warnke, Trans.). Cambridge, MA: MIT Press.

Aristotle (1996). *Poetics* (Malcolm Heath, Trans.). New York: Penguin.

Asimov, Isaac (1966). *Foundation.* New York: Avon Books.

(1994). Spell my name with an S [1958]. In *The complete short stories* (Vol. I, pp. 397–414). London: Doubleday.

Attridge, Derek; Bennington, Geoff; & Young, Robert (1987). *Post-structuralism and the question of history.* Cambridge: Cambridge University Press.

Ben-Menahem, Yemima (1997). Historical contingency. *Ratio, 10,* 99–107.

Bentley, Michael (1999). *Modern historiography: An introduction.* London: Routledge.

263

Berlin, Isaiah (1960). History and theory: The concept of scientific history. *History and Theory, 1*, 1–31.
  (1969). Historical inevitability. In *Four essays on liberty.* Oxford: Oxford University Press, 41–117.
Bloch, Marc (1967). A Contribution towards a comparative history of European societies. In J. E. Anderson (Trans.), *Land and work in medieval Europe: Selected papers by Marc Bloch.* (pp. 44–81). New York: Harper & Row.
Bopp, Franz (1845). *A comparative grammar of the Sanscrit, Zend, Greek, Latin, Lithuanian, Gothic, German, and Sclavonic Languages* (Lieutenant Eastwick M.R.A.S Trans.). London: Madden and Malcolm.
Boudin, Raymond (1988). Will sociology ever be a normal science. *Theory and Society, 17,* 761–5.
Breslauer, George W. (1996). Counterfactual reasoning in Western studies of Soviet politics and foreign relations. In Philip E. Tetlock & Aaron Belkin (Eds.), *Counterfactual thought experiments in world politics: Logical, methodological, and psychological perspectives* (pp. 69–94). Princeton: Princeton University Press.
Brockmann, Stephen (1990). The politics of German history. *History and Theory,* 29 (2), 179–189.
Brodbeck, May (1966). Methodological individualism: Definition and reduction. In William Dray (Ed.), *Philosophical analysis and history* (pp. 297–329). New York: Harper & Row.
Bunzl, Martin (1997). *Real history: Reflections on historical practice.* New York: Routledge.
Burke, Peter (1990). Ranke the reactionary. In Georg G. Iggers & James M. Powell (Eds.), *Leopold von Ranke and the shaping of the historical discipline* (pp. 36–44). Syracuse: Syracuse University Press.
  (1991). Overture: The new history, its past and its future. In Peter Burke (Ed.), *New perspectives on historical writing* (pp. 1–23). Cambridge: Polity Press.
Butler, Pierce (1940). *Origins of printing in Europe.* Chicago: University of Chicago Press.
Butterfield, Herbert (1955). *Man on his past: The study of the history of historical scholarship.* Cambridge: Cambridge University Press.
Campbell, Keith (1997). The metaphysics of abstract particulars. In D. H. Mellor & A. Oliver (Eds.), *Properties* (pp. 125–139). Oxford: Oxford University Press.
Carr, David (1986). *Time, narrative and history.* Bloomington: Indiana University Press.
Carr, E. H. (1987). *What is history?* Harmondsworth, Middlesex: Penguin.
Carter, Thomas Francis (1955). *The invention of printing in China and its spread westward* (2nd ed. rev. by L. Carrington Goodrich). New York: Ronald Press.
Cartwright, Nancy (1983). *How the laws of physics lie.* Oxford: Oxford University Press.

(1989). *Nature's capacities and their measurement.* Oxford: Oxford University Press.

Caws, Peter (1986). The scaffolding of psychoanalysis. *The Behavioral and Brain Sciences, 9,* 230.

(1991). Committees and consensus: How many heads are better than one *Journal of Medicine and Philosophy, 16,* 375–391.

Cebik, L. B. (1969). Colligation and the writing of history. *The Monist, 53,* 40–57.

Cederman, Lars-Erik (1996). Rerunning history: Counterfactual simulation in world politics. In Philip E. Tetlock & Aaron Belkin (Eds.), *Counterfactual thought experiments in world politics: Logical, methodological, and psychological perspectives* (pp. 247–67). Princeton: Princeton University Press.

Chartier, Roger (1988). *Cultural history: Between practices and representations* (Lydia G. Cochrane, Trans.). Cambridge: Polity Press.

Chatto, William Andrew (1861). *A treatise on wood engraving, historical and practical.* London: Chatto and Windus.

Churchland, Paul (1985). Reduction, qualia, and the direct introspection of brain states. *The Journal of Philosophy, 82,* 8–28.

Churchland, Paul. M., & Churchland, Patricia S (1995). Intertheoretic reduction: A neuroscientist's field plan. In J. Cornwell (Ed.), *Nature's imagination: The frontiers of scientific vision* (pp. 64–77), Oxford: Oxford University Press.

Clark, J. C. D. (1997). British America: What if there had been no American revolution? In Niall Ferguson (Ed.), *Virtual history: Alternatives and counterfactuals* (pp. 125–74). London: Picador.

(2000). *English society 1660–1832: Religion, ideology and politics during the Ancien regime* (2nd ed.). Cambridge: Cambridge University Press.

Coady, C. A. J. (1992). *Testimony: A philosophical study.* Oxford: Oxford University Press.

Cohen, I. Bernard, & Westfall, Richard S. (Eds.) (1995). *Newton: Texts, backgrounds, commentaries.* New York: Norton.

Collingwood, R. G. (1956). *The idea of history.* Oxford: Oxford University Press.

Coveney, Peter, & Highfield, Roger (1996). *Frontiers of complexity: The search for order in a chaotic world.* London: Faber & Faber.

Danto, Arthur (1985). *Narration and knowledge: Including the integral text of analytical philosophy of history.* New York: Columbia University Press.

Darnton, Robert (1991). History of reading. In Peter Burke (Ed.), *New perspectives on historical writing* (pp. 140–65). Cambridge: Polity Press.

Davidson, Donald (1980). *Essays on actions and events.* Oxford: Oxford University Press.

Davis, John Francis (1857). *China: A general description of that empire and its inhabitants with the history of foreign intercourse down to the events which produced the dissolution of 1857.* London: J. Murray.

Dennett, Daniel C. (1996). *Darwin's dangerous idea: Evolution and the meaning of life.* New York: Touchstone.

DeVinne, Theodore Low (1876). *The invention of printing: A collection of facts and opinions descriptive of early prints and playing cards, the block-books of the fifteenth century, the legends of Lourens Janszoon Coster of Haarlem, and the work of John Gutenberg and his associates.* New York: Francis Hart & Co.

Dilthey, Wilhelm (1988). *Introduction to the human sciences: An attempt to lay a foundation for the study of society and history* (Ramon J. Betanzos, Trans.). Detroit: Wayne State University Press.

Donagan, Alan (1966). The Popper-Hempel theory reconsidered. In William Dray (Ed.), *Philosophical analysis and history* (pp. 127–59). New York: Harper & Row.

Dray, William (1957). *Laws and explanation in history.* Oxford: Oxford University Press.

(1980). *Perspectives in history,* London: Routledge.

(1981). *La philosophie de l'histoire.* Ottawa: Editions de l'Université d'Ottawa.

(1989). *On history and philosophers of history.* Leiden: Brill.

(1993). *Philosophy of history* (2nd ed.). Upper Saddle River, NJ: Prentice Hall.

(1995). *History as re-enactment: R. G. Collingwood's idea of history.* Oxford: Clarendon Press.

Dretske, Fred I. (1981). *Knowledge and the flow of information.* Cambridge, MA: MIT Press.

Duhem, Pierre (1954). In Philip P. Wiener (Ed.), *The aim and structure of physical theory.* Princeton: Princeton University Press.

Dummett, Michael (1978). *Truth and other enigmas.* Cambridge, MA: Harvard University Press.

Dupré, John (1995). *The disorder of things: Metaphysical foundations of the disunity of science.* Cambridge, MA: Harvard University Press.

Earman, John (2000). *Hume's abject failure: The argument against miracles.* New York: Oxford University Press.

Elster, Jon (1978). *Logic and society: Contradictions and possible worlds.* Chichester: Wiley.

(1989). *Nuts and bolts for the social sciences.* Cambridge: Cambridge University Press.

Elton, G. R. (1969). *The practice of history.* Glasgow: Collins.

Ereshefsky, Marc (1992). The historical nature of evolutionary biology. In Matthew H. Nitecki & Doris V. Nitecki (Eds.), *History and evolution* (pp. 81–99). Albany: State University of New York Press.

Evans, Richard J. (1999). *In defense of history.* New York: Norton.

Fales, Evan (1980). Uniqueness and historical laws. *Philosophy of Science, 47,* 260–276.

Ferguson, Niall (Ed.) (1997). *Virtual history: Alternatives and Counterfactuals.* London: Picador.

Fetzer, James (1975). On the historical explanation of unique events, *Theory and Decision, 6,* 87–97.

Feyerabend, Paul (1962). Explanation, reduction, and empiricism. In Herbert Feigel et al. (Eds.), *Minnesota studies in the philosophy of science* (Vol. III, pp. 28–97). Minneapolis: University of Minnesota Press.

(1981). *Philosophical papers.* Cambridge: Cambridge University Press.

Finkelstein, Israel, & Silberman, Neil Asher (2001). *The Bible unearthed: Archaeology's new vision of ancient Israel and the origin of its sacred texts.* New York: The Free Press.

Fischer, David Hackett (1989). *Albion's seed.* New York: Oxford University Press.

Forster, Malcolm R. (1988). Sober's principle of common cause and the problem of comparing incomplete hypotheses. *Philosophy of Science, 55,* 538–59.

Fredrickson, G. M. (1980). Comparative history. In Michael Kammen (Ed.), *The past before us: Contemporary historical writing in the United States.* Ithaca: Cornell University Press, 457–473.

Friedman, Richard (1987). Route analysis of credibility and hearsay. *Yale Law Journal, 96,* 667–742.

Fukuyama, Francis (1992). *The end of history and the last man.* New York: The Free Press.

Fulbrook, Mary, & Skocpol, Theda (1984). Destined pathways: The historical sociology of Perry Anderson. In Theda Skocpol (Ed.), *Vision and method in historical sociology* (pp. 170–210). Cambridge: Cambridge University Press.

Gadamer, Hans-Georg (1989). *Truth and method* (Joel Weinsheimer & Donald G. Marshall, Trans.). London: Sheed & Ward.

Ginzburg, Carlo (1983). *Night battles: Witchcraft and agrarian cults in the sixteenth and seventeenth centuries* (John Tedeschi & Ann Tedeschi, Trans.). Baltimore: Johns Hopkins University Press.

Glymour, Clark (1980). *Theory and evidence.* Princeton: Princeton University Press.

Goldhagen, Daniel Jonah (1997). *Hitler's willing executioners: Ordinary Germans and the Holocaust.* New York: Vintage Press.

Goldman, Alvin (1987). Foundations of social epistemics. *Synthese, 73,* 109–44.

Goldman, Alvin I. (1999). *Knowledge in a social world.* Oxford: Oxford University Press.

Goldstein, Doris S. (1990). History at Oxford and Cambridge: Professionalization and the influence of Ranke. In Georg G. Iggers & James M. Powell (Eds.), *Leopold von Ranke and the shaping of the historical discipline* (pp. 141–53). Syracuse: Syracuse University Press.

Goldstein, Leon J. (1976). *Historical knowing.* Austin: University of Texas Press. (1996). *The what and the why of history: Philosophical essays.* Leiden: Brill.

Gooch, G. P. (1959). *History and historians in the nineteenth century.* Boston: Beacon Press.

Gould, Stephen Jay (1989). *Wonderful life: The Burgess shale and the nature of history.* New York: Norton.

Grafton, Anthony, Most, Glenn W., Zetzel, James E. G. (1985). Introduction. In F. A. Wolf, *Prolegomena to Homer* (pp. 3–35). Princeton: Princeton University Press.

Greene, Jack P. (1988). *Pursuit of happiness.* Chapel Hill: University of North Carolina Press.

Greg, W. W. (1927). *The Calculus of Variants: An essay on textual criticism.* Oxford: The Clarendon Press.

Grew, Raymond (1980). The case for comparing histories. *American Historical Review, 85,* 763–78.

Gulya, Janos (1974). Some eighteenth century antecedents of nineteenth-century linguistics: The discovery of Finno-Ugarian. In Dell Hymes (Ed.), *Studies in the history of linguistics traditions and paradigms* (pp. 258–76). Bloomington: University of Indiana Press.

Gurr, Ted. R. (1970). *Why men rebel.* Princeton: Princeton University Press.

Habermas, Jürgen (1971). *Knowledge and human interests* (Jeremy J. Shapiro, Trans.). Boston: Beacon Press.

(1990). *On the logic of the social sciences* (Shierry Weber Nicholson & Jerry A. Stark, Trans.). Cambridge: Polity Press.

Halevi, Judah (1964). *The Kuzari (Kitab al khazari): An argument for the faith of Israel* (Hartwig Hirschfeld, Trans.). New York: Schocken Books.

Hamilton, Gary G. (1984). Configuration in history: The historical sociology of S. N. Eisenstadt. In Theda Skocpol (Ed.), *Vision and method in historical sociology* (pp. 85–128). Cambridge: Cambridge University Press.

Hammond, Michael (1977). Weighing causes in historical explanation. *Theoria, 43,* 103–128.

Hanson, Norwood Russell (1958). *Patterns of discovery: An inquiry into the conceptual foundations of science.* Cambridge: Cambridge University Press.

Haslam, Jonathan (1997). Stalin's war or peace: What if the Cold War had been avoided? In Niall Ferguson (Ed.), *Virtual history: Alternatives and counterfactuals* (pp. 348–67). London: Picador.

Hay, Cynthia (1980). Historical theory and historical confirmation. *History and Theory, 19,* 39–57.

Hayek, F. A. (1973). *Law, legislation and liberty.* Chicago: University of Chicago Press.

Hempel, C. G. (1965). *Aspects of scientific explanation.* New York: The Free Press.

Hitchcock, Christopher (1998). The common cause principle in Historical Linguistics. *Philosophy of Science, 65,* 425–47.

Hobbs, Jesse (1993). Ex post facto explanations. *Journal of Philosophy, 90,* 117–36.

Hoenigswald, Henry M. (1974). Fallacies in the history of linguistics: Notes on the appraisal of the nineteenth century. In Dell Hymes (Ed.), *Studies in the history of linguistics traditions and paradigms* (pp. 346–58). Bloomington: University of Indiana Press.

Hausman, Daniel M. (1998). *Causal Asymmetries.* Cambridge: Cambridge University Press.

Hoyningen-Huene, P. (1989). Epistemological reductionism in biology: intuitions, explications, and objections. In Paul Hoyningen-Huene & Franz M. Wuketits (Eds.), *Reductionism and system theory in the life sciences: Some problems and perspectives* (pp. 29–44). Dordrecht, Kluwer.

Hull, David (1975). Central subjects and historical narratives. *History and Theory, 14,* 253–74.

(1984). Informal aspects of theory reduction. In Elliott Sober (Ed.), *Conceptual issues in evolutionary biology* (pp. 462–76). Cambridge, MA: MIT Press.

(1992). The particular-circumstance model of scientific explanation. In Matthew H. Nitecki & Doris V. Nitecki (Eds.), *History and evolution* (pp. 69–80). Albany NY: State University of New York Press.

Hume, David (1988). *An enquiry concerning human understanding*. Amherst, NY: Prometheus Press.

Humphrys, Henry Noel (1868). *A history of the art of printing, from its invention to its wide-spread development in the middle of the sixteenth century*. London: Bernard Quaritch.

Hunt, Lynn (1984). Charles Tilly's collective action. In Theda Skocpol (Ed.), *Vision and method in historical sociology* (pp. 244–75). Cambridge: Cambridge University Press.

(1989). Introduction: History, culture, and text. In Lynn Hunt (Ed.), *The new cultural history* (pp. 1–22). Berkeley: University of California Press.

Huntington, Samuel P. (1997). *The clash of civilizations and the remaking of world order*. New York: Simon & Schuster.

Iggers, Georg G. (1985). *New directions in European historiography*. Middletown, CT: Wesleyan University Press.

(1995). Historicism: The history and meaning of the term. *Journal of the History of Ideas, 56*, 129–52.

Iggers, Georg, & von Moltke, Konrad (Eds.) (1973). *The theory and practice of history: Leopold von Ranke*. Indianapolis & New York: Bobbs-Merrill.

Jackson, Alvin (1997). British Ireland: What if Home Rule had been enacted in 1912? In Niall Ferguson (Ed.), *Virtual history: Alternatives and counterfactuals* (pp. 175–227). London: Picador.

Jackson, Frank, & Pettit, Philip (1992). Structural explanation in social theory. In D. Charles & K. Lennon (Eds.), *Reduction explanation and realism* (pp. 97–131). Oxford: Clarendon Press.

Jardine, Nicholas (1991). *The scenes of inquiry: On the reality of questions in the sciences*. Oxford: Clarendon Press.

Jegalian, Karin, & Lahn, Bruce T. (2001). Why the Y is so weird. *Scientific American, 284* (2), 56–61.

Jenkins, Keith (1991). *Re-thinking history*. London: Routledge.

Jervis, Robert (1997). *System effects: Complexity in political and social life*. Princeton: Princeton University Press.

Johnson, Chalmers (1966). *Revolutionary change*. Boston: Little & Brown.

Joynt, C. B., & Rescher, N. (1961). The problem of uniqueness in history. *History and Theory, 1*, 150–62.

Jones, Sir William (1967) [1786]. The third anniversary discourse, on the Hindus. In Winfred P. Lehmann (Ed. and Trans.), *A reader in nineteenth-century historical Indo-European linguistics* (pp. 10–20). Bloomington: Indiana University Press.

Jordanova, Ludmilla (2000). *History in practice*. New York: Oxford University Press.

Judt, Tony (2001). New York diarist. Burst. *New Republic on Line* (Sept. 24, 2001). From: *http://www.tnr.com/092401/judt092401.html*

Kant, Immanuel (1998). *Critique of pure reason* (Paul Guyer & Allen W. Wood, Trans.). Cambridge: Cambridge University Press.

Kellert, Stephen H. (1993). *In the wake of chaos: Unpredictable order in dynamical systems.* Chicago: University of Chicago Press.

Kennedy, Paul M. (1989). *The rise and fall of the great powers: Economic change and military conflict from 1500 to 2000.* London: Fontana.

Kershaw, Ian (1998). *Hitler 1889–1936, hubris.* New York: Norton.

Kincaid, Harold, (1996). *Philosophical foundations of the social sciences: Analyzing controversies in social research.* Cambridge: Cambridge University Press.

Kiparsky, Paul (1974). From paleogrammarians to neogrammarians. In Dell Hymes (Ed.), *Studies in the history of linguistics traditions and paradigms* (pp. 331–45). Bloomington: University of Indiana Press.

Khong, Yuen Foong (1996). Confronting Hitler and its consequences. In Philip E. Tetlock & Aaron Belkin (Eds.), *Counterfactual thought experiments in world politics: Logical, methodological, and psychological perspectives* (pp. 95–118). Princeton: Princeton University Press.

Köhnke, R. C. (1991). *The rise of Neo-Kantianism: German academic philosophy between idealism and positivism* (R. G. Hollingdale, Trans.). Cambridge: Cambridge University Press.

Kosso, Peter (1992). Observation of the past. *History and Theory, 31,* 21–36.

 (1993). Historical evidence and epistemic justification: Thucydides as a case study. *History and Theory, 32,* 1–13.

 (2001). *Knowing the past: Philosophical issues of history and archeology.* Amherst, NY: Humanity Books.

Krieger, Leonard (1977). *Ranke: The meaning of history.* Chicago: University of Chicago Press.

Kripke, Saul (1981). *Naming and necessity.* Oxford: Blackwell.

Kuhn, Thomas S. (1977). *The essential tension,* Chicago: University of Chicago Press.

 (1996). *The structure of scientific revolutions* (3rd ed.). Chicago: University of Chicago Press.

Kunz, Diane (1997). Camelot continued: What if John F. Kennedy had lived? In Niall Ferguson (Ed.), *Virtual history: Alternatives and counterfactuals* (pp. 368–91). London: Picador.

Lakatos, Imre (1978). *The methodology of scientific research programmes* (John Worrall & Gregory Currie, Eds.) Cambridge: Cambridge University Press.

Langlois, Ch., & Seignobos, Ch. (1926) *Introduction to the study of history* (G. G. Berry, Trans.). New York: Henry Holt & Co.

Laplace, Pierre Simon Marquis de (1951). *A philosophical essay on probabilities* (Frederick Wilson Truscott & Frederick Lincoln Emory, Trans.). New York: Dover.

Laudan, Larry (1984). *Science and values: The aims of science and their role in scientific debate.* Berkeley: University of California Press.

(1998) [1990]. Demystifying underdetermination. In Martin Curd & J. A. Cover (Eds.), *Philosophy of science: The central issues* (pp. 320–53). New York: Norton.

Laudan, Larry & Leplin, Jarrett (1991). Empirical equivalence and underdetermination. *The Journal of Philosophy, 88,* 449–472.

Laudan, Rachel & Laudan, Larry (1989). Dominance and the disunity of method: Solving the problems of innovation and consensus. *Philosophy of Science, 56,* 221–37.

Laudan, Rachel (1992). What's so special about the past? In Matthew H. Nitecki & Doris V. Nitecki (Eds.), *History and evolution* (pp. 55–67). Albany: State University of New York Press.

Laufer, Berthold (1973) [1931]. *Paper and printing in ancient China.* New York: Burt Franklin.

Lebow, Richard, Stein, Ned & Janice Gross (1996). Back to the past: Counterfactuals and the Cuban missile crisis. In Philip E. Tetlock & Aaron Belkin (Eds.), *Counterfactual thought experiments in world politics: Logical, methodological, and psychological perspectives* (pp. 119–48). Princeton: Princeton University Press.

Lefebvre, Georges (1971). *La naissance de l'historiographie moderne.* Paris: Flammarion.

Le Goff, Jacques, (1992). *History and memory* (Steven Rendall & Elizabeth Claman, Trans.). New York: Columbia University Press.

Lehrer, Keith & Wagner, Carl (1981). *Rational consensus in science and society: A philosophical and mathematical study.* Dordrecht: Reidel.

Levi, Giovanni (1991). On microhistory. In Peter Burke (Ed.), *New perspectives on historical writing* (pp. 93–113). Cambridge: Polity Press.

Levi, Isaac (1985). Consensus as shared agreement and outcome of inquiry. *Synthese, 62,* 3–11.

Lewontin, R. C. (1994a). Facts and the factitious in the natural sciences. In James Chandler, Arnold I. Davidson, Harry Harootunian (Eds.), *Question of evidence: Proof, practice, and persuasion across the disciplines* (pp. 478–91). Chicago: University of Chicago Press.

(1994b). A rejoinder to William Wimsatt. In James Chandler, Arnold I. Davidson, Harry Harootunian (Eds.), *Question of evidence: Proof, practice, and persuasion across the disciplines* (pp. 504–9). Chicago: University of Chicago Press.

Lipton, Peter (1991). *Inference to the best explanation.* London: Routledge.

(1998). The Epistemology of testimony. *Studies in History and Philosophy of Science, 29,* 1–31.

Lloyd, Christopher (1993). *The structures of history.* Oxford: Blackwell.

Longino, Helen E. (1990). *Science as social knowledge: Values and objectivity in scientific inquiry.* Princeton: Princeton University Press.

(1994). The fate of knowledge in social theories of science. In Frederick F. Schmitt (Ed.), *Socializing epistemology: The social dimensions of knowledge* (pp. 135–57). Lanham, MD: Rowman & Littlefield.

Lorenz, Chris (1994). Historical knowledge and historical reality: A plea for "internal realism." *History and Theory, 33,* 297–327.

McCloskey, Donald N. (1991). History, differential equations, and the problem of narrative. *History and Theory, 30,* 21–36.

McCullagh, C. Behan (1998). *The truth of history.* New York: Routledge.

Maas, Paul (1958). *Textual criticism* (Barbara Flower, Trans.). Oxford: Clarendon Press.

Mandelbaum, Maurice (1977). *The anatomy of historical knowledge,* Baltimore: Johns Hopkins University Press.

Manicas, Peter (1981). Review of Skocpol's states and social revolutions. *History and Theory, 20,* 218–31.

Martin, Raymond (1989). *The past within us: An empirical approach to philosophy of history.* Princeton: Princeton University Press.

Marwick, Arthur (1993). *The nature of history* (3rd ed.). London: Macmillan.

Marx, Karl (1978a). The class struggles in France, 1848–1850. In Robert C. Tucker (Ed.), *The Marx-Engles Reader* (2nd ed., pp. 586–93). New York: Norton.

(1978b). The Eighteenth Brumaire of Louis Bonaparte. In Robert C. Tucker (Ed.), *The Marx-Engles reader* (2nd ed., pp. 594–617). New York: Norton.

Maudlin, Tim (2000). The character of chaos. Paper delivered at the Annual Meeting of the American Philosophical Association in New York, December 2000.

Meinecke, Friedrich (1972). *Historicism: The rise of the new historical outlook* (J. E. Anderson, Trans.). New York: Herder & Herder.

Metcalf, George J. (1974). The Indo-European hypothesis in the sixteenth and seventeenth centuries. In Dell Hymes (Ed.), *Studies in the history of linguistics traditions and paradigms* (pp. 233–57). Bloomington: University of Indiana Press.

Miliband, Ralph (1977). *Marxism and politics.* Oxford: Oxford University Press.

Mill, J. S. (1976). A system of logic. In John M. Robson (Ed.), *The collected works of J. S. Mill.* Toronto: University of Toronto Press.

Miller, Constance R. (1983). *Technological and cultural prerequisites for the invention of printing in China and the West* (Asian Library Series; no. 21 Studies in East Asian Librarianship). San Francisco: Chinese Materials Center.

Miller, Richard W. (1987). *Fact and method: Explanation, confirmation and reality in the natural and social sciences.* Princeton: Princeton University Press.

Milligan, John D. (1979). The treatment of an historical source. *History and Theory, 18,* 177–96.

Momigliano, Arnaldo (1977). *Essays in ancient and modern historiography.* Middletown, CT: Wesleyan University Press.

Mommsen, Wolfgang J. (1990). Ranke and the Neo-Rankean school in Imperial Germany: State-oriented historiography as a stabilizing force. In Georg G. Iggers & James M. Powell (Eds.), *Leopold von Ranke and the shaping of the historical discipline* (pp. 124–49). Syracuse: Syracuse University Press.

Murphey, Murray G. (1973). *Our knowledge of the historical past.* Indianapolis & New York: Bobbs-Merrill.

(1994). *Philosophical foundations of historical knowledge.* Albany: State University of New York Press.

Nagel, Ernst (1961). *The structure of science.* New York: Harcourt, Brace & World.

Nickels, T. (1973). Two concepts of inter-theoretic reduction. *The Journal of Philosophy, 70*, 181–201.

Nozick, Robert (1974). *Anarchy, state, and utopia.* New York: Basic Books.

Oakeshott, Michael (1985). *Experience and its modes.* Cambridge: Cambridge University Press.

Okruhlik, Kathleen (1994). Biology and society. *Canadian Journal of Philosophy,* Supple. Vol. *20*, 21–42.

Oppenheim P. & Putnam H. (1958). Unity of science as a working hypothesis. In Herbert Feigel et al. (Eds.), *Minnesota studies in the philosophy of science* (Vol. II, pp. 3–36). Minneapolis: University of Minnesota Press.

Partner, Nancy F. (1995). Historicity in an age of reality-fictions. In Frank Ankersmit & Hans Kellner (Eds.), *A new philosophy of history* (pp. 21–39). London: Reaktion books.

Peirce, C. S. (1957) [1883]. The general theory of probable inference. In J. Buchler (Ed.), *Philosophical writings of Peirce* (pp. 190–217). New York: Dover.

Percival, W. Keith (1974). "Rask's view of linguistic development and phonetic correspondences. In Dell Hymes (Ed.), *Studies in the history of linguistics, traditions and paradigms* (pp. 307–14). Bloomington: University of Indiana Press.

Pettit, Philip (1993). *The common mind: An essay on psychology, society, and politics.* Oxford: Oxford University Press.

Pirenne, Henri (1939). *Mohammed and charlemagne.* New York: Norton.

Plato, (1981). Meno. In *Five dialogues* (G. M. A. Grube, Trans.) (pp. 59–88). Indianapolis: Hackett.

Pompa, Leon (1981). Truth and fact in history. In L. Pompa & W. H. Dray (Eds.), *Substance and form in history: A collection of essays in philosophy of History* (pp. 171–186). Edinburgh: Edinburgh University Press.

Popper K. R. (1964). *The poverty of historicism.* New York: Harper & Row.

Poulantzas Nico (1978). *Political power and social classes.* London: Verso.

Putnam, Hilary (1975). *Mind, language and reality, philosophical papers,* Cambridge: Cambridge University Press.

(1990). *Realism with a human face* (James Conant, Ed.). Cambridge, MA: Harvard University Press.

Quine, W. V. O. (1960). *Word and object,* Cambridge MA: Harvard University Press.

(1975). On empirically equivalent systems of the world. *Erkenntnis, 9,* 313–28.

(1980). Two dogmas of empiricism. In *From a logical point of view* (pp. 20–46). Cambridge, MA: Harvard University Press.

Quine, W. V. O. (1985). Epistemology naturalized. In Hilary Kornblith (Ed.), *Naturalizing epistemology* (pp. 15–29). Cambridge MA: MIT Press.

Ragin, Charles (1982). Comparative sociology and the comparative method. In J. Michael Armer & Robert M. Marsh (Eds.), *Comparative sociological research in the 1960s and 1970s*. Leiden: Brill.

Ranke, Leopold (1981). *The history of the popes, their church and state, and especially their conflicts with Protestantism in the sixteenth & seventeenth centuries* (E. Foster, Trans.) (3 vols). London: George Bell & Sons.

(1909). *History of the Latin and Teutonic nations (1494 to 1514)* (G. R. Dennis, Trans.). London: George Bell & Sons.

(1981). Introduction to the history of the Latin and Teutonic Nations. In Roger Wines (Ed. & Trans.), *Leopold von Ranke, the secret of world history: Selected writings on the art and science of history*. New York: Fordham University Press.

Rappard, V. P. (1993). History and system. *Annals of Theoretical Psychology, 9*, 1–40.

Rask, Rasmus (1967) [1818]. An investigation concerning the source of the old Northern or Icelandic language. In Winfred P. Lehmann (Ed. & Trans.), *A reader in nineteenth-century historical Indo-European linguistics* (pp. 31–7). Bloomington: Indiana University Press.

Reichenbach, Hans (1956). *The Direction of Time*. Berkeley: University of California Press.

Reisch, George A. (1991). Chaos, history, and narrative. *History and Theory, 30*, 1–20.

Reisch, George (1995). Scientism without tears: A reply to Roth and Ryckman. *History and Theory, 34*, 45–58.

Renfrew, Colin (1988). *Archeology and language: The puzzle of Indo-European origins*. New York: Cambridge University Press.

Rescher, Nicholas (1993). *Pluralism: Against the demand for consensus*. Oxford: Clarendon Press.

Resnik, David B. (1989). Adaptationist explanations. *Studies in History and Philosophy of Science, 20*, 193–213.

Rickert, Heinrich (1962). *Science and history: A critique of positivist epistemology* (George Reisman, Trans.). Princeton: D. Van Norstrand Company.

Ringer, Fritz (1997). *Max Weber's Methodology: The unification of the cultural and social sciences*. Cambridge, MA: Harvard University Press.

Roberts, Andrew (1997). Hitler's England: What if Germany had invaded Britain in May 1940? In Niall Ferguson (Ed.), *Virtual history: Alternatives and counterfactuals* (pp. 281–320). London: Picador.

Rogerson, John (1985). *Old Testament criticism in the nineteenth century*. Philadelphia: Fortress Press.

Rorty, Richard (1979). *Philosophy and the mirror of nature*. Princeton: Princeton University Press.

Ross Taylor, Lily (1966). *Roman voting assemblies: From the Hannibalic War to the dictatorship of Caesar*. Ann Arbor: The University of Michigan Press.

Rotenstreich, Nathan (1958). *Between past and present.* New Haven, CT: Yale University Press.

Roth, Paul A. (1987). *Meaning and method in the social sciences.* Ithaca: Cornell University Press.

Roth, Paul A., & Ryckman, Thomas A. (1995). Chaos, clio, and scientific illusions of understanding. *History and Theory, 34,* 30–44.

Rouse, Joseph (1987). *Knowledge and power: Toward a political philosophy of science.* Ithaca: Cornell University Press.

Ruben, David-Hillel (1990). Singular explanation and the social sciences. In Dudley Knowls (Ed.), *Explanation and its limits* (pp. 95–117). Cambridge: Cambridge University Press.

Rueschemeyer, Dietrich (1984). Theoretical generalization and historical particularity in the comparative sociology of Reinhard Bendix. In Theda Skocpol (Ed.), *Vision and method in historical sociology* (pp. 129–69). Cambridge: Cambridge University Press.

Ruse, Michael (1984). Reduction in genetics. In Elliott Sober (Ed.), *Conceptual issues in evolutionary biology* (pp. 446–61). Cambridge, MA: MIT Press.

(1989). Sociobiology and reduction. In P. Hoyningen-Huene & F. M. Wuketits (Eds.). *Reductionism and system theory in the life sciences: Some problems and perspectives* (pp. 45–83). Dordrecht: Kluwer.

Ryan Alan (1975). *John Stuart Mill.* London: Routledge.

Salmon, Wesley (1984). *Scientific explanation and the causal structure of the world.* Princeton: Princeton University Press.

Salmon Wesley C. (1998) [1990]. Rationality and objectivity in science or Tom Kuhn meets Tom Bayes. In Martin Curd & J. A. Cover (Eds.), *Philosophy of science: The central issues* (pp. 551–83). New York: Norton.

Santamaria, Ulysses & Bailey, Anne M. (1984). A note on Braudel's structure as a duration. *History and Theory, 23,* 78–83.

Sarkar, Husain (1997). The task of group rationality: The subjectivist's view– part II. *Studies in History and Philosophy of Science 28,* pp. 497–520.

Schaffner, Kenneth (1984). Reduction in biology: Prospects and problems. In Elliott Sober (Ed.), *Conceptual issues in evolutionary biology* (pp. 428–445). Cambridge MA: MIT Press.

Scholderer, Victor (1963). *Johan Gutenberg, The inventor of printing.* London: British Museum.

Scriven, Michael (1966). Causes, connections and conditions in history. In William Dray (Ed.), *Philosophical analysis and history* (pp. 238–64). New York: Harper & Row.

Shapin, Steven & Schaffer Simon (1985). *Leviathan and the air-pump: Hobbes, Boyle, and the experimental life.* Princeton: Princeton University Press.

Shapiro, Robert (1992). *The human blueprint: The race to unlock the secrets of our genetic script.* London: Cassell.

Sharpe, Jim (1991). History from below. In Peter Burke (Ed.), *New perspectives on historical writing* (pp. 24–41). Cambridge: Polity Press.

Shermer, Michael (1995). Exorcising Laplace's demon: Chaos and antichaos, history and metahistory. *History and Theory, 34,* 59–83.

Simmel, Georg (1977). *The problems of the philosophy of history: An epistemological essay* (Guy Oakes, Trans.). New York: The Free Press.

Sklar, Lawrence (1967). Types of inter-theoretic reduction. *British Journal for the Philosophy of Science, 18,* 106–24.

Skocpol, Theda (1979). *States and social revolutions.* Cambridge: Cambridge University Press.

Skocpol, Theda, & Somers, Margaret (1980). The uses of comparative history in macrosocial inquiry. *Comparative Studies in Society and History, 22,* 174–97.

Smart, J. J. C. (1990). Explanation – Opening address. In Dudley Knowls (Ed.), *Explanation and its limits* (pp. 1–19). Cambridge: Cambridge University Press.

Smith, Peter (1998). *Explaining chaos.* Cambridge: Cambridge University Press.

Smith, Roger (1997). *The Fontana history of the human sciences.* London: Fontana Press.

Sober, Elliott (1988). *Reconstructing the past: Parsimony, evolution, and inference.* Cambridge, MA: MIT Press.

(1989). Independent evidence about a common cause. *Philosophy of Science, 56,* 275–87.

(1999). Modus Darwin, *Biology and Philosophy, 14,* 253–78.

(2001). Venetian sea levels, British bread prices, and the principle of the common cause. *British Journal for the Philosophy of Science, 52,* 331–46.

Solomon, Miriam (2001). *Social empiricism.* Cambridge, MA: MIT Press.

Spence, Donald P. (1994). *The rhetorical voice of psychoanalysis: Displacement of evidence by theory.* Cambridge, MA: Harvard University Press.

Spitzer, Alan B. (1990). John Dewey, the "Trial" of Leon Trotsky and the search for historical truth. *History and Theory, 29,* 16–37.

Stoianovich, Traian (1976). *French historical method: The Annales paradigm.* Ithaca: Cornell University Press.

Swadesh, Morris (1972). *The origin and diversification of language.* London: Routledge.

Tennessen, Herman (1969). History is science. *The Monist, 53,* 116–33.

Tetlock, Philip E., & Belkin, Aaron (1996). Counterfactual thought experiments in world politics: Logical, methodological, and psychological perspectives. In Philip E. Tetlock & Aaron Belkin (Eds.), *Counterfactual thought experiments in world politics: Logical, methodological, and psychological perspectives* (pp. 1–38). Princeton: Princeton University Press.

Thagard, Paul (1993). *Computational philosophy of science.* Cambridge, MA: MIT Press.

(1998) [1978]. Why astrology is a pseudoscience. In Martin Curd & J. A. Cover (Eds.), *Philosophy of science: The central issues* (pp. 27–37). New York: Norton.

Tilly, Charles (1984). *Big structures, large processes, huge comparisons.* New York: Russell Sage.

(1988). Future history. *Theory and Society, 17,* 703–12.

Troy, Christopher S., MacHugh, David E., Bailey, Jullian F., Magee, David A., Loftus, Ronan T., Cunningham Patrick, Chamberlain, Andrew T., Sykes, Bryan C., & Bradley, Daniel G. (2001). Genetic evidence for Near-Eastern origins of European cattle. *Nature, 410* (April 26), 1088–1191.

Tucker, Aviezer (1990). Some methodological notes on the explanations to the invention of printing. *History and Technology, 7,* 73–89.

(1993). Plato and Vico: A platonic reinterpretation of Vico. *Idealistic Studies, 23,* 139–50.

(1998). Unique events: The underdetermination of explanation. *Erkenntnis,* 48–1, 59–80.

(1999a). The genealogy of incommensurability in psychoanalysis. In Eric J. Engstrom, Matthias M. Weber, Paul Hoff (Eds.), *Power and knowledge: Perspectives in the history of psychiatry, Proceedings of the third triennial conference of the European association for the history of psychiatry* (pp. 197–207). Berlin: VWB – Verlag für Wissenschaft und Bildung.

(1999b). [Review of the book *Roger Smith, The Fontana history of the human sciences.* London: Fontana Press, 1997] *The British Journal for the History of Philosophy, 7,* 365–367.

(2000). *Networking* [Review of the book *David Stark & László Bruszt, postsocialist pathways: Transforming politics and property in East Central Europe.* Cambridge: Cambridge University Press. 1998]. *East European Constitutional Review, 9* (1–2), 107–112. From: *http://www.law.nyu.edu/ eecr/vol9num_onehalf/reviews/networking.html*

(2001). The future of philosophy of history. *History and Theory, 40,* 37–56.

(2002). Kripke and fixing the reference of "God." *International Studies in Philosophy, 34* (4), 155–160.

(2003). The epistemic significance of consensus. *Inquiry, 46,* 501–521.

Valla, Lorenzo (1922). *The treatise of Lorenzo Valla on the donation of Constantine* (Christopher B. Coleman, Trans.). New Haven, CT: Yale University Press.

van Fraassen, B. (1980). *The Scientific Image.* Oxford: Clarendon Press.

Vico, Giambattista (1984) [1725]. *The New Science* (Thomas Goddard Bergin & Max Fisch, Trans.). Ithaca, Cornell University Press.

von Laue, Theodore H., (1950). *Leopold Ranke: The formative years.* Princeton: Princeton University Press.

Wade, Nicholas (2003). In click languages, an echo of the tongues of the ancients. *The New York Times,* March 18, F2.

Wallace, Edwin R., IV (1985). *Historiography and causation in psychoanalysis: An essay on psychoanalytic and historical epistemology.* Hillsdale, NJ & London: The Analytic Press.

Walsh, W. H. (1966). The limits of scientific history. In William Dray (Ed.), *Philosophical analysis and history* (pp. 54–74). New York: Harper & Row.

Weber, Max (1949). *The methodology of the social sciences* (Edward A. Shils & Henry A. Finch, Trans. and Eds.) New York: The Free Press.

Weinryb, Elazar (1975). The justification of a causal thesis: An analysis of the controversies over the theses of Pirenne, Turner, and Weber. *History and Theory, 14,* 32–56.

White, Hayden (1973). *Metahistory*. Baltimore: Johns Hopkins University Press.
    (1978). *Tropics of discourse*. Baltimore: Johns Hopkins University Press.
    (1987). *The content of the form*. Baltimore: Johns Hopkins University Press.
White, Morton (1965). *Foundations of historical knowledge*. New York: Harper & Row.
Wilson, Adrian (1993). Foundations of an integrated historiography. In Adrian Wilson (Ed.), *Rethinking social history: English society 1570–1920 and its interpretation*. Manchester, Manchester University Press, 293–335.
Wimsatt, William (1984). Reductive explanation: A functional account. In Elliott Sober (Ed.), *Conceptual issues in evolutionary biology* (pp. 478–508). Cambridge, MA: MIT Press.
    (1994). Lewontin's evidence (that there isn't any). In James Chandler, Arnold I. Davidson, Harry Harootunian (Eds.), *Question of evidence: proof, practice, and persuasion across the disciplines* (pp. 492–503). Chicago: University of Chicago Press.
Winch Peter (1958). *The Idea of a Social Science*. London: Routledge.
Windelband, Wilhelm (1980). Rectorial address, Strasbourg, 1894 (Guy Oakes, Trans.) [Translation of: Geschichte und Naturwissenschaften, *History and Theory 19*, 169–85. In *Praludien*, Vol. II, 136–60: Verlag von J. G. B. Mohr, Tübingen].
Wittgenstein, Ludwig (1953). *Philosophical Investigations* (G. E. M. Anscombe, Trans.) Oxford: Blackwell.
Wolf, F. A. (1985) [1795]. *Prolegomena to Homer*. (Anthony Grafton, Glenn W. Most, & James E. G. Zetzel, Trans.). Princeton: Princeton University Press.
Wright, Crispin (1984). Second thoughts about criteria. *Synthese, 58*, 383–405.
Wylie, Alison (1995). Unification and convergence in archeological explanation: The agricultural "wave-of-advance" and the origins of Indo-European languages. *The Southern Journal of Philosophy, 34* (supple.), 1–30.
    (1999). Rethinking unity as a "working hypothesis" for philosophy of science: How archaeologists exploit the disunities of science. *Perspectives on Science, 7*, 293–317.

Notes

Chapter One

1. Note that this explanation is not necessarily a causal explanation. Some philosophers may object to considering an aspect of the cause as its effect. Shared knowledge implies analytically shared beliefs, since all knowledge is composed of beliefs. Shared beliefs, however, do not imply common knowledge, so this explanation does not beg the question.

2. "Face" in the original.

3. Formally, if C stands for a consensus; K stands for knowledge; $B_1, B_2 \ldots B_n$ stand for different biases, Pr stands for the probability of $\ldots$, and the vertical line | expresses "given," then for Solomon to be right: $Pr\ (C|B_1) \times Pr\ (C|B_2) \times \ldots Pr\ (C|B_n) > Pr\ (C|K)$. For this to be the case, the likelihood of the consensus given each of the biases must be higher than its likelihood given common knowledge. This can be the case only if the likelihood of the consensus given all the biases is extremely high, or if the prior probability of common knowledge is extremely low.

4. Helen Longino (1994) also thought that consensus on beliefs results from a wide distribution of personal differences. She added however a Habermasian stipulation that the consensus must result from critical deliberation among individuals and groups from different points of view, an "interactive dialogic community" (pp. 142–3). Longino stipulated further the properties of the community that can transmute subjective points of view into scientific objectivity. There must be public fora for criticism; the community must be responsive to criticism; there must be revisable public standards, cognitive values, for which participants in the discourse can appeal to reach agreement; and the community should be intellectually egalitarian, where decisions about beliefs are not taken by appeal to authority. Critical discourse should explain how different biases and point's of view are transformed into a consensus on beliefs. However, Rescher's

279

criticism is just as relevant here: Longino cannot be interested in consensus per se, but in an ideal process for generating knowledge. The conditions she stipulated have never been satisfied in any historical case of consensus, and are of doubtful usefulness in explaining actual historical cases of consensus on beliefs.

5. Putnam (1990, pp. 135–41, 163–78) avoided the conclusion that knowledge is relative to cognitive values. If a culture upholds certain values, it does not imply that these values are not objective, in the sense of being valuable for what Putnam following Aristotle called "human flourishing." Cognitive values make an indirect contribution to human flourishing, through the acquisition of knowledge. The acquisition of knowledge helps us to orient ourselves in the world and consequently should improve our chances for survival and flourishing. Still, in some historical contexts, cognitive values detract from what many would consider human flourishing (Tucker, 2003).

Chapter Two

1. Some contemporary Russian xenophobic historians similarly claim that the entire Western historiography was fabricated recently to obscure the superiority of the Byzantine and later Russian civilizations.

2. Dretske (1981, pp. 104–5) wrote of the same process when he noted that equivocation (lost information) accumulates.

3. Current archeology found further evidence for this hypothesis in remains of polytheistic worship in virtually all Hebrew settlements dating to the period of the first temple (Finkelstein & Silberman, 2001).

4. Wolf also supported his hypotheses by demonstrating their consistency with other views of the Homeric poems: The Jewish historian Josephus Flavius wrote in the first century CE that the Homeric poems were initially memorized and only later were they written. Cicero held that the Homeric codex was collected by Pisistratus. But Wolf's translators note (Wolf, 1985, p. 145 note a) that Wolf did not adhere to strict critical methods when he used such late sources. He conflated their testimonies and did not consider whether they had an earlier common source.

5. The inference of etymologies from similarities in sound survived the establishment of scientific comparative linguistics. Heidegger attempted to infer etymologies of important metaphysical terms in Latin and Greek according to similarities in sound.

6. Another precursor was the Hungarian Gyarmathi who noticed in his 1799 publication the similarities between Hungarian (excluding Hungarian words borrowed from Turkish), Finnish, and Estonian. Gulya (1974) suggested that external factors such as absence of demand in Hungary for this type of research prevented the establishment of a Fino-Ugarian community of scholars. In Germany there was much interest in early German history, and fascination with possible common religious and intellectual origins shared with the ancient conquerors of India. In Hungary there was

no romantic allure for the discovery of a connection with "fish eaters" like the Lapps or nations of limited glory in the eighteenth century such as the Finns and Estonians.

7. Similarly, continental European legal systems, for example, in Germany, unlike common law systems, admit hearsay evidence because in nonjury legal systems professional judges are expected to examine critically hearsay evidence and distinguish credible elements from intentional lies or unintentional corruptions.

8. This approach is currently associated with "Realist theory" in International Relations, founded in the United States by German émigrés like Hans Morgenthau and advocated by political scientists turned politicians like Henry Kissinger, who argued that states have and should have interests dictated by their geopolitical situation. Irrespective of their ideologies, states such as Russia, China, and Iran are forced to have a continuous foreign policy. In its transplanted American context, the statist, yet antiromantic and antinationalist aspects of realist theory are often ignored.

9. None of these disciplines, including evolutionary biology, is purely cladistic, branchlike, because the various branches can and apparently often did get "entangled" together. Documents, species, and languages can and did influence each other after their historical separation. The proper model would then look more like a bush than a tree. Cladistic models are therefore simplified, idealized, hypothetical descriptions of historical reality.

Chapter Three

1. David Carr (1986) considered historiography to have a narrative form. Yet, Carr also thought that it is a true story because historiographic narratives are isomorphic to an independently existing historical narrative. Carr claimed that time and collective action, as they are experienced, have a narrative structure. We have an experience in common when we grasp a sequence of events as a temporal configuration. Its present phase derives its significance from its relation to a common past and future (Carr, 1986, p. 127). Each community has a narrative that constitues it. This narrative is the unity of story, storyteller, audience, and protagonist. Storytellers tell stories in which the protagonist is the communal we of their audience, the community. A second order, historiographic, narrative is told by historians. It might have, for cognitive or aesthetic reasons, a different content from a first order narrative. But if both narratives share an identical subject, the narrative forms remain isomorphic. I do not think Carr was successful in presenting a convincing account of historiographic truth. Historians do not wish always to talk about communal subjects that were present in the consciousness of a historical community. Social historians may write legitimately about social categories whether or not the historical subjects of these categories were conscious of them. Carr's model of historiography does not fit historiography that does not deal with the phenomenology of consciousness of historical communities through time.

Nor did Carr suggest criteria for choosing between competing isomorphic second order historiographic narratives. Still, Carr's account of narrative historiography proves that the form of historiography does not determine its epistemology.

2. Friedman (1987) analyzed legal testimonies by using the full Bayesian formula. However the legal approach to evidence is different from the scientific-historiographic one. The question in criminal court is whether the accused did it or not. What is the posterior probability of the guilty hypothesis? The prosecution argues that it is high and the defense claims that there is insufficient evidence for it, or that he did not do it. The defense does not have to offer an alternative hypothesis to the one offered by the prosecution. The defendant has the right to remain silent. Still, sometimes the defense does offer an alternative hypothesis to the prosecution's because the negation of the guilty hypothesis is more convincing if there is a convincing alternative hypothesis that explains the evidence better than the guilty hypothesis.

3. Greg (1927) grouped variational groups of documents in binary sets according to a single variable with a binary choice of affirmative presence of it or negative absence of it. Such two groups may be divided further by two according to as many variables as necessary. In information theory, each such division generates one bit of information by eliminating alternative possibilities (Dretske, 1981). Consistent grouping according to all variables implies that membership in one group excludes membership in the other group, and the same goes for subgroups within each binary based grouping. Consistent groupings in relation to different variables indicate that the similarities may result from a common cause.

Chapter Four

1. Though Quine discussed the underdetermination of theory by its *observable logical consequences*, following Laudan and Leplin's (1991) criticisms and Murphey's (1994) interpretation, I substitute *evidence* for it.

2. "... a remarkably successful development of the universalizing logic. If anyone emphasizes structural circumstances favoring revolutions, Theda Skocpol is the one" (Tilly, 1984, p. 105); "... excellent... very sophisticated, both methodologically and substantially" (Manicas, 1981, p. 204).

3. Skocpol compounded the vagueness of the theory by adding a teleological stipulation to her definition of the revolutions. Her definition "makes *successful* sociological transformation – actual change of state and class structures – part of the specification of what is to be called a social revolution." Because "successful social revolutions probably emerge from different macro-structural and historical contexts than do either failed social revolutions or political transformations that are not accompanied by transformations of class relations" (1979, p. 5). Teleological definitions of types of historiographic events are based on the logical fallacy of affirming the consequent, that all the causes of a single token effect must be

identical. Successful revolution may have different causes, while unsuccessful revolutions may fit Skocpol's model, save for a single intervening variable.

4. Skocpol asked why the 1917 Russian peasant revolution resulted in the leveling of landed property, while in revolutionary France an identical cause benefited the well-to-do peasants? Auxiliary ad hoc hypotheses favor two factors (Skocpol, 1979, pp. 137–40): (1) In Russia the returning soldiers destabilized traditional society and led to land redistribution. (2) The Russian *Obshchina* was traditionally hostile to private property while the French village assemblies had a tradition of limited authority and respect for private property. The choice of these two factors among the myriad differences between France and Russia to account for the difference between the post-revolutionary agrarian structure in France and Russia is purely ad hoc. Skocpol (1979, pp. 190–3) attempted to explain the peculiarly French fall of the Jacobinic regime. While the Bolsheviks and Chinese Communist regimes survived. Skocpol added an auxiliary hypothesis to explain the anomaly: The decentralized structure of the economy prevented the Jacobins from solving France's economic problems, Skocpol thought that the Soviet and Chinese Communists "solved" the economic problems of their countries. Consequently, the Jacobins lost their political support among the peasantry. However, identical conditions of peasants' and workers' discontent were also present in Russia in 1921, and are therefore insufficient to explain the fall. Another group of ad hoc hypotheses must be added: As "the party of the proletariat," operating in a twentieth-century society that already had large-scale, modern industries, the Bolsheviks enjoyed two advantages: They possessed both an ideological self-justification and a realistic organizational basis for a political mission that could sustain their movement in state power [The Montagnard had neither]" (Skocpol, 1979, p. 192).

5. The pragmatic and semantic features of psychoanalysis resemble traditionalist historiography. Edwin R. Wallace IV (1985) noted the parallels between the methodologies of psychoanalysis and historiography, as well as the communication problems among psychoanalysts. Theoretical psychologists recognize the theoretical fragmentation of psychology and the problems of communication among psychologists. Compare the symposium in *Annals of Theoretical Psychology*, volume 9 (Rappard, 1993). In psychology, as in historiography, theoretical proliferation cannot remain on the institutionalized school level. Clinical psychologists must confront individual cases. The grand theories of psychology (Freud, Adler, Jung; Gestalt, Behaviorism, Cognitive, and others) cannot be applied without interpretation to individual cases. Practicing psychologists interpret the theories they adopt ad hoc differently, and have communication problems like historians (Tucker, 1999a, 1999b).

6. Chartier actually did not substantiate the connection between the introduction of the book and Christianity because according to the first definition Hindus, Confucians, and Jews had books prior to Christianity.

Chapter Five

1. Arguably, it is possible to limit reenactment to the realm of rational acts, in the sense of rationality as explicated by modern rational choice theory. Rules of rational behavior in addition to descriptions of historical states and agents' preferences as initial conditions may infer the rational reasoning of historical agents, as chess players reenact the rational calculations of their opponents. Collingwood, Popper, and Hempel thought that people share at least a potential for rationality, and therefore it is possible to understand the thoughts of other people as problem solving. Such reenactment is of impersonal rational moves. This method is limited to the extent that historical agents behaved rationally. In the social sciences, where debates on rational choice theory are far more extensive than in historiography due to the radiating dominance of rational choice theories from economics through political science outward to the other social sciences, it has been argued that social agents behave often irrationally. Jon Elster, an early advocate of rational choice theory has devoted most of his many books to examining its limitation (Elster, 1989, pp. 13–88). Dray (1995) made an important observation when he stressed that in historiography rationality is discovered rather than assumed or deduced a priori. In historiography rationality has to be established through the evidence. There is also plenty of evidence for irrational, confused, inadvertent, and arbitrary actions in history.

Chapter Six

1. Mill's model of the evolution of the sciences is inferred from a single case, the history of physics and what he regarded as applied physics, astronomy. On the basis of this evolutionary model, Mill predicted that sociology will "take its place among the sciences. When this time shall come, no important branch of human affairs will be any longer abandoned to empiricism and scientific surmise and the circle of human knowledge will be complete" (Mill, 1976, VI: X, p. 8). Ryan (1975, pp. 179–80) found this prediction puzzling. How can human knowledge be on the one hand, complete, and on the other hand, expanding? I think that when Mill referred to complete, he meant theoretical completion, the discovery of all the laws that govern the phenomena. Still, new phenomena will be discovered, explained, and predicted, using the old precise laws. Ryan wondered why Mill expressed in this paragraph the belief that sociology would be able to predict the future of society just as Newtonian mechanics can predict the course of the planets, while in his discussion of the social sciences, Mill was careful to abstain from such confident statements about the capacity of the social sciences to subject human phenomena to laws and predict them. This apparent discrepancy is resolved if we recall that Mill predicted here the far future of the social sciences, when they reach the third phase in their evolution and become an exact science, while the bulk of his discussion Mill was concerned with preparing the transformation of the social

sciences from the first prescientific stage to the second inexact scientific stage.

2. Hayek argued that since a social science is impossible, any claim for its discovery, most notably Marxism, must be fraudulent. Marxism and alchemy share in Hayek's opinion a claim for control of a realm of nature founded on a pseudotheory. I agree with Hayek that Marx's social theory is not a theory in the scientific sense, in my opinion because it is too vague and given to conflicting interpretations. But Hayek's necessary link between a scientific theory of society and political utopianism is as tenuous as the relation between a cosmological theory of the universe and control of the evolution of the universe. It is quite possible to advocate a scientific theory of the evolution of society without inferring any practical means to engineer it.

3. Mathematicians suggested a number of methods for deciding whether a system is chaotic or not. A useful though not fail-safe method is by using Lyapunov exponents: Measurements of a time-series of values for one of the variables of the system that can be periodic, intermittent, or irregular. Irregularity indicates chaos. In dissipative systems, the reconstruction of *strange attractors* out of the same series indicates a chaotic system (Kellert, 1993, pp. 23–8).

4. Windelband foreshadowed Hempel's covering law model of explanation: "Every causal explanation of any historical occurrence presupposes general ideas about the process of things on the whole...natural laws of events...of mental events or psychological processes" (Windelband, 1980, pp. 182–3). Windelband held that causal explanation of events assumes a syllogism whose major premise is nomothetic (a law of nature) and minor premise is ideographic (conditions). Windelband was inconsistent since the description of events as minor premises in scientific syllogism must use the conceptual framework of the covering law to connect with it, therefore it cannot be ideographic in Windelband's sense of offering an exhaustive description (Fetzer, 1975).

5. Asimov envisioned a statistical historiographic science and even historiographic engineering. Still, to connect science with engineering in historiography, which Hayek and Popper took for granted, following the Marxists, Asimov had to give his scientific historians/scientists mind reading and mind controlling powers.

Index

Alter, Stephen, 85–7
Annales, 84, 165, 170, 172, 220, 226
archives, 76–7, 84
Aristototle, 92
Astruc, Jean, 53
Augustine, 16

Bayesian
  analysis of counterfactuals, 231
  analysis of knowledge of history, 95–100, 120
  case study of historiographic knowledge, 134–40
  reason for historiographic underdetermination, 150
Beard, Charles, 4
Ben-Menachem, Yemima, 221, 224
Berlin, Isaiah, 17, 42, 75, 208, 211, 213–14
  esotericism of, 19
Berlin, University of, 60, 67, 76, 78
biblical criticism, 53–9, 74
Bloch, Marc, 84, 132, 170
Bopp, Franz, 67–8
Braudel, Ferdinand, 170–1
Burckhardt, Jacob, 84, 138
Burke, Peter, 69, 168
Butterfield, Herbert, 69–70, 177

Carr, David, 281
Carr, E. H., 5
Caws, Peter, 28, 166
chaos, 222–5
Chartier, Roger, 171–2, 181–2
Clark, Jonathan, 201–2, 221, 226, 228, 236
Classical philology, 59–63, 73, 74
cliometrics, 228
cognitive values, 36–9, 42, 47, 145, 146, 254–5
  accuracy, 147, 148, 149, 152
  complexity *see* simplicity
  consilience, 148, 149
  consistency, 160
  critical, 48, 53, 79
  scope, 147, 148, 152
  simplicity, 149, 152, 154
  traditionalist, 38–9, 47, 48, 49–51
coincidence, 218–20
colligation, 137–8
Collingwood, R. G., 15, 17, 48, 132–3, 200 *see also* self-consciousness
  understanding re-enactment, 202–3, 204–7
common cause, 74, 87, 100–34 *see also* separate causes
  alternative, 116–17, 119

common cause (*cont.*)
  as an explanation of descriptions
    of events, 199–200
  five kinds of, 103
  particular vs. general, 103–4, 113,
    119–20
  type vs. token, 100–1, 113, 116–17,
    119
communication, 179–81
  within historiographic schools,
    179, 181–2
  within historiography, 179–83
  within science, 179
Comparative history *see*
  historiography, comparative
Comparative Linguistics, 63–8, 74,
    86, 88–90
  prescientific, 64–5
  scientific, 65–8, 124
Comte, August, 16
consensus on beliefs, 24, 88, 204
  cognitive values and, 36–9
  debate on epistemic significance
    of, 25–7
  dissent from, 39–44
  epistemic significance of, 27–8
  scope of, 46
  unique and heterogeneous, 29–34
  usefulness of, 34–5
Constructionism, 255–6, 257, 258–60
  see also Realism
contingency and necessity, 220–39
counterfactuals, 226–39
credibility *see* fidelity
Croce, Benedetto, 15

Danto, Arthur, 12–14, 138–9, 163,
    213
Darwin, Charles, 85–7, 148
determinism, 221
DNA, 124–6, 128
Dray, William, 17, 93, 137, 163, 194,
    219
  on Collingwood, 204–5
Dretske, Fred, 18, 94, 106 *see also*
  epistemology

Earman, John, 99
Eichhorn, J. G., 55–6
Elster, Jon, 160, 227–31
Elton, Geoffrey, 5, 129, 133, 190
epistemology
  Dretske's, 18
  individualistic, 51
  naturalized, 9–10
esotericism, 19
Evans, Richard J., 26, 123
evidence, 8–10, 17–93
  correlated *see* similar
  fixed, 144, 146
  independent, 119, 123
  insufficient, 142
  internal vs. external, 123
  new, 134–7, 145
  non-intentional, 76
  public, 74, 142
  similar, 75, 100
  and theory, 18–19, 75, 93, 95, 98
    see also Bayesian analysis of
    historiographic knowledge
evolutionary biology, 85–8
expectancy (Bayesian logic), 97
explanation, 185–284
  atomic, 187–8, 191, 199–200, 207,
    243
  covering law model of, 188–90,
    242–3
  ex-post-facto, 190–1
  inference to the best, 186,
    191–2
  singular causal, 191
  traditionalist, 197–9

fallacies *see* Clark, Jonathan;
    counterfactuals; Martin,
    Raymond
Feyerabend, Paul, 179
fidelity, 106–7, 121–34
  constant rates of, 124–7
Fukuyama, Francis, 16, 209

Gadamer, Hans Georg, 48, 184, 203,
    204

genetic group, 105 *see also* variational
group
Gesenius, Wilhelm, 58
Ginzburg, Carlo, 137
Glymour, Clark, 33, 131, 145
Goldman, Alvin, 24, 27, 28, 121
Goldstein, Leon
on coherence of beliefs, 120
on historiographic explanation,
163, 189, 190
on historiography and evidence,
4, 17, 92, 93, 94, 95, 142
on superstructure-infrastructure
distinction in historiography,
6–7, 168
Gottingen, University of, 69–70
Gould, Stephen Jay, 148, 236–9
Gramberg, C. P. W., 58–9
Grimm, Jacob, 68

Haeckel, Ernst, 87
Halevi, Judah, 48
Hempel, Carl Gustav, 5, 188, 209
see also explanation, covering
law model of
Hegel, Georg, 15, 16, 202, 203
Herder, Johann Gottfried von, 16
historikerstreit, 43
historiography
comparative, 151–60, 250, 252
critical, 74–6
definition of, 1–2
demographic, 84
Enlightenment, 51
legitimate, 40, 41–2 *see also*
consensus on beliefs
philosophy of, 2, 6, 46, 261–2
philosophy of scientific, 3–6,
210–15, 240, 252–3
revisionist, 42–4
scientific, 1, 2, 68–85, 208–15,
249–53
serial, 84
textbooks, 4, 6–7, 168, 190, 193,
256
therapeutic, 40–1, 79, 262

traditionalist, 47–8, 79, 155, 167,
183–4, 209–10, 213 *see also*
traditionalist science; schools in
historiography
underdetermined, 146–51,
162–6
world, 84, 219
history
definition, 1–2
complexity of, 215–18
philosophy of, 14–17, 183 *see also*
self-consciousness
Huizinga, Johan, 84
Humboldt, Wilhelm, 60
Hume, David, 51, 52
on miracles, 99
Huntington, Samuel, 16, 209

Ibn Khaldun, 16
Iggers, Georg, 39, 132, 189, 200
Indo-European hypothesis, 63, 67–8,
85, 88, 118
information, 75, 94, 106, 121, 228,
260
nested, 106
interpretation, 1–2, 10–14, 141

Jardine, Nicholas, 6
Jervis, Robert, 161–2, 213, 218,
233

Kant, Immanuel, 5, 11, 15, 16
Kennedy, Paul, 16
Kocka, Jurgen, 43
Kosso, Peter, 8, 33, 94, 120, 123, 132
Krieger, Leonard, 68, 69
Kripke, Saul, 48
Kuhn, Thomas, 6, 11, 24, 36, 144,
167
on pre-science, 179

Laet, Johannes de, 65
Lakatos, Imre, 29, 179
Langlois & Seignobos, 4, 8, 17, 75
Laplace, Pierre Simon, 52
Laudan, Larry, 3, 36, 96, 142

Lefebvre, Georges, 70–1
Le Goff, Jacques, 23, 50, 172
Leipzig, University of, 73
likelihood (Bayesian logic), 97
  comparison of, 99, 109, 115–17
  of evidence given counterfactual, 231
  of variational group given common cause, 111
Lloyd, Christopher, 19, 143, 147, 175, 179, 210
  analysis of the structure of social historiography, 170
Locke, John, 51
Longino, Helen, 30

Martin, Raymond
  confusions of, 193, 195
  esotericism of, 19
  logical fallacies of, 193, 194
Marwick, Arthur, 1, 41, 122–3, 194
Marx, Karl, 15, 16, 173–4, 211
Marxist historiography
  as a historiographic school, 157, 165, 169–70, 172–3, 220, 226 *see also* schools, in historiography
  doctrinaire, 211
  within legitimate historiography, 12, 41, 42, 201 *see also* historiography, legitimate, scientific
Masaryk, Tomáš G., 41
Meier, Christian, 43
methodological individualism vs. holism, 212–13
Mill, John Stuart, 16, 189, 215–17
Momigliano, Arnaldo, 72–3
Mommsen, Theodor, 136–7
Murphey, Murray
  on evidence, 17, 121, 129
  on explanation, 185, 186, 244
  on historiography, 4, 9, 150–1, 178, 180, 250

Narrative, 7–8, 12–14, 44–5, 92, 138–9, 281

necessity *see* contingency and necessity
Neo-Kantian philosophy *see* Rickert; Simmel; Windelband
Neo-Rankeans, 81–4
Newton, Isaac, 3, 246
Niebuhr, Barthold Georg, 71–3
Nolte, Ernst, 42–3

Okruhlik, Kathleen, 30
opinion, in historiography, 141
other minds, problem of, 205–6

path dependence, 233
Peirce, Charles, 26, 99
Pettit, Philip, 212
phenomenology *see* Hegel; Gadamer
Plato, 23
Pompa, Leon, 93–4
Popper, Karl, 17, 208, 214, 217
posterior probability (Bayesian logic), 98
primary sources, 122–3
prior probability (Bayesian logic), 97
  of common cause hypotheses, 110–11, 120
Putnam, Hilary, 35–6

Quine, W. V. O., 9, 143–4
  holism, 120, 143
  indeterminacy of translation, 180

Ranke, Leopold, 73–80, 226
  paradigm, theories, and methods, 73–4, 76, 77–8, 79, 242
  spread of paradigm, 80–1
  works of, 76–7, 78
Rask, Rasmus, 66–7
Realism, 255, 257 *see also* Constructionism
reduction, 211–12, 247–52
  explanatory methodological, 247–8
  inter-theoretical, 248

of descriptions of properties,
248–9
ontological, 247
weak, 248
re-enactment *see* Collingwood
Reichenbach, Hans, 102, 104
realiability *see* fidelity
Rescher, Nicholas, 25, 26–7, 180
Rickert, Heinrich, 10–11, 200, 211,
241–2
Rotenstereich, Nathan, 15, 16
Roth, Paul, 24, 189, 204

Salmon, Wesley, 99, 100, 103,
116–17, 119
Sarkar, Husain, 34, 37
Schleicher, August, 88–9
Schools, 166–8
in biology, 147
in historiography, 143, 150, 163,
170, 172, 175
in psychoanalysis, 147, 283
self-consciousness, 15–16, 183, 202,
203, 204 *see also* history,
philosophy of
separate causes, 112–115 *see also*
common cause
Simmel, Georg, 10
Skepticism, 19, 44–5, 51–2,
141–2
Skocpol, Theda, 154–60
Sober, Elliott, 99, 126
on common causes, 100, 103,
104–5, 107, 110, 112, 116, 120
social science theories, 96, 160–2
sociology, 160
historical, 153–4
of knowledge, 28
Solomon, Miriam, 31–2, 35–6
speculative philosophy of history
see history, philosophy of
Spencer, Herbert, 16
Spengler, Oswald, 16
substantial philosophy of history
see history, philosophy of
Swadesh, Maurice, 90, 124

Thagard, Paul, 148–9
Theory, 138, 162, 166
accuracy *see* cognitive values
ad hoc, 148, 150, 153, 155, 163,
164
common sense, 75
consilience *see* cognitive values
conspiracy, 105
grand-scope and vague, 162
historiographic, 143, 177–9
in international relations,
161–2
mediating, 149
middle-range, 160
scope *see* cognitive values
simplicity *see* cognitive values
underdetermination, 143–8,
149
Toynbee, Arnold, 16
traditionalist science, 167–77
see also historiography,
traditionalist

understanding, 199–200, 207, 214
unique events, 240
unique hypotheses, 244–7

Valla, Lorenzo, 50
van Fraassen, Bass, 101, 162, 177,
192
variational group, 105, 114, 118
see also genetic group
verstehen see understanding
Vico, Giambattista, 15, 118, 203

Walsh, W. H., 11–12, 14
wave theory of language, 89–90, 118
Weber, Max, 165, 175
Wette, W. M. L. de, 56–8
Whewell, William, 87, 137
White, Hayden, 44
Windelband, Wilhelm, 241, 285
Wittgenstein, Ludwig, 183, 204, 205
Wolf, Friedrich August, 59–63, 72,
203
Wylie, Alison, 33, 127, 131